Donald Dinnie sporting a selection of his medals and an extraordinary sporran.
Courtesy: Robert Dinnie

Contents

The St Fillans Highland Games in 1828

Introduction

Donald Dinnie – A Sporting Colossus. That was the headline of Ian Archer's lengthy book review in the Glasgow Herald of November 1973. "For a week now," he wrote, "I have been leaving home and returning time and time again to one of the most important tomes on Scottish sport ever to be dumped on my doormat – and reading over and over again about Donald Dinnie, the great 'heavy' of the Highland Games."

Although Archer praises the 'affectionate portraits' of Bill Anderson and other athletes, it was clearly Donald Dinnie who captured his imagination. His was a common response.

David Webster, author of the book Scottish Highland Games to which Ian Archer refers, was inundated with requests for more information about Donald Dinnie and was glad when the clamour died down. Nearly quarter of a century later along came Gordon Dinnie, born 19th June 1939 in Cambuslang, Glasgow, and remotely related to the great athlete. A more dedicated Dinnie fan would be impossible to find. He has a marvellous collection of newspaper and magazine cuttings pertaining to his hero and he had a driving ambition to see his predecessor get the full credit due to him. Gordon believed that had Dinnie lived in this age of the Internet and television the whole world would know him to be the greatest athlete that ever lived.

After lengthy discussion Gordon Dinnie and David Webster decided they would write a book. David had unearthed a long forgotten life story of Donald Dinnie, written by Donald himself after his travels were over.

This and Gordon's superb collection gave the pair more information than had ever been available before, and this new work is the result of their combined efforts.

Charlie Allan, a leading professional Highland Games athlete of the 1960s and '70s, expressed an interest in the proposals and after discussion agreed to publish the book.

Dinnie was persuaded in 1912 to write his autobiography for Health and Strength Magazine as a source of inspiration for the youth of the nation, particularly young sportsmen. The grand old athlete was then nearly 76, and during his life had met the best and strongest men of his time; therefore his reminiscences, as well as being personal, constituted a classic athletic history of an early pioneer in international sport.

The greater part of the narrative was Donald's own, but it became clear his modesty was obscuring the enormity of his accomplishments and underplaying his role in developing heavy events and international Highland games. To remedy this E. Stewart Smith, the editor of Health and Strength Magazine, who knew him well and wrote with authority, took up the narrative so we have an authentic contemporary account which will provide source material for students of sport and Scottish culture.

Unfortunately this format was not considered suitable for book publication at that time and a contributory factor may have been that he did not bow to popular publishing demand and titillate readers with details of his colourful private life. In such matters Dinnie was uncompromising; his entertainment was above reproach and suitable for youngsters, adults, grannies and granddads. His manuscript was the same – it would not offend Mary Whitehouse or the most sensitive maiden aunt.

For example, Donald Dinnie would sometimes relate a tale of how when he was young he had two sweethearts at the same time. When they heard of his duplicity, they confronted him and said he must make his choice. Depending on the company Donald would embellish the story in different ways.

However research has shown that his father Robert Dinnie often told an almost identical tale.

"I could not make up my mind which I liked most," Robert would explain. "One sweetheart lived up the road and the ither lived doon the road.

"I decided that I would dress up in my best claes (clothes) and gang to the middle o' the road, throw my stick into the air, and then whichever way the point o' my stick would lay when it fell, I would follow it. It pointed doon and I followed it."

"But ye had a gey good guess what way the stick would fa'," commented his spouse, "and ye never regretted it."

In Donald's version he used to say he threw his bonnet in the air and the girl nearest to where the feathers pointed he would marry.

We, Gordon Dinnie and David Webster, now rectify the lack of a Dinnie biographical book. Additional information has been added to give a more comprehensive overview and to show how widely his talents were recognised. We draw from many fine periodicals and publications to show how writers and historians perceived him, and acknowledge with gratitude those who helped us in our task.

We thrill – the pulses quicken at the sight
Of him who was the King of Human Might
When Dinnie trod of old the rural sward
No rival could his royal course retard
'Twas first in wrestle, caber, throw or sprint
He 'scapes ere burnished shield receives a dint
Still King of Might, he sought the distant shores
Of foreign lands, where wild Niagara roars
Again the laurels full he did attain
And home the hero came without a stain
God grant that while his sun doth slowly set
His latter days with plenty will be met
For while the British are a virile race
For him to 'want' is a national disgrace.

Gwelkin Graham, Duncraig, Barnhill

A Scotsman's heart is just as wide as any heart could be,
Yet feels a pardonable pride a brither brave to see,
In front of all, a good spear's length, our Dinnie takes his stand
And 'gainst the world for feats of strength upholds his native land.

J. Rae

Enthusiast J. Rae's poem appeared in the Melbourne Northern Star in 1884 when Donald Dinnie, then making triumphal progress round the world, visited that great city. To the present generation the wonderful feats of this great Scottish athlete, whom many hail as the best all-round athlete the world has ever known, come as an echo – but a stirring echo.

Dinnie was the first sporting superstar. There were heroes in Greek Olympics, true to the best amateur traditions in competing for a crown of olive leaves, and, perhaps for the greatest, their statues on the perimeter of the arena. There were highly acclaimed gladiators in ancient Rome, often slaves fighting for freedom or criminals fighting for their lives. Medieval knights jousted for honour or tokens from favoured ladies.

All were superb in their own ways but none can approach the multi-faceted career of Donald Dinnie.

It was widely accepted that during Donald Dinnie's glorious career this virtually invincible athlete won nearly 11,000 competitions. A newspaper report published in 1898, announcing his impending return to Scotland, stated the figure as 10,895 up until 1895. Since he competed at Highland games for another 15 years, plus wrestling, and stage contests at his own promotions, it is estimated that the figure topped 11,000. In round figures he won more than 2,000 hammer throwing contests, over 2,000 wrestling matches, 1,800 in putting the stone, 1,800 in jumping, 1,400 in caber tossing, 300 in weight throwing, over 200 in weightlifting, and approximately 500 in running and hurdles. However, he also won many prizes for pole vaulting, highland dancing, shooting, quoiting, club swinging and even elocution.

In one day he could earn more than a workman could in several years. A conservative estimate of his cash winnings is £25,000, to which must be added appearance money and proceeds from displays and shows which he organised.

These facts alone made him a superstar, but there is further confirmation. He endorsed commercial products, one of these being Scotland's other national drink, Barr's Iron Brew, now known as Irn Bru. Dinnie's image was used on the bottle labels of this popular beverage and in newspaper and magazine advertising and shown in TV programmes 100 years after his record-breaking sprees.

Donald Dinnie was a household name. Postcards of him sold briskly and his portrait was featured on cigarette cards. During World War I a 60-lb mortar shell was named after him and as these missiles screeched overhead soldiers in the trenches would crouch down and say: "There goes another Donald Dinnie."

In the 1950s Canadian fiddler Dan Rory MacDonald and pianist Marie MacLellan included a Strathspey called Donald Dinnie on a recording of Scottish country music.

And a champion Australian ram was given the name. The stock-getting power of this Donald Dinnie was remarkable and at market it fetched the princely sum of 1200 guineas. The Pastoralists' Review enthuses: "He weighed 248-lb and cut 33-lb of bright lustrous fleece of beautiful character."

The real Donald Dinnie had to suffer many wise cracks because of this prolific namesake.

Imagine Donald Dinnie if you can; a dark complexioned, muscularly built professional athlete with eyes as piercing as a hawk, his moustache carefully waxed at the points. Regardless of the occasion, or the country, he wore his national dress with pride. Adventuring round the world, challenging all comers, whether on the field of sport, tramping the hills or riding horseback, he favoured the kilt, of Clan Hay tartan. It was said that he never owned a pair of trousers.

A colourful character, then. But let Donald Dinnie tell his own story.

The Braemar Gathering at Invercauld House in 1848

Dinnie's Own Story

To be invited to contribute my reminiscences is, sir, an honour I esteem very highly indeed, and if my story should be the means of helping the young men of the present day to excel in the field and in the battle of life I shall be content.

If now and then I appear to be a trifle egotistic you must forgive me, for as I am writing about myself I am bound, of course, to talk about myself.

I first saw the light of day at Balnacraig, in the east end of the parish of Aboyne, on the 8th day of June, 1837, just a few days before the Coronation of Queen Victoria. Nearly thirty years earlier my father, Robert Dinnie[1], was born within two miles of my birthplace. He was a man of great physical strength and a notable athlete in his day. At wrestling or fighting – 'rough and tumble' – he excelled and was, indeed, so I have been told, the champion of Deeside. He started life as a stonemason's apprentice but when quite a young man he struck out for himself as a contractor, builder and architect and his power to lift very heavy stones placed him at a great advantage.

In the Deeside district there are many stories told of his extraordinary feats. Just let me tell you one.

On the granite stone bridge that crosses the River Dee at Potarch there were, and still are, two large stones weighing about 8cwt the pair, placed in a recess[2]. In the early 1830s massive iron rings were placed in them, to which ropes were fixed so that scaffolds could be attached for pointing the bridge. Now, one of these stones was somewhat heavier than the other. Very few strong men of that day could lift the heavy one with both hands, but my father could raise one in each hand with apparent ease, and could throw the heavier stone of the two on to the top of a parapet wall of the bridge.

On one occasion, I have been told, he took one stone in each hand and carried them both to the end of the bridge and back – a distance of 100 yards. This achievement has been pronounced the greatest feat of strength ever performed in Scotland.

Those stones are still on the bridge and I myself lifted one in each hand on many occasions and one market day, I carried them across the bridge and back, some four to five yards. I did not, however, attempt to go to the end of the bridge, as my father had done.

About three years ago, one of the strongest athletes of the present day heard of these feats whilst on a visit to Aberdeen. There upon he

[1]For further information on Robert Dinnie, see page 141

[2]Further information on the Dinnie Stones appears in Appendix 1, page 152

motored to Potarch Bridge to see "the stones" and have a go at them, but it is said that he only succeeded in raising the two clear of the ground.

My father Robert Dinnie was also great at pulling the 'swee tree'[1], and throwing the hammer, though no records of distances are preserved. The missiles were rarely weighed in those days, and the weights, as a rule, were mason's or blacksmith's hammers, with handles from two to three feet long, yet my father had usually the best of all comers until I came along in 1852 and bowled him out.

My father seemed literally made of sinews and muscles and in build I was certainly a chip of the old block, though more rounded on the shoulders. He was over 6ft in height, and weighed 15st. He was well known in his day as an antiquary and historian and he could write poetry too. So you see I had every reason to be proud of my old dad, and I'm not ashamed to boast about him either.

In 1833 my father Robert was happily married to Miss Celia Hay. At 5ft 7in in height she was a beautifully formed, physically strong woman, endowed also with quite superior intelligence. They had six sons and four daughters. All the former are strong and athletic, and have been prize-winners at athletic sports. The youngest, Walter, who joined the detective force at Scotland Yard, was a front-rank, all-round athlete, winning many trophies in the amateur ranks at putting the weight, vaulting, running, leaping, etc.

An average taken of the six sons would work out at over 6ft in height and 15st in weight. This, to the Eugenic Society, would, I am sure, be most interesting, for as you will recollect, those were my father's measurements. Five of the boys took up the stonemason's trade. All married, and all have large families. After 59 years of happy married life my father and mother both died in 1891, within a few months of each other, so that it might almost be said, "in their death they were not divided".

I recall with pleasure many incidents of my early infancy. In 1841, when I was a child of four, my dad drove me by mail coach to

[1]This event is also called the swingle tree and in the Gaelic *Ceapan Togail*. Two competitors sit on the ground, each placing the soles of his feet against those of his opponent. They grasp a short stick (*rachd*) or similar object and on a signal try to pull the other off the ground. More than a century ago this was a popular activity in Argyleshire, the Western Isles and elsewhere in Scotland. Hefty farmhands used part of the harness for paired horses for this test of strength.

This is not to be confused with the 'swinging tree'. The Argyleshire Folklore Society circa 1893 described this dangerous trick played by mischievous lads in the days when a swee (Gaelic - *slabhraidh*) hung over every fireplace for cooking purposes. When parents were not present they grabbed the opportunity offered to put their feet in the hook of the swee and grasping the chain, or the spar to which it was attached, would swing themselves to and fro over the fire.

The Marquis of Huntly tries the weight of the heavier Dinnie Stone

Aberdeen, and I took up my abode with William Hay, a brother of my mother, who dwelt in the Backwynd of Union Street. At a public school hard by I learnt the alphabet, but two years later my father called again and carried me back to Deeside. I recollect with what glee I welcomed him, and the prospect of another long coach ride of 26 miles.

I also clearly recall an incident, which happened some year later, when, as a schoolboy, I had a very narrow squeak.

The school nearest to Balnacraig was at Kincardine O'Neil, some way over a mile, and across the River Dee. A Mr James Hogg was then schoolmaster, a front-rank scholar and most earnest teacher, though sometimes exceedingly hard on boys who misbehaved. The quill pens were then used for writing, and at preparing them and writing copperplate with them Mr Hogg was second to none. He taught me to write, and to write well. At boys' outdoor sports such as bowls, football, etc, I was always keen.

While attending this school, when about nine years of age, I was nearly drowned in the Dee, in an attempt to wade across, as the scholars often did during the summer, when the river was low. On this occasion the river was swollen, but as an old boy about 18 years of age had led the way, I did not feel disposed to give in without a trial. I followed on at once, but in the deepest part the water was too strong for my weight. I was swept down, and only rescued in the nick of time by my companion, who, after a very severe struggle, pulled me to the bank. I had become quite insensible whilst in the water, and fancied all the time that I heard the bagpipes play a stirring march.

But I loved the River Dee, as I always shall, and an accident such as that I have just described could not keep me away from it. In the winter of that year, when it was frozen over, I remember what jolly hours we boys enjoyed upon the ice. But here again I had a narrow escape. The river was only partly frozen over, but we boys made for the ice that was there. A crash, a shriek, and we were floundering together in the water. Luck was with us, and a boatman who had seen the accident came to our rescue. If he had not done so there would have been no Donald Dinnie records.

I admit that after this, but while still a lad, I sometimes supplemented our domestic supplies of porridge and brose with a salmon from the Dee. We had many an expedition near the Bridge of Potarch, where there are many fine pools that the fish lie in. We used to catch them with a spear. I remember one night we got eleven fish, all weighing between 20 - 40-lb. There was a man named E... who was a regular champion at the game. He would sit on a tree and when the fish appeared he would fling his spear and he hardly ever missed. Of course the watchers saw us, but they didn't interfere. They might have got a good steeping in the river if they had!

When I was about ten years of age my teacher proposed to my father that I should learn the rudiments of the Latin language. Father readily agreed to this, and at twelve years of age I understood the now-despised dead language pretty well. Just about this time my father bought a long lease of a piece of land nearly a mile farther to the south end of the parish, and there built a nice seven-roomed house, which, on account of its beautiful sylvan surroundings, he named Wood Cottage. In consequence of this removal I was transferred to the school of Birse, which my brothers and I attended for many years.

Aberdeen in Dinnie's day – 1840. Courtesy: Aberdeen City Arts Department

Highland Games

At the age of fifteen I was apprenticed to the granite stone mason trade. At that time a lad, Alexander George, from Cromarty, some eight years older than I, and an older brother of the noted athlete, John George, gave me my first lesson at putting the stone. The sport fascinated me so much that I practised it every day. When I met my preceptor some two years later I showed over him some ten feet, and in the same year won my first prizes in open competitions for putting, hammer-throwing, running, leaping and wrestling.

About this time I contested my first wrestling match for money. Perhaps the best all-round athlete in the Deeside district at that time was David Forbes, of Aboyne. His father was then keeper of the toll-gate of the village. At a Feeing Market at Kincardine O'Neil, Forbes was offering to wrestle anyone for £1 a side. I was then sixteen years of age, and when they urged me to take on the challenger I hung back a bit. I was, however, accompanied by a young farmer who knew what both of us could do. Well, he offered to back me, and, the preliminaries being over, we adjourned to a level spot on the turnpike to settle matters.

We wrestled five falls in the back-hold style. Forbes proved himself both smart and scientific. I was no match for him at all in science, but I had developed extraordinary strength, and I do not think my agility was a thing to be despised. Anyway, with only three minutes' interval between each fall, I won all the five falls inside twenty minutes.

On the following Christmas Day – 'Auld Yule', as it was called in the North in 1853 – I attended the games at Fordoun. I won the hammer-throwing, stone-putting, and caber-tossing contests, also the short race and high leaping.

Then at the wrestling, for which I was most eager, I met one Taylor, who had won this prize previously on many occasions, and who that day was not only surprised but also annoyed to find that a boy of 16 years could throw him sure of every fall.

After the games were over, and as we were on our way home, he asked me to have another try, as, until that time, he had never met anyone who had had the best of him at wrestling. I very willingly took him on, for I felt confident that, having beaten him at our first meeting, I was sure of success ever after. Fortune favoured me, and I was there and then able to prove to Taylor that he could never have the least chance of winning a fall.

I was still serving my time to the mason trade, but attended many of the best sports in the North during the summer months

The earliest photograph of Donald Dinnie, taken in 1855 when he was 18.
Courtesy: Suzanne Jane Griffiths (nee Dinnie)

Early Athletic Associates

In 1854 I went as a spectator to Banchory Games, then the best meeting in Aberdeenshire. I was somewhat lame, having sustained an accident at my trade, so I did not compete, but I was surprised and delighted to see there Little Willie Stewart, of Perth, a man only 5ft 6in in height, and $10^1/_2$ stone in weight. His name was known all over the country as one of the greatest putters of the day. His memorable matches v. Lait and Haggart were then much talked of in athletic circles, and undoubtedly he was the greatest putter at his weight the world has ever seen.

At Banchory the stone weighed precisely 28-lb 4oz and Stewart won easily with a great put of 32ft 5in. This on ground practically level was an extraordinary effort for a man of $10^1/_2$st [147-lb or 67kg]. I have seen him put a commercial 56-lb weight over 20ft on many occasions. He was also a first-class, short-distance runner, and latterly one of our front rank quoit players. It was in 1856, at Forfar Games, that he was seen putting against the big soldier, George Bell, who stood 6ft 4in in height, and weighed $19^1/_2$ st. He was nearly twice Stewart's weight, yet 'Little Willie' beat him by 6in. George Bell died through some accident 35 years ago, but Little Willie Stewart, of Perth, crossed the River Jordan only some nine years ago, and must have been well over 80 years old.

About the year 1856, I joined the Perth Highland Society and competed at their games that year, when I and Little Willie Stewart made a close contest at putting the stone, the former winning the first prize by one inch, and the latter the champion medal by a similar advantage. Stewart was 15 years older than I, but I do not hesitate to say that it was he who, as I kept on improving, helped me to beat him.

About this time there was another rising athlete, James Paton of Murthly, who was four years older than I, who made a close match for me for a few years.

It was often remarked that James Paton was the best looking and finest made Highlander who ever appeared on any stage. He was 6ft in his shoes and over 15st in weight. He was also one of the best Highland dancers extant, his perfectly moulded form giving him great advantage in showing the best positions.

In those days swordsmanship was looked on as one of the leading contests at Highland Games, and at this James Paton was second to none – a basket handle and a cane some 3ft long being used for the competition. The scientific feat of 'hitch and kick' was also contested at that time. It was a very attractive feat to spectators, and required a large share of agility.

James Methven, of Lundie Mill, Fife, was the leading athlete in this department. He was perhaps the most regular and consistent all-round leaper we have seen in Scotland.

His usual performances were: At high leap, from 5ft 10in to 6ft; at 'hitch and kick', from 9ft 8in to 9ft 11in; at pole-vaulting, from 10ft to 10ft 10in; at long leap with run, from 21ft to 22½ft; at 'hop, step and leap' from 46ft to 48ft. Then he often won prizes for throwing the hammer and putting the stone, and was also a first-class runner up to 440 yards. In fact, he was a splendid all-round athlete. He had an opponent who used to travel the round of the sports with him, named Tivendale; who often pushed him close, more especially at long leap and hop, step and leap.

However, during that same period Scotland's best all-round athlete was John Tait, the oldest of the athletic family of that name, who could push Methven very close at the leaping, beat him at both flat and hurdle running, and easily at all weight-throwing and feats of strength. John was all-round champion of Britain from 1846 till 1856, when his brother William took his place, showing even greater ability than John.

In the 1860s

The Northern Meeting 1860

"The great Donald Dinnie won the two hammer events, tossing the caber, putting the stones, 150 yards race and the hurdle race. The caber was 20ft long." Sir Ivan Colquhoun of Luss.

About the beginning of the Sixties the Sports Committee at Coatbridge offered a silver trophy for the best all-round athlete. This was open to all comers.

After a close and very interesting contest I proved the winner by three points, scoring 31 to Tait's 28. For many years afterwards, up to 1868, in fact, I improved so much that Tait had to be content with second place all round.

About the middle of the Sixties another – afterwards noted – athlete was beginning to show extra abilities, particularly at putting the stone and tossing the caber. This was the late James Fleming of Tullymet, who for some eight or ten years kept in the front rank with me. He was some three years younger.

In 1867, in the spring months, I contracted a severe attack of influenza, which reduced my usually good condition very much, and when he attended his first games at Maryhill that season James Fleming won both putting stones and hammer-throwing. However, though very weak, I succeeded in winning the caber-tossing and Cumberland wrestling, even against one of the best heavy-weights in England – Collins, of Newcastle. This being the largest prize offered that day, I was fortunate in having won most money for the day.

By the end of the season I had nearly regained my lost form, and kept in front ever after. My next year, 1868, was the best in my life for great feats. My first meeting with Fleming that year was at Coupar Angus, where I put a 24-lb ball, on level ground, 37ft 9in, to Fleming's 35ft 5in. James expected to win, as he said afterwards that he had improved a little during the winter, and he was greatly surprised, remarking to me: "You are away and left me with the putting altogether this year!"

During that time I easily kept my lead, and was never afterwards the least pushed at stone, hammer, caber or wrestling. It was that same year I made my greatest [high jump] effort of 6ft 1in at Turriff, Aberdeenshire. To make all correct, a level was sent for, and it was found I was rising from the ground over one inch lower than where the measure was taken. This is not a world's record leap, yet nothing better was ever done in Scotland on level ground.

Dinnie As An Innovator

It was in 1867 that I invented the present style or mode of professional hammer-throwing. Previous to this the hammer was thrown by the pendulum or figure 8 swing and with very short handles. It came about in this way. I had just recovered from a severe attack of influenza when I began to practise in the early spring, and, feeling my back became somewhat weak after I had let the hammer back in the pendulum style, it had to be suddenly pulled forward to give force to the delivery.

To save the waste of strength it struck me that by allowing the hammer to go round the same swing till delivery, it would be at least much easier for the athlete, so after a few trials I got up to my former mark, and by still persevering at this style I shot a few feet ahead of my former distance. As, however, the handle was only the usual pendulum length, it occurred to me that a few inches longer would be a great improvement, so I made one over 4ft in length. By the end of that season I had added from four to five yards to my best distance.

An early photograph of Donald Dinnie

The following year many of the best athletes adopted this new style of hammer throwing, and all admitted it was a great improvement, more especially when longer handles were supplied. It was, however, not until many years later that games committees could be persuaded to provide the long handle. The hammers of that period were similar to those used for breaking stones, or for a blacksmith's anvil; in fact, such hammers were often brought to sports meetings for use there.

At Inverness, the greatest meeting for athletic games in Scotland, which has been held annually for over a century, blacksmith's hammers were used. I supplied them with two proper round ones about 1871.

It was in 1868 that I made my great 'rut' on Lord Charles Kerr's Bowling Green, Kinoull, Perth. I put a stone weighing 16-lb 2oz 49ft 6in – equal to over 50ft with the real weight – and also made my greatest high leap of 6ft 1in. The same year I made an off-hand match with Fleming that with a 22-lb stone I would beat him 1ft 6in on level ground, and send each put over 39ft with three trials only. Fleming accepted and after the three trials each, Fleming's best was 38ft 3in, Dinnie 39ft 3in, 39ft 6in and 39ft 8in, thus losing one by 1in and winning the other by 3in.

My Other Contemporaries

It was some time after the beginning of the 1860s when another of Scotland's greatest athletes first appeared in the North. John George of Cromar, Tarland, which is in the Dee valley in Aberdeenshire, was a front-rank, all-round athlete. Putting the ball was, perhaps, his speciality, yet he was well to the front at hammer-throwing and caber-tossing, a good runner and leaper, and a fair wrestler.

He attended College some two or three years in Aberdeen. His father was at that time a contractor and builder and he took him to learn his trade. But John did not fancy hard work of that kind, so left and went south to Dumbarton and joined the police force. While at College he had found time to practise athletics, which he still kept up. He was a good model for an athlete, being about 6ft in height and close on 15st in weight, very broad shouldered and with red, rosy cheeks and very dark hair. When in his best form he could put a 22-lb ball over 38ft and a 16-lb ball 45ft on the level.

John George threw the hammer by the old pendulum style, consequently he never made a throw worthy of comparison with the present style, though he has done over 100ft with a 16-lb by the old style. He was a good caber-tosser.

Being in the police for many years, he could not attend so many sports as he might otherwise have done. It appears that he stopped competing around 1870, at which time he could beat Peter McHardy and William Tait, who were the two next ranking throwers.

Residing in Edinburgh for some time, J. George often met Owen Duffy, a great ball-putter from Ireland and who joined the police in Edinburgh about the end of the 1860s.

Duffy could put the 22-lb ball about equal to George or Fleming, but with a 16-lb ball he could beat them from three to four feet.

One day, at Tranent, he had won over Fleming by 3½ft with the light

16-lb ball though Fleming had won the heavy by 1in. Fleming remarked to Duffy that he would get his match at the 16-lb ball when he met Dinnie. Duffy replying that he would be pleased to meet him.

Duffy was a big, powerful man, standing over 6ft 2in and 17½st in weight. He had a splendid style of putting, which, combined with his stalwart build, gave him much advantage. He was said to be longing to meet and get a win over me, of whom he had heard so much. In 1871 an opportunity came.

I had engaged to appear at the games in Falkirk. On seeing this advertised, Duffy made up his mind to attend. Kenneth McRae and John Anderson also entered for that day's sports – the greatest putting day ever known to Auld Scotia.

Duffy was very particular. He insisted upon each put being measured precisely at the spot where the right foot finished the effort. The ground was particularly level, and after we had each had three trials the results were registered as follows: Dinnie, 49ft 9in; Duffy, 48ft 6in; McRae, 41ft 10in; Anderson, 41ft 8in.

However, as Duffy was dissatisfied, three other attempts were made. At the third put he was three inches over my best, the distance being precisely 50ft. Now, as you may guess, I was not going to leave matters thus. I made up my mind to have another go. I claimed the same number of trials as Duffy, and at my second put sent the ball the extraordinary distance of 50ft 6in! I was thus the victor still, with a trial in reserve. The ball weighed 16-lb. As a proof of this, I may mention the fact that McRae and Anderson, who were certainly good second-class putters, were nearly three yards behind.

Duffy and I met at some sixteen sports in all, two of which Duffy won the light ball by a few inches, though I made sure to lift the ball and send it over him with an extra trial to which Duffy did not often respond. 'Putting' was the feat at which Duffy excelled, he being only third class at any other.

Kenneth McRae was just attaining to his best athletic form at this time, but was always considered a better hammer-thrower than putter for not until a year or two later did he make his record throw of 120ft 6in with a 16-lb hammer. This was at Inverness Northern Meeting. That throw has not since been approached by any of our young athletes.

I threw the same hammer across the top of the field, where it was more level, 124ft 6in and at Golspie, on level, 130ft 6in, with three trials only.

All these throws were done with a very thick, stiff handle, as in those days handles were not prepared so well as they are now.

George Davidson, the front-rank, all-round athlete, appeared only at local sports until 1876, but that season he came out in his very best form, though only 22 years of age. We saw him putting the 22-lb ball at Coupar Angus, on level 38ft 4in, a record which he attained on several occasions during his somewhat short career.

He was generally close on me with the heavy stone, but a long way behind Duffy and me with the light stone. At hammer-throwing Davidson and McRae usually made a very close competition, the former having a shade the best at heavy and the latter at the light.

Kenneth McRae

In 1878, at Fochabers Games, 4in only divided the pair, I being 15½ft in front. At Oban Highland Gathering that same year, 4in again divided Davidson and McRae, and on that occasion I won easily, with 14ft 8in to spare, with an 18-lb hammer, though at putting a 24-lb stone I won by only 9in from Davidson. I also won the caber-tossing and wrestling easily.

James Fleming of Tullymet

I assure you, I never travelled with a more likeable or straightforward man than James Fleming of Tullymet. He was a handsome man, with fair, curly hair, and graceful in style in the arena. James stood 6ft in his shoes, and weighed close upon 15st. He was three years younger than I, and in his forty-eighth year when he died.

It was in the year 1870 that the Caledonian clubs of America, recognising my athletic abilities, invited me to contend against the best of the American and Canadian athletes. I was not slow to accept the invitation, and set sail, in company with George Mitchell, then the Chief of the New York Caledonian Club, by the S.S. Anglia, of the Anchor Line. I was readily engaged by all the principal Caledonian clubs in the United States and Canada, and was well paid for my trouble. In fact, it was like exhibitions, as I had usually but small effort to make to win, except at the running and leaping, and I generally won from twelve to sixteen events at each meeting.

An American Tour

This section is introduced by an unnamed old schoolmate of Donald Dinnie, working in conjunction with E. Stewart Smith, editor of Health and Strength Magazine. It was written some 85 years before this book. The compilers of this book in 1999 note that there is another report, circa 1900, which seems to indicate R. R. McLennan's exhibition related below may be from the tour of 1872 rather than Dinnie's first relatively short visit in 1870. However Dinnie did compete in Toronto during his first tour, attracting a crowd of some 15,000. Our research continues.

It should be mentioned that our champion met one great athlete at Toronto who hailed from Glengarry, Canada. He was undoubtedly the greatest hammer-thrower by the 'run' or 'turn' ever seen. The Caledonian Club rules are the same as in Scotland, but they sometimes offer extra prizes for the 'turning' style to get the great R. R. McLennan to exhibit.

McLennan did not compete at the 'fairstand' style with others, but along with a brother gave an exhibition at the 'turning' style, both at hammer and weight-throwing. The Caledonian Club rules state that the hammer head must be the precise weight without the handle, which at that date did not weigh less than from 1½-lb to 2½-lb as they were very thick though only 4ft long.

At their exhibition R. R. McLennan threw the heavy hammer, which must have weighed, including handle, close to 24-lb, the wonderful distance of 130ft 4in. The same weight with a wire handle, similar to the amateurs', would have been sent by the same effort close to 160ft.

The light hammer, with a similar handle, must have weighed about 18-lb, which he sent 179ft. Bear in mind, these feats were done with little effort, as he had only a younger brother against him, who was some 30ft behind.

They then gave an exhibition at throwing the 56-lb weight by the turning style, when R. R. McLennan took only one try and though the weight was only a commercial one, with one small ring, without taking off his coat and with one turn only, sent it 37ft 6in. There is not the least doubt but that, by a weight with chain, as used in Scotland, he could easily have thrown it over 50ft. Yet we are told by our Scottish would-be record takers that 34ft 1in is the world record because it was made in Scotland.

Donald Dinnie picks up the story again.

The same day, at Toronto C.C. Games, I won the 56-lb weight-throwing 'fair-stand' at 26ft 9in, the ring being too small for a proper effort. I also won the heavy and light hammers, heavy and light stones, caber-tossing, wrestling, 100 yards race, and high leap. The committee and spectators also were somewhat disappointed that they could not see a real contest between me and their native McLennan.

It may be remembered by some of our old athletic-inclined countrymen that close on 50 years back one named Thomas Rice or Jarmey came to Scotland and challenged all comers at throwing a 12-lb hammer in the 'turning style'. As turning had been stopped through an unfortunate accident, in which two gentlemen were hit. Thomas Rice could find no opponent except old John Tait, who had just retired in favour of his brother William. But as John had practised the 'turn' in his day, he accepted the challenge, and the match took place on the Stonefield Recreation Grounds, Glasgow. Rice, being a one-handed thrower, would only use a 12-lb hammer, and allowed 12ft to Tait, he being a veteran.

This was all right had they shown up on equal terms, but, though Tait came to the mark with the usual stiff ash handle, not over 4ft in length, Rice had his handle rolled up like a ball in his pocket, some 5ft long, and a knob at the end to keep the hand from slipping, so, there being no restrictions about handles, Rice won easily by 11ft.

Under the circumstances however, Tait could not be expected to rest satisfied, and he tried hard for a return match with common wooden handles. Rice however, refused to give away his chance so J. Tait started to practise with the whip handle, and during the same season

The Caledonian Club of San Francisco's games at Sausalito on May 23, 1868

made a second match on even terms, and won by several feet, thus proving that it is the handle mainly and not the weight that makes the distance.

Rice, finding no other opponent at this style, left the following season for America. On hearing of R. R. McLennan, he at once put out a challenge to all-comers to throw a 12-lb hammer. This challenge was at once accepted by McLennan, who, though not in practise with such light hammers, understood the advantage of the long thin handle.

Though Rice had all as he desired, McLennan won by over 30ft. Aye, and without exerting himself. It is quite safe to say that no one who ever lived could take so little as a 30ft start and have the least chance of a win. McLennan was a miracle at his own speciality, having practised this style until he could turn steady, getting faster, each turn till the last effort, when the hammer left his hand as if fired from a cannon. He was certainly the most wonderful hammer-thrower by the turn the world has ever seen.

Canada's Wonder

George McKenzie Ross, who spent some six or eight years among the American athletes, corroborates my statement that if R. R. McLennan had used a wire handle with lead head, similar to that used by the amateurs, he could have thrown a 16-lb hammer over 220ft on level ground. He was made all over an athlete, standing 6ft 4in, and weighing 17st, and could do over 20ft at long leap. He had a brother who stood 6ft 4in and weighed 18½st who could put the weights better than Rory. He had, however, to give in to James Fleming, our Perthshire athlete, by nearly 2ft. To him, as well as to McLennan, I have previously alluded.

I met several good athletes in America on my first visit. These included Thomas Russell, one of our best vaulters and leapers in Scotland during the Sixties, and also Thomas Aitken, the front rank hop, step and leaper, whom I met at Boston, where the greatest Caledonian Games in the world are held. I also met John Anderson, the noted ball putter of Edinburgh, on several occasions, and John Mackay, a noted weight thrower during the Sixties and beginning of the Seventies. He was a native of Argyleshire.

I returned from America by the SS Columbia of the Anchor Line, after an extraordinary rough passage of 19 days between New York and Glasgow. I was very sick, and unable to eat one meal all the way. Though when I left I was in my usual good form, weighing 220-lb, I arrived in Glasgow weighing only 195-lb. I was, of course, very weak, and not until after some eight months' regular training did I get back my lost condition.

A New Decade

In June 1871, I was again the leader of athletics all over the United Kingdom. J. Fleming took a trip to America that season, and I had no particularly close opponents at putting the ball except Owen Duffy.

William Fleming, a distant relation of the famous James, was well up at the throwing feats, and also tossing the caber.

There were also William Bremner, from Aberdeenshire, and G. Glen, a soldier, who were both well up at stone and hammer-throwing. They generally made a very close match. Their average distance with a 16-lb hammer was 110ft and with a 16-lb ball 43ft. William McCombie Smith, a middle-weight athlete, sometimes in absence of a better came in for a third place, but could rarely pass 100ft with the 16-lb hammer, and 37ft with a 16-lb putting ball. One heavy-weight athlete who sometimes came close to Fleming at stone, hammer and caber, also at leaping, about that date, was Donald McDonald, of Murthly. He was a man of about 6ft in height, and 15st in weight, growing steadily heavier until around 1907 and still competing, he weighed 17st [238-lb – nearly 109 kg].

Fleming and Dinnie in their early touring days

In 1872 Fleming and I, finding America the best place for athletes and money, made arrangements to again visit that country, this time together. We were both engaged by all the Caledonian Clubs. We were paid a good salary for the use of our names, and all we could win in prizes. I generally won at leaping and short distance running, averaging from 12 to 16 first prizes at each meeting and Fleming in most cases, made sure of a close second.

Before this season was more than halfway through an unfortunate accident befell me at Buffalo Caledonian Club Games, where I contested in the pole-vaulting competition. By losing my balance when crossing the bar I sprained my left

hand and wrist very severely, thus spoiling my work to a very considerable extent for the remainder of that season.

This accident happened in the second week of August, and many of the best sports of the season were yet to follow, so that I was not a little disappointed at being so put out. My friend, Fleming, had to take my place and do his best to support the fame of Scotland's athletes. Jamie did well, and only on one occasion did he lose one of the laurels which might have been won by me. This was at Toronto, where he met the great R. R. McLennan, of Glengarry, who won the heavy hammer by some 6ft from Fleming. But Jamie had his revenge by winning against him at both heavy and light putting balls and caber-tossing.

With my left arm still in a sling, I tried only the light hammer with one hand, for which McLennan did not compete, and I won easily by 7ft. Fleming did not suffer any reverses after that till the end of the season, and by then I was putting the weights, as well as throwing the light hammer. However, my sprained wrist did not fully recover till next year.

We left America on our return journey with more gold in our pockets than we could have found in Britain in three seasons. We went out by the Cunard SS Scotia, the only paddle steamer crossing the Atlantic. Before leaving Liverpool we were engaged to give exhibitions at the opening of the Sefton Park, where two days' sports were held. We returned by the Anchor Line to Glasgow in October, and, after getting clear of the seaweed, we toured through Britain in the music hall line, challenging all comers at feats of strength.

William McCombie Smith

It was about this date that the middle-weight, W. McCombie Smith, while practising with me, his tutor, expressed the opinion that he could throw a hammer a greater distance, in comparison to his weight, than any other man. I replied that I was quite ready to match him on that condition.

"And how much do you say I should give you of a start with a 16-lb hammer?" I said to Smith.

After calculating it over, Smith said "You should give me 28ft."

"All right," said I, "I'll give you, say, 30ft and we can throw the match on the level mound at Banff, at McLeod's Games, and let it be for only £1 a side to suit your purse."

The match was duly advertised to take place at Banff, as proposed. The competition was left open to all comers. There were several entries, and a very large crowd turned out to witness the sports. Smith and I were well prepared for our match. Smith having practised some six weeks with my thin, hickory-handled hammer, which weighed precisely 16-lb 2oz. It being an open competition, three trials each only were allowed, and Smith reached the creditable distance (for his weight) of 99ft 8in. I proved too much for him, however, for at my third effort I got up to 133ft 10½in, still nearly 5ft short of my best record with the same hammer I had used at Coupar Angus.

Smith was not at all pleased at the result of this match, as he had not seen me doing my best records, and did not believe I had so much to spare. Anyhow, I tempted him with a 33ft start, but he had lost enough. The fact is, at that date I could easily beat anyone according to weight. My style was very similar to that of our present all-round champion, John McKenzie, and his agility has been compared to mine. Then close on 2st more weight of muscle is much to be reckoned on at hammer-throwing.

Donald Dinnie's personal writings conclude here, but he provided much of the information which follows. Direct quotes are given where these were recorded and whenever possible contemporary features and eye-witness accounts form the basis of our work.

America Once More

Donald Dinnie made a third trip to North America, appearing there in 1882 and 1883. In 1882 he won the all-round athletic championship of America at Lucknow, Canada. The best of seven events was needed to win, but Dinnie annexed the whole seven and, in addition, won a 100yd scratch race.

Robert C. M. Auld of New York, who knew the Dinnie family well, wrote in a letter to the Sun on 10th December 1935 that the tour was managed for Dinnie by the late James Kennedy. Such personal correspondence often contains interesting information and this one states that Donald Dinnie never drank anything but milk from the bar.

In the same season of 1882 the great athlete won the important Police Gazette Championship Medal for mixed style wrestling. These were considered world championships by many people, not least by Richard K. Fox, the flamboyant publisher of the Police Gazette. The competition was held at Plainfield, New Jersey, with Dinnie winning four of the five styles contested with Duncan C. Ross and Captain J. Daly. Later during the same season he, along with D. C. Ross, matched two noted athletes, Messrs Lynch and Daly, for an all-round athletic contest at Philadelphia and it turned out an easy win for the Scottish Champions.

Duncan C. Ross, who teamed up with Dinnie

Dinnie and Ross attended all the principal Caledonian Club meetings. With the exception of the first, when Dinnie was only a few days off his sea voyage and out of form, he invariably won all heavy-weight events, including wrestling.

The games held at Boston at that time were regarded as the largest and best Caledonian meeting in the world. The open prizes were from £10 to £15 for each first and £5 to £25 for each second. In addition to all the prizes they could win, the leading athletes were also paid from $100 to $500 in appearance money, depending on their advertising value.

On the morning following the games a Boston Herald contributor wrote: "Donald Dinnie is the champion of the world in throwing heavy weights, wrestling, etc. He is a man of splendid physique and, although all the noted athletes of America were present, they became diminutive when compared with him."

It must be borne in mind that this was 12 years after the champion had first contested at Boston Caledonian Games in his best form, when he won several leaping and running events, as well as heavy feats and dancing.

The Montreal Caledonian Club games was also a highlight of the season. All the finest athletes attended, including Dinnie, Ross and McDonald. The leading paper remarked that "Donald Dinnie, the world's champion athlete, was present, and maintained his reputation by winning all the principal events on the programme against the best athletes of America."

A Tricky Situation

After the Caledonian games were finished for the season, Dinnie received an offer from the Thistle Club, San Francisco, to attend their games of 1883, and, after fixing terms with them, he made arrangements to give exhibitions of weight-lifting, etc, at all the principal music halls on his long journey to California.

The first incident worthy of mention was at St Louis, where he had two weeks' engagement at a fair salary per week. After the first week's show Donald did not call for his pay till Monday night. He was then told that Thursday was pay day, but an advance could be given at a charge of 25 per cent. Donald, in his usual outspoken way, said he could not stand that as "it would be like a swindle". At this the proprietor pulled out his pistol, saying: "Do you call me a swindler?"

Donald Dinnie, not to be messed with.
Courtesy: Caledonian Club San Francisco

But as he took aim Donald coolly hit the pistol with such sudden force that it landed at the other end of the saloon.

However, as Donald observed a waiter lifting the pistol, no doubt to return it to the landlord, he thought it the best part of valour to walk from the presence of such a dangerous character. He left and called on a friend who, like himself, belonged to Deeside, Aberdeenshire and was chief of the Caledonian Club of St. Louis. After hearing Dinnie's account of the pistol attack, Mr Mitchell objected to his returning to the hall and offered any money he required to continue his journey across the States. He also made terms with Dinnie to return from California to attend their Caledonian Club games the following season.

Although a peace-loving man, Donald Dinnie was always prepared to meet trouble half way and in his earlier days he might not have been able to walk away.

Dinnie described an encounter with the noted pugilistic champion Jem Mace. "Jem," he said "was with a circus company at Stonehaven, and began blackguarding us Scotch folk. He was angry about something, and called us all the nasty things he could lay his tongue to." Dinnie accepted Mace's challenge and the fighting rules of those days, such as they were, included a blend of wrestling and boxing.

"I knew I had no chance against Mace if he got a fair smack at me, but I managed to slip in behind him and get a good hold. Then I lifted him up like a baby and dashed him face downward on the ground. That settled Jem for the time being and he talked quite civilly when he got his wind again." Yes, such treatment could have quite a calming effect.

Jem Mace, pioneer of gloved boxing

Jem Mace was born in Beeston, Norfolk, on 8th April 1831. He was one of four brothers, three of whom were blacksmiths. Jem became a cabinet-maker by trade but led a very varied life, becoming an itinerant fiddler. Travelling to fairgrounds with his dog and violin, he learned boxing in the booths and at the age of 24 could hold his own with almost anyone regardless of weight.

Though he was often described as a Romany or gypsy, his family denied there were any such links in their past. Mace first won the British middle-weight crown and later, on 18th June 1861, became the British heavyweight champion. He went on to many international victories overseas and was recognised as a very important world champion, being a pivotal figure in the change from bare-fist prize fighting to the widespread use of gloves, from 1863-1885. Without doubt as a scientific boxer he was well ahead of all his rivals and he did more to foster boxing as an art than any man of that era.

Held in the highest esteem, he fought and promoted in the Antipodes, America and England, being at his peak around 1870, although quoted as being world champion 1883-1885.

He remained active and continued to challenge in booths at fairs or circuses, dying nearing 79 years of age on 30th November 1910.

As Donald now had a week to spare, and was then a widower (Elizabeth Birss Dinnie died at Auchenblae, Aberdeenshire, on 18th November 1882), Mr Mitchell introduced him to a nice, young, rich widow, with over £30,000 in cash. Though she seemed pleased with her new acquaintance, Donald did not care to cultivate his opportunity lest she might imagine he was only in love with her fortune. At that time he had never been very hard up. He may later have hankered after a life of health and prosperity, instead of the hardship that was his lot after his return to Scotland in 1899.

However, to continue his tour through the United States, he duly arrived at Kansas City, the home of Clarence Whistler, then the champion catch-as-catch-can and Graeco-Roman wrestler of America. He and Tom Cannon travelled together for some time, giving exhibitions, though Tom admitted Whistler had the better of him at these two styles.

Dinnie and the latter met at his own native city when Dinnie offered to win ten falls by the Scotch style, while Whistler gained five by the catch-as-catch-can style. The match took place in the Colosseum and, unfortunately for Whistler, Dinnie threw him so hard in his third fall that his right arm was dislocated at the shoulder. A doctor came on the stage and pulled it in again, and he gamely started to wrestle again. But, Dinnie being in great form that night, some two falls later, he doubled Whistler back, and, falling on him, put out his knee joint. After the injury was put right Whistler was plucky enough to try again, but his seconds, on seeing his knee swollen, took him away, and, of course, the match was awarded to Dinnie.

Dinnie then journeyed west to Denver, Colorado, where he exhibited for a week, and had a joyful reunion with several old Scottish friends. He then took a train for Salt Lake City, en route for California. After visiting the lake, with its briny waters, he passed over the Rocky Mountains, or rather through them, as many miles near the top are like passing through a long tunnel, being covered alternately with wood and rock. After leaving the heights and running down the Californian side, he passed the memorable gold diggings of that state, and then Sacramento, which was once a famous centre in connection with the diggings.

Dinnie's first engagement, however, being with the Thistle Club of San Francisco, he passed on and arrived a few days before the games. He first installed himself comfortably in the popular Russ House, in Montgomery Street, and while looking round for the secretary of the Thistle Club he met William Muldoon, the Graeco-Roman wrestler, whom he had before met in the East.

William Muldoon was America's Father of Wrestling. The historian Nat Fleischer, hailed him as 'the first Idol of Wrestliana'. Muldoon's parents came from Galway, Ireland, although he was born in Belfast, New York, on 25th May 1845. At 15 he fought in the American Civil war and then the Franco-Persian war and on returning to America, from 1876 to 1881, he became a policeman. He was vociferously supported by his colleagues at all matches and a German champion grumbled: "To beat Muldoon I would have to throw the whole police force of New York City."

From 1880 he was recognised in America as the World Champion, having victories over Thebaud Bauer, Andre Christol, Prof Miller, Tom Cannon and other leading wrestlers of that time. Muldoon wrestled several draws with Clarence Whistler, his greatest rival. At his best wrestling weight of 200-lb, Muldoon was a fine specimen of manhood, strong, fast and agile – qualities he cherished until he retired from wrestling in 1887. He was an honest, robust dominator, still in fine shape when he died in his 88th year.

Muldoon, who was engaged as 'Charles the Wrestler' at a theatre, proposed a wrestling match with Dinnie and he, knowing Muldoon was not such a powerful wrestler as Whistler, agreed to a match on similar conditions to those on which he wrestled the latter. They met next day at a newspaper office to settle preliminaries and lay a deposit. The match was for £50 a side.

Unfortunately for Dinnie, it was found that no date would suit Muldoon's engagements so well as the evening of the Thistle Club games day. Dinnie had there to meet all comers at throwing the hammer, putting the stone, tossing the caber, leaping, wrestling, etc. However, as Dinnie did not want to miss a chance of meeting Muldoon, he agreed to wrestle, and undertook to throw Muldoon twice for his once at Scotch and Graeco-Roman styles, or ten falls to Muldoon's five.

William Muldoon – American Wrestling Champion

The Grand Opera House was engaged for the match, and although the largest in the city except for the Pavilion, there was no room for more than two-thirds of the attendance. The lowest admission was two dollars and some £900 was taken.

£320 in One Day

The match proved very exciting, each doing his utmost to win the fall in the shortest time possible. After the first three falls on each side, Dinnie was much ahead with time, but had difficulty in countering Muldoon's strangleholds, a move banned in other wrestling codes. Being tired out by his big day's exertions at the games, the Scot was getting much slower towards the end.

The result was that when Muldoon had won five falls in the Graeco-Roman style, Dinnie had won nine in the Scotch style, and failed by only three seconds to gain the tenth. One account of the match said that Dinnie threw his opponent for the winning fall as the gong sounded. Officially, a result which Donald accepted without complaint, Muldoon won the match. Dinnie's mistake was allowing too much of a handicap after such a hard day's work. But he at least had the satisfaction of pocketing his record takings for athletics in one day – £320. At Boston the year previous he had earned £220 for one day's games alone. And this at a time when a farm labourer was paid around 10 shillings a week.

A historic photograph of Davidson & Dinnie about 100 years ago

Dinnie some time later arranged a mixed wrestling match with an Irish-American named Nolan at the best of the three styles: catch-as-catch-can, collar-and-elbow, and American side-holds. This also took place in the Grand Opera House, for £50 a side, but drew only a fair house, as it was generally expected that Nolan was no match for Dinnie. Sure enough, Dinnie won with straight falls.

Although Donald Dinnie was now in this 47th year, he was in great form, so since the California climate is one of the best all the year round, Dinnie proposed leaving a few American all-comers records behind him. It was arranged that these should be attempted on a level green on the Mission of San Francisco. The editor of the principal sporting paper of the west coast arranged for six capable, experienced judges to authenticate weights, levels, measurements etc, and Dinnie left at least two records which American athletes aimed to exceed for a long time after.

Record-making

The Caledonian Club rules of those days stated the 16-lb hammer-head must weigh precisely that, so with a stiff 4ft handle the weight would have been close to 18-lb and the handle, being shorter than the preferred length, also reduced the possible distances.

At that time the record was only 102ft, made by D. C. Ross, in New York. Here Dinnie made 113ft 8in on the Mission under American rules, and his hammer being $^1/_4$-lb overweight makes it even better.

With the 56-lb weight he did a standing throw of 29ft 7in and, contrary to the present rules, neither foot was moved until after the weight was delivered. This beat his old world record of 29ft 3in, done with this style. Instead of a weight with ball and chain, a standard commercial block ring weight was used, the overall length being under 14in. Using the more common triangular handle and chain, and still with the standing style, Dinnie had thrown 56-lb a distance of 40ft 6in.

Some of Donald's records were not recognised in Scotland for various reasons. The most legitimate of these was that the powers that be did not have access to the documentattion regarding the level of the ground and weighing of the implements. It was good publicity when records were broken and Dinnie's records made it difficult for other athletes at the time to earn any exposure. An old school pal, whose name unfortunately was not recorded at the time, waxed eloquent in Health and Strength Magazine about the ludicrous situation in Scotland where the record with the 56-lb was said to be 34ft 1in. This ignored the fact that those such as Rory McLennan in Canada and many Americans had greatly exceeded this figure. Big Rory would get all three attempts over

45ft in most competitions and would have many backers to beat 50ft using a chain and triangle 56, as was used in Scotland at that time. There was a general recognition of the need for accurate weights and level ground, but Dinnie's supporters emphasised the importance of the type, lengths and shapes of the handles and weights. He pointed out that just prior to the turn of the century, George Hardy Johnstone of Aberdeen did a 16-lb hammer throw of 119ft $1^1/_2$ in at Stirling in a record attempt with a common iron head and stiff wooden handle. Eight years later Alexander Anthony Cameron of Lochaber, for some reason always called A. A. Cameron, did 122ft 10in with a hammer of the same weight. But this implement had a compact, lead head and a thin cane handle, ideal for long throws.

By this date the passing of the years had taken its toll on Johnstone and his hammer was usually around 109-111ft, yet with the same pliable shaft and smaller hammer head, he managed to throw 119ft 3in, thus improving on his previous best. It was thought that with such a hammer at the height of his powers Johnstone could have thrown around 127ft. He was thought to be the best hammer thrower between the time of Donald Dinnie and World War One.

G. H. Johnstone of Aberdeen

James Morrison, of Partick, was another first class hammer-thrower

James Morrison

for a few years, and about the beginning of 1900 he pushed Johnstone close before he began to fail. However, Morrison did not keep up his good form long, and after his marriage in 1901 he did not attend to his training properly, and fell back a few yards at the hammer.

He improved considerably for a spell around 1910 but never repeated his old records. Like Johnstone, Morrison was a fine physical specimen, 6ft tall, 16st and with a 45in chest. He could easily have doubled for Johnstone.

Morrison was born on 7th July 1874 at Drumore, Killearn, Stirlingshire. On leaving school he became a farm hand and until the age of 20 was a ploughman, like his father William before him. He moved to Clydebank to join the Dunbartonshire Police on 17th November 1894 but left on 15th August 1895 to become a blacksmith. He rejoined the police on 9th May 1898, this time at Partick, a Glasgow precinct, which greatly encouraged athletes. As a constable he received £1.20 weekly and by 1910 he was getting £1.65 per week. He claimed a world record in hammer throwing in 1901 and was also good at Cumberland wrestling and caber tossing. He began competing at wrestling in 1895 and moved on to the Highland heavy events. He competed very successfully throughout Scotland in what was a boom period for the games and his competitions with G. H. Johnstone were considered classics.

For a short period tights were allowed instead of kilts and Morrison's bright red tights showed off his massive legs, with thighs measuring 26½in and calves 18in. He was 6ft tall and weighed 16 stones. A newspaper in the summer of 1908 reported him appearing at the Games Park, Lochy Bridge, Thornton, Fife, one of the best attended Highland games for a great many years. The report says that 70,000 attended and although Morrison was by then well past his prime, many came to see him throw the hammer as one of the most famous athletes in Scotland.

After retiral from the sporting arena he became a much respected judge at Highland games. He lived in Clydebank, where he died in 1945.

About the end of July, 1883, Dinnie and Duncan A. McMillan, his closest opponent on the West Coast of America at weight-throwing, wrestling, etc, after attending Stockton and Sacramento Caledonian games, took a train for the East, calling at Leadville and Denver, Colorado. There Dinnie wrestled two mixed matches with an elder brother of McMillan. The champion won two straight falls in the first, and two from three in the second.

They then made for St Louis Caledonian Club games, where they annexed first and second prizes in all the principal events. As usual, Dinnie came out on top. As they had engaged to give exhibitions in the northern part of the West Coast, they returned by train direct to San Francisco, then took a steamer for Portland, Oregon, where they first attended games. Dinnie again won all weight-throwing events, wrestling, etc. They then gave exhibitions in the Portland Theatre of Varieties.

The athletes went north by Tacomba, Seattle, and Victoria, British Columbia, wrestling several matches in the Cornish and collar-and-elbow styles at various games. After meeting Muldoon in an exhibition match at Portland, they returned to

OGDEN'S CIGARETTES

Donald even appeared on cigarette cards
Courtesy: David Horne

San Francisco, where Dinnie was engaged to give exhibitions of dumb-bell lifting and dancing for ten minutes on Sunday afternoons, his remuneration being five dollars per minute.

There he met several Scotsmen from the Australian Colonies, who strongly advised him to make a tour of the southern hemisphere. Believing he could make it a profitable tour, about a month later he set sail for Honolulu and Auckland, leaving the steamer at Auckland to catch one at Onehunga for the South Island of New Zealand. The object was to arrive in good time for the Dunedin Caledonian Club Games in 1884, where they held three days' sports. Although it rained hard on all three days, they took more money at the gates than at any previous meeting, which was no doubt owing to the announcement that the world's champion all-round athlete was engaged to attend.

Down Under With Donald

Dinnie's first engagement in New Zealand was at Ashburton with the Caledonian Society sports, held on 17th December 1883. There he received £25 appearance money and won eight prizes worth about £20.

In those days the first week of the New Year was looked on as a holiday week in New Zealand, the principal attraction being the annual Caledonian Society's games at Dunedin. The town, one of the largest in the most populous district, had more Scottish inhabitants than any other part of New Zealand. They flocked from all parts of the South Island to attend the New Year Sports at Dunedin, and as the best prizes were offered there, the leading athletes came to compete.

Donald Dinnie's terms were £50 for his name to be advertised and the chance of all prizes he could win. He won all the weight throwing events each day – that is, stone, hammer and caber – with ease, some 18 firsts in all. He left the wrestling to be divided among the local men, which was won on the last day by William Hudson, from Cumberland. He was only a middle-weight, yet a very scientific wrestler in Cumberland style.

Dinnie had over £90 for his share at the games. Afterwards he got a three-style wrestling match fixed with the winner at the sports. This came off in the Music Hall two weeks later, when Dinnie won easily. Hudson was hurt during the second fall and had to retire. With stakes and a share of house, the winner pocketed £50 10s.

At Dunedin his engagement fee was £50 and the chance of wins, which amounted to over £40. This was his most profitable day in New Zealand. Then at Balclutha he was engaged for a Scottish concert at £15 for one ten-minute turn. From there he went to Riverton Caledonian

Games, where he won ten first prizes and was paid £25. Then the Invercargill Caledonian Society paid him £25 for his name, and he won eight first prizes, to the value of £30. The same evening he wrestled H. Harper, of local fame, and won easily by two straight falls.

His next engagement was at Blue Spur, where he received £15 for his name and won ten first prizes. Wyndham Caledonian Society's games was his next engagement, for which he received £25 and won nine first prizes. His next was at Palmerston Caledonian Sports, where he was paid £15 and won nine first prizes. For appearing at a concert at Gore he was paid £20. At Riverside Caledonian Games he was paid £16, then at Lumsden he got £20 appearance money and won ten first prizes.

A rare life study of Donald

Dinnie then journeyed north by Otago for the Oamaru Caledonian Sports, where he was paid £20 and won 15 events, amounting to close on £30. Timaru was his next engagement, where he made £35, winning over a dozen first prizes.

The Christchurch Caledonian Society organised a special day's sports for Donald Dinnie that he might exhibit his wonderful powers there before leaving New Zealand. He received £35 for his name and the chance of all he could win in prizes, which amounted to £28.

In the wrestling he beat a big 260-lb Maori[1], who had won at Dunedin 15 years in succession.

Donald made preparations to visit by first boat the land of the kangaroo. Before leaving he did not forget to send a substantial cheque home to the less fortunate members of his family in Scotland. This had been his aim when leaving his country some two years earlier. In addition to the financial support to his family, he also deposited some £400 in

[1]Perhaps it was 19th century racism, but the reporters thought it was not necessary to give the Maori's proper name.

the bank at $7^1/_2$ per cent interest and, transactions completed, sailed from the Bluff for Melbourne about the middle of March 1884, calling at Hobart, Tasmania, during the journey.

A few days after arriving in Melbourne on 22nd March 1884 he began his engagement with Pickersgill and Willis, giving exhibitions of weightlifting in the Victoria Hall, and within a week he was challenged by Professor William Miller for a match at dumbbell lifting. Miller is now recognised as the Father of Australian Physical Culture and was then champion of Australia at weightlifting and wrestling in the Graeco-Roman style.

He was not a professor in the university sense but a great teacher and master of his arts. He always signed himself Professor Miller, champion athlete of the world.

Miller was born in Cheshire, England, in 1846, and went to Australia in 1851. As an adult he travelled the world competing in boxing, wrestling, weightlifting, even fencing (his father had been an English fencing champion) and long distance walking. In USA in 1879 he walked 102 miles in 24 hours. His gym at 216 Swanston St, Melbourne, was the colony's prime fitness facility, accepted by people from many

Prof. William Miller, the 'father of Australian Physical Culture'

walks of life. His best lift was a two-hands anyhow with 160-lb in right hand and 60-lb in his left. At 37 he was 5ft 9in, 191-lb (87 kg) and had a 41in chest. Miller died in Baltimore in 1939.

Dinnie accepted his challenge and they met to settle preliminaries. It was agreed that the stakes should be £50 a side, and each to choose five feats of strength with dumbbells.

Miller's feats were: Putting up a one-handed dumbbell at five different weights: 120-lb, 130-lb, 140-lb, 150-lb and 160-lb, the number of times from shoulder to stretch of arms to count.

Dinnie chose: supporting a 56-lb dumbbell on palm of hand, arm horizontal, against time; pushing up two 56-lb dumbbells, one in each hand, to stretch of arms, number of times; pushing up a two-handed dumbbell above head, number of times, of 220-lb weight; same feat with dumbbell weighing 230-lb; same feat with dumbbell weighing 240-lb.

The match took place in the Melbourne Exhibition Buildings, and drew perhaps the largest crowd ever seen at a dumbbell lifting match, as £671 5s was taken for admission.

Great Weightlifting and Wrestling

The match caused great excitement, and all through the different trials of strength Dinnie, though the stranger, was the favourite. Although Miller failed to equal Dinnie at either of his own feats, and Dinnie put up his opponent's 120-lb dumbbell twice oftener than Miller, the referee decided that Miller's style was better, and gave him the decision. Then, again, at the 140-lb dumbbell, Miller did six times and failed at his seventh attempt, while Dinnie, amid great applause, put it straight up seven times. The referee again gave Miller the verdict on style.

At the last trial, the 160-lb dumbbell, Miller put it up to stretch of arm once, and left it, expecting Dinnie would fail at this weight; but Dinnie, after rubbing his hand with turpentine[1], with one pull snatched the weight straight to arms length overhead.

However, Monsieur Victor, the referee, again decided that Miller's style was the fairest and best. So the match ended in a draw, at which Dinnie was much dissatisfied. He pushed Miller hard for another match at the same feats with a different referee, but Miller would not agree.

Subsequently, however, he agreed to wrestle Dinnie a match, for £50

[1]Highland Games athletes still have their own special home-made preparations to assist in obtaining a firm grip. The most popular, known as 'tacky', is made by mixing melted resin with Venice turpentine.

a side, at Graeco-Roman and Scottish styles, three falls at each. The Exhibition building was again secured for this match, at the rent of £100. As a referee to satisfy all concerned could not easily be found, Prof. Miller again chose Monsieur Victor. Dinnie, however, chose J. Thomas, a noted Cumberland wrestler, to act on his behalf, and if any disagreement occurred a third party to decide.

Miller stood 5ft 9in, and weighed over 17st, while Dinnie stood 6ft and weighed as usual 15st 10-lb of bone and hard muscle. They tossed for choice of first style, and on winning Miller chose the Graeco-Roman.

As soon as time was called, they clasped each other and Dinnie lifted his opponent up and swung him round, but could only put him on all fours. Miller then tried hard to pull Dinnie over, but found it a hard job. He reversed his hold many times, but Dinnie was quick to evade, and on getting clear he several times lifted Miller bodily and swung him in space, but failed to turn him properly over on the required two points. Dinnie then tried to roll Miller over by the half-nelson, but failed. Miller got a good hold on his opponent's arm and pulled him down on one shoulder. By gradually pushing all his weight on his chest he wore the other shoulder to the carpet, thus winning the first fall in nine minutes.

The next fall was in the 'Scotch' style, as they called it in those days, and Dinnie won it cleverly in 30sec. The third was in the Graeco-Roman style, which, after a severe and lengthened struggle of over 15min, was won by Miller. The next fall being Scotch, Dinnie again won easily inside 30sec. The third and last fall at Graeco-Roman was a surprise and misfortune for Miller. After the usual five minutes' rest, Dinnie appeared to come out very fresh, and as time was called he rushed in and lifted Miller clean over his head, and, turning quickly round, endeavoured to throw him on his back, but he came down on one leg with such force that the bone was broken at the ankle. Dinnie at first was inclined to rush on top and put the two shoulders down, but on seeing Miller's plight he stood back and called for a doctor at once.

After the doctor's inspection, a door was obtained, and Miller was taken to the dressing-room, Dinnie being foremost to assist with the trouble. Thus the match ended in a win for Dinnie, and he allowed the stakes to remain at the Sportsman office for a deciding match.

The deciding wrestling match took place in April 1884, with a record crowd. Miller was given the verdict but although not publicly making a fuss the Scot was not at all happy with Australian refereeing. The same month Dinnie was engaged for the Scottish games held on the Melbourne Cricket Ground, where he made some extraordinary perfor-

DONALD DINNIE

WILLIAM MILLER

WRESTLING CONTEST BETWEEN
PROFESSOR WILLIAM MILLER AND DONALD DINNIE
THE AUSTRALIAN AND SCOTTISH CHAMPIONS.

"MELBOURNE 1884"

mances at weight-throwing; in fact, not far short of what he did with similar weights in his best day, some 17 years previous.

Five pounds and a gold medal were offered for throwing the 16-lb hammer, and, to encourage entries, the champion had to allow all comers a 20ft start. The hammer weighed precisely 16-lb and had a rather stiff handle, only 4ft over all.

His nearest opponent, a young blacksmith from the country, registered 92ft, while Dinnie's third throw measured 126ft 6in. This, considering the short handle, was not many feet short of his best.

At putting the stone he made 39ft 9in with the heavy, and 49ft 6in with the light. The stones were found to weigh respectively 21-lb and 15-lb, but the ground was quite level.

Dinnie also won throwing the 56-lb weight, tossing the caber, hurdle race and 120 yards handicap from scratch; winning also the high leap, and first for wrestling. He was awarded the prize for the best all-round athlete, winning ten events in all. He gave one exhibition throw of the same hammer, 16-lb and made 144½ft with two turns.

He next wrestled a match with Monsieur Victor, in the latter's own style (Graeco-Roman) in the Victoria Hall, Melbourne. Dinnie easily won two straight falls in three minutes.

The champion then went travelling with Pickersgill and Willis's Company to Geelong, Ballarat and Allandale, also through Gippsland, winning 16 contests for weight-lifting and wrestling.

Then came trouble with the manager of the company. To save time and the expense of a lawsuit, Dinnie engaged the company on his own behalf, and toured the remainder of Victoria and New South Wales to Sydney, drawing crowded houses in every town along the way.

On 9th December 1885 Donald married Melbourne actress Eleanor Bagley in her home town. Donald was 24 years her senior.

Their daughter, Eva Lena Ida Dinnie, was born in Melbourne on 24th June 1887.

A Clash with the Police Farce

On this trip there were one or two amusing incidents. One evening while Dinnie was directing business before the show started, a man attempted to pass the ticket office without paying.

"Please get your ticket there, sir," said Dinnie, at the same time pointing to the box office.

To which the man replied, "I am a policeman, sir." Just at that moment there came a drunken man, attempting to get a free seat also.

Dinnie, having already asked for proof of the alleged policeman's assertion, on the impulse of the moment said, "Well, if you are a Bobby[1], please take that drunken man away."

To this the man replied angrily "What do you call me – a 'Bobby'? I'll make you pay for that," and with this he turned on his heel and left.

A day or two later, when Dinnie and his company were many miles on their tour, he received a summons to attend court on a charge of having assaulted a policeman. As the company's time was entirely filled up, Dinnie ignored the summons, leaving the court to decide his fate. He was fined £2 and costs, which was a flea-bite to the expense of attending court.

But it was not the end of the affair. After Dinnie finished this 12-month tour he bought an historic hotel in the suburbs of Melbourne.

The Croxton Park Hotel was built in 1850, probably by Mr Duff who operated it when it was known as the Pilgrim Inn. When Mr Goyder became the licensee he changed the name to the Red House after a celebrated sporting inn in England. The hotel was taken over by Mr Hutchins, a famous billiards champion, about 1878, who remodelled it and renamed it Croxton Park. Dinnie took over circa 1886.

The police in the locality, having strong objections to sport and sporting men, opposed the granting of Dinnie's licence. On hearing this the champion engaged a solicitor and, as was the custom, the local policeman attended the Licensing Court to support the objection to Dinnie's licence being granted. They argued that Donald, being a fighting and wrestling man, would encourage all the larrikins of Melbourne about the place. To prove that Dinnie was a dangerous person, the police brought the policeman previously mentioned some 200 miles to testify that Dinnie had assaulted him and been fined.

When this policeman was put into the witness box Dinnie's solicitor asked him if the champion had knocked him down.

"No," he replied.

"Did he hit you very hard?"

He again replied, "No."

"Then what did he do?" asked Donald's solicitor.

"He-he called me a 'Bobby'," stuttered the embarrassed cop.

"And is that not correct?" asked the solicitor, to roars of laughter. Dinnie was granted the licence.

[1]The word 'Bobby' is still widely used in Scotland to refer to a policeman. The term stems from Robert (Bobby) Peel, the originator of the police force.

Touring in Australia

While on tour Dinnie challenged all comers at wrestling, weightlifting and athletics. At Narandra he met Pedan, a big strong Irishman some 6ft 3in in height, who offered to match him at collar-and-elbow style wrestling for £15 a side. Dinnie accepted and at Donald's show the following night, the Scot won two straight falls in 12min.

About a week later he arrived at Goulburn, where his old friend, Charles McHardy, had joined the police in 1882. Dinnie arranged to have athletic sports there, and McHardy was his closest opponent. Dinnie threw the 16-lb hammer 123ft to McHardy's 103ft.

At this time he was in his 48th year, while McHardy was only in his 24th, and when they met on the same field some six years later, with a 16-lb hammer and a short handle of 3ft 7in, McHardy made 107ft, Dinnie 100ft 4in, and D. C. Ross 100ft. McHardy was now nearing 30 years of age, and at that time had a strong claim for the all-round athletic championship of the world. He won putting both heavy and light balls, and also the weight-throwing that day. He broke the world record with 14-lb ball, Irish style, beating Mitchell's 15-year-old record of 59ft 5in, by 4ft 6in, doing 63ft 11in at his first attempt.

Continuing his first tour of the Australian Colonies, Dinnie pro-

James Fleming, said to be the subject of this statue owned by Charlie Allan

ceeded to Sydney in time to fulfil a two weeks' engagement with Matthews circus. There he met his closest friend, James Fleming, who came from Scotland as much for the sake of his health as to travel as Dinnie's advance agent.

After making all necessary arrangements they started by boat for Newcastle in September. After showing two nights to crowded houses they took a train for Glen Innes, showing at Maitland and all towns en route. At Glen Innes, then the terminus of the railway, they did good business for two nights, and made an engagement to show at athletic sports at Inverell on their return journey.

They travelled by coach to Stanthorpe, the border of Queensland, where they gave one night's show before taking trains towards Brisbane. They did a series of one-night stands showing in all towns on the route and arriving in Brisbane in time for the Caledonian Club Games.

A few days later Dinnie engaged in a wrestling match with Stables, the Queensland champion, laying £20 to £10 that Stables, who had wrestled in England before emigrating and kept a store in Stanley Street, could not win two falls from seven in any style. Stables elected for Cumberland wrestling and the match took place in the Town Hall before a crowded house. Stables failed to win one fall, and gave up after losing five. Apparently Dinnie could throw him when and where he wished.

The group now toured north by Maryborough, where Dinnie organised games which were well patronised. He allowed long starts to all comers with hammer and in the put, and an Irishman there named McMahon came well up at putting, being within 3½ft of the champion. The company showed in the hall that same evening to a crowded house, and were enthusiastically received, Dinnie's wonderful feats of strength attracting very much attention. Every evening throughout his tour he offered £500 to anyone who could equal them. He generally found a few strong men to attempt them. The most amusing feat was the 56-lb weight, which he held out with his hand level with the shoulder, asking any of the competitors to put it on the palm of his hand. He would keep it steady there for from 25 to 45 seconds, and then offered £1 for every second any other man could support it. But he didn't find one man in the Colonies who could support it fairly for one second. In his contest with Prof. Miller, however, the latter was awarded 13sec, but Miller had his wrist bent upwards, shortening the leverage by 3 to 4 inches! This is not a feat of science, but of strength of muscle only.

Dinnie and his company then showed at Gympie, where he held athletic games. He was received by a great crowd of some two to three thousand people, and was greatly applauded for his wonderful feats at hammer, stone and caber. He allowed long starts to all comers, yet came in first, seemingly with ease. He also showed two evenings in the hall to crowded houses and was again awarded much applause. He gave all comers an opportunity of making money at every show, either for lifting his dumbbells or wrestling in any style.

He then left Gympie for Bundaberg, where he had a cousin, Robert Dinnie, who owned a sugar plantation. One of his old schoolmates, William Davidson, owned another sugar plantation on the opposite side of the town.

Athletic games were organised and a large crowd turned out to see the champion at the hammer, stone and caber-throwing. His old schoolmate came nearest to Dinnie at stone and hammer, he being a very tall, strong man of over 16st. Donald's cousin and Davidson had come out together from Deeside some time during the 1860s, and were by this time well acclimatised to the heat of Queensland.

The champion, with his company, then took a boat for Rockhampton, where they showed two nights, and one night at Mount Morgan, a great gold-digging locality some 16 miles inland from Rockhampton. Meantime, Dinnie had sent Fleming, his advance agent, still farther north by Townsville and Charters Towers. There it was discovered that owing to the slow steamboats on that route the company could not travel so far north and return in time to fulfil the engagement Dinnie had made to attend sports at Inverell at the New Year.

Donald wired Fleming to return by Brisbane and Stanthorpe to Glen Innes, where Dinnie supplied him with a horse and gig. This was necessary as Jamie had now to advertise the show throughout the East Coast, where at that time there was no railway and the roads were very poor.

Tough Journeys

It is very easy to overlook the difficulties of long distance travelling in those days before roads and rail-tracks were developed and the hardships Dinnie and his company met along the way make the tribulations of modern air travel seem very insignificant.

The gold rushes a few years earlier had resulted in a great many widely dispersed townships with small populations, the vast majority unable to support a permanent theatre.

In those days before TV, cinema and even before radio, road shows were the only professional entertainment seen by many of the rural communities. Itinerant troupes made difficult and tedious journeys, stopping along the way at isolated hamlets and fragmented settlements. Leaving the ill-made roads to try a short cut was not only hazardous but also dangerous. Pioneer showmen sometimes faced hacking their own paths, encountering major unexpected problems.

Dinnie returned to Brisbane with his colleagues, and after buying horses and a suitable wagon to take the company and luggage over many bad roads, they started for Inverell, showing at Warwick, by the way. The Caledonian Society of Warwick held their games at this time, where Dinnie was paid £20 for his name, and won ten first prizes, amounting in all to £45. They also showed in the hall at night to a full house, and were well received. Compared with the takings of other ethnic shows and well documented travelling circuses, these were major takings in those days.

They had yet the great hill of Bolivia to cross, which lies between

Queensland and New South Wales, Dinnie feared it would take hard pushing to get there in time, so he had the company prepared to make an early start for the hills the following morning.

Rising before dawn, they got over the roads well for the first 50 miles of the journey, but on the second day one of the horses, having been fed on grass for some time previous to Dinnie purchasing it, began to weaken at so much uphill work. Dinnie, wishing to reach Inverell in time to fulfil his engagement, hired other horses to assist them over the Bolivia Hill at the first opportunity. It became a race against time and only by travelling day and night did they reach Glen Innes very late the night before the Inverell Caledonian Games.

It had been a wearing, stressful journey but the great Scot took it all in his stride. Such a journey on horseback was certainly not the best preparation for an important competition.

There was a record attendance at the sports, and Dinnie won all the heavy events easily, also leaping and hurdle race. After he had won the Scotch wrestling a middle-weight Irishman, Pat by name, entered the arena and challenged Dinnie Irish style. Donald, typically, refused to wrestle unless there was a bet or a prize, but since the Irishman could not, or would not, back himself against Dinnie, the Scot offered to back his wrestling-partner, Jack Graham, to throw the Irish wrestler in any style he wished for the small stake of 6d.

The committee requested Dinnie to wrestle Pat, to which Dinnie

replied: "If he succeeds in throwing my man I'll be pleased to give him all he wants." However Pat failed to win one fall from Graham, although he tried all he knew.

Afterwards Dinnie asked Graham to take a final fall with him, to which he agreed and they had no sooner caught hold when Dinnie, with one great swing and sudden twist, laid his man flat on his back, almost as quickly as he used to throw Clogger Currie of Alexandria[1], in the Cumberland style.

Dinnie and company left Glen Innes next day for Grafton on the East Coast and on the banks of the Clarence River. They had to cross from Glen Innes over a very long hill, it being from seven to eight miles from top to the bottom where Grafton lies. It was extremely steep in many places and on such occasions all the horses had to be used to pull the heaviest wagon and then go back for the next. Going downhill on the other side, Dinnie found it necessary to trail large trees to his wagons to slow them down and keep them from running over the precipice.

The company showed two nights at Grafton to crowded houses. They then travelled south, showing at all towns between there and Newcastle. The roads were the worst they had encountered and they often had to hire six or seven oxen to pull their wagon through heavy clay. Near the mouth of the rivers the wheels would sink to the axle in sand and the end result was that there was but a very small profit for such an arduous tour.

Bushwhackers were amongst the hazards of that era and these outlaws sometimes preyed on road shows. Some years earlier Johannes Wirth and his troupe of German entertainers were journeying northwards and were held up by Fred 'Thunderbolt' Ward, leader of a notorious band of bushwhackers. He had been on the lookout for a group returning with the racehorse which had won the principal event of the Tamworth races.

---

[1]James 'Clogger' Currie, born in Ecclefechan, Dumfriesshire in November 1847, was one of Scotland's best known wrestlers in Victorian times. He was a fine figure of a man, one of 12 athletes selected to represent Scotland at the world's first international team bodybuilding championship, which they won. This took place at the Paris Exposition in 1889.

Clogger was near 6ft tall, with good posture, deep chested and with massive shoulders. He had thick hair and mutton chopped whiskers framing his rubicund face, which always seemed to wear a smile. The Clogger was beaten by Donald after a Titanic struggle at Alexandria Games, near where Currie lived. He got his revenge at Luss when after 90 minutes of hammer-and-tongs combat Clogger gained victory.

He claimed the Scottish championship for 20 years and once won the all-weights wrestling in the famous ring at Carlisle. He got his nickname from his trade as a clog-maker. When he won a caber competition he would demand the caber as a trophy and would use it to produce clogs. He died quite suddenly on 4th July 1903.

Stopping the Wirths, he demanded all their money, amounting to some £20, then bid them entertain him and his men.

After the performance, which was much enjoyed, the Teutons explained they were poor people and they, along with their women and children, would suffer badly as a result of this robbery. The bushwhacker took note of their address and said if he was successful in his plan to intercept and seize the champion racehorse he would return their money. The sceptical show folks went on their way very depressed by the incident but on eventually returning home were surprised and delighted to find £20 awaiting them.

Perhaps not surprisingly, although Dinnie and his team of hard men were always on the lookout for robbers, they were never troubled in this way.

A Sydney Challenge

After showing one night in Newcastle the company took a boat for Sydney, where they settled for a week to prepare for a continuation of the tour. Dinnie had noted in a Sydney paper that Larry Folley was ready to fight both him and Jack Graham in one afternoon for £500 a side, so he at once visited the newspaper office and deposited a cheque for £650, offering to knock out Larry inside ten minutes in a go-as-you-please fight, which is certainly the fairest way to find the best man. Larry, however, would not be caught and, advised by Prof. Miller, preferred to spend money on a few bottles of champagne to make friends rather than be annihilated inside ten minutes.

Here, again, Dinnie remembered his family and friends in Auchenblae, Scotland. In spite of reduced profits he had sent them £100 en route and now from Sydney he sent a cheque for £50.

For the accommodation of his horses, Dinnie had taken lodging in the suburbs of Sydney, and one day, having to meet a friend in a hotel in George Street, he took a good trotting mare he purchased in Brisbane for £55 and rode in at the appointed time, 3pm, fixing his animal to a place for that purpose at the back of the hotel. Though he was absent for only some seven or eight minutes, Dinnie found that the mare, with a new, first-class saddle he had just purchased, had been stolen.

The company then toured the south-east coast from Liverpool by Cowra, Bomballa, Queenbeyan, Goulburn, Wagga Wagga, Albury, Deniliquin and Bendigo, to Melbourne. At Bomballa the company were well received by a very large and appreciative audience.

The next town of much importance was Queenbeyan, where there lived an extraordinary strong man named Maxwell, and as Dinnie, as usual, had advertised that £500 would be paid to anyone who could do their feats of strength, it was expected by the natives that Maxwell would make a good thing of it, as he could lift a dray with twelve men on it. He was also said to be a great wrestler.

The show opened, as usual, at 8pm, and Maxwell was there as expected. But, we fear, only to be greatly disappointed. Dinnie's first feat, for which he offered £100, was to hold arm and hand horizontal and support a 56-lb weight laid on the palm over 30sec. He then offered £1 per second for the same feat, but Maxwell found he was not strong enough to do any fraction of a second to save his life. He was then offered £400 to lift from stage to stretch of arms overhead a dumbbell weighing 250-lb, but failed to lift it even to his shoulders.

He then wished to show his hand at wrestling. Dinnie put forward Graham, who was ready to tackle him, but he said: "No, I'll wrestle only a good man," and would not be convinced Graham was so. To satisfy him, Dinnie at once offered him a fall, at any style.

"Well, let each wrestle as he likes," Maxwell responded.

Dinnie agreed, although such "all-in wrestling" was not to his liking. The challenger grabbed Donald by the throat, but Dinnie took matters coolly, and after getting a secure hold of his fingers, pulled them from his throat and doubled them back till at least two of them were broken, when Maxwell fell against the wall, saying: "That's enough."

Dinnie's motto was always, *Nemo me impune lacessit.*

– Nobody provokes me with impunity.

It was 1884, and the company travelled on by Goulburn, Wagga, and Hay. At Goulburn his old friend, Charles McHardy, was pleased to meet him on his return from a successful tour, and gave an exhibition with him that evening at dumbbell lifting and wrestling.

At Wagga in New South Wales, some admirers there offered to present him with a gold medal if he would make a record for Australia for holding a 56-lb weight on palm of hand, arm horizontal. When showing that evening, Dinnie made a successful effort by registering 45sec – equal to his previous best done in his native country. He got the gold medal and this enormous feat was also recorded for posterity in one of the ten moulded plaques of the magnificent silver belt[1] awarded as a tribute and testimonial on his return to Britain. Knowledgeable enthusiasts of today are bound to question the ability of anybody to do a hold-out

[1]Further information on this remarkable belt appears in Appendix 2, page 154

like this, but Dinnie did incredible times and weights many times, under strict conditions, to win his place in the record books.

Eight days later the company's tour was finished at Melbourne, and Dinnie at once set about trying to fix a second match at wrestling with Prof. Miller. The prof's leg was quite healed, over 12 months having passed since his accident. The stakes were still at the Sportsman office; so the two men met to arrange preliminaries. Miller objected to so many falls being gone through again, stating that three were quite enough. Dinnie did not object to this, only he said one of the three would require to be in some other style. Miller admitted the fairness of this, yet thought it would be hard to come to an agreement about the third fall. Dinnie replied that as they were to wrestle for the stakes he had already won, he ought to have the choice.

Miller would not agree to this, so Dinnie offered Miller the choice of the third fall on condition that in the event of Dinnie being the loser Miller would, for similar stakes, wrestle him a third match of five styles, Miller again being allowed choice of the fifth style. This was considered by the Sportsman a very favourable offer for Miller, who could not well refuse, so before leaving the office, articles were signed and a deposit laid on the second match, which was also to be for £50 a side.

The Bijou Theatre was engaged for the first match, which took place in July 1885. Though tickets cost from 5s to 30s each, the theatre was crowded and hundreds were refused admission. Between £550 and £600 was taken at the doors.

This match proved the closest between the men. Miller won by securing the third fall by a narrow margin after 35 minutes' of hard wrestling, as Dinnie was still improving at this style. Just two weeks later their second match of five styles was wrestled in the Victoria Hall, when Dinnie won rather easily by three falls to one, amid much applause.

Clarence Whistler

Wrestlers Galore

On their arrival in Melbourne from their long tour Dinnie had rented Khartoum House, a nice six-bedroomed building near the Cyclorama, with ground and stables, where Fleming and he stayed close on 12 months. After settling there with horses and traps, Dinnie again sent to his family in Scotland, through a cousin, Alexander Dinnie, an order for £100. This brought to £550 the total he had sent from foreign lands to Scotland within three years.

About this time the American champion wrestler at catch-as-catch-can and Graeco-Roman styles, Clarence Whistler, visited Australia ready to wrestle all comers at these styles.

Whistler's first match in Melbourne was against J. Thomas, of Eaglehawk, Bendigo, a first-class Cumberland wrestler, but the match had to be catch-as-catch-can, with not more than three minutes' wrestling on the ground or carpet. It proved a very close contest. Thomas threw his opponent twice from the feet with one shoulder down, but failed to flatten both at one time.

Whistler succeeded in struggling round and pushing his opponent over on both shoulders, thus winning two falls after a very short – six minutes – and desperately severe struggle.

Whistler and Dinnie then met at the Sportsman office and made terms to wrestle a mixed match, Dinnie allowing his opponent to choose three falls to his two. This was also to be for £50 a side. Whistler chose Graeco-Roman, catch-as-catch-can and Cornish, while Dinnie chose Scotch and collar-and-elbow. This match took place in the Victoria Hall and drew a crowded house.

At their appearance on the stage both men were loudly applauded, and on tossing for first fall Dinnie won and chose Scotch style, which he won easily inside half a minute. After the five minutes' interval Whistler chose Graeco-Roman, which proved very close and prolonged, till Whistler, getting his opponent in a suitable position, put on his favourite hammer-lock and pressed both shoulders to the carpet; time, 16min 10sec.

Dinnie next named collar-and-elbow, and in one minute and five seconds had his opponent flat on his back by a clever twist and smart cross-buttock. Dinnie had now won two falls and Whistler one, and as the next was the latter's choice he named catch-as-catch-can. This turned out to be the most severe trial of the whole. Dinnie had the best of it from the feet, but Whistler seemed invincible on the floor. They started this fall at 11.12pm, and as the hall had to be closed at midnight they had just 48 minutes to decide the fall. Yet when time was called they were no further advanced, so had to postpone for another date, which had to be at least three weeks later, as Prof. Miller and Whistler had previously agreed to a match in the Graeco-Roman style the following week.

The Miller v Whistler match proved a great success for Whistler, as the hammer-lock was then unknown to Miller. At the first opportunity Whistler applied it quickly, and had Miller fixed so he had to give in or go down. Not caring to have an arm dislocated, he at once gave way.

After five minutes' rest they again met, and Whistler, seeing that his opponent had little or no idea of the hammer-lock, at once applied it when on their feet, pushing his arm up his back, while he kept the other shoulder, so that Miller had again to give in to save worse trouble.

Clarence Whistler was born near Delhi, India, in 1856 from pure American stock. He went to New York just before John L. Sullivan made his first appearance as a boxer. Billed as the Omaha Demon, and sometimes the Kansas Demon, he was 5ft 10½in and weighed in around 180-lb. When he went to New York around 1880 he challenged all the best wrestlers and had an impressive list of victories over such notables as James Quigley, the Graeco-Roman Champion of the famed NY Police Dept, Theodore Bauer, the champion of France and Henry Moses Dufur (aka Dufer and eventually Dupher), the American style collar and elbow wrestler. His real name was Eliphalet Dunn. Whistler went on to challenge Muldoon and their five-hour draw gained him world recognition.

He was a distant relative to the renowned artist James McNeil Whistler and well connected with the theatre, being a competent actor and associate of Maurice Barrymore, who went with him to Australia in 1885.

An Unequalled Wrestling Feat

A company of Melbourne sporting men decided to promote a wrestling tournament at the Melbourne cricket grounds during four evenings of the Melbourne Cup racing week. A great innovation was the all-round lighting of the grounds by electricity, and to add variety to the programme other athletic feats were held. £25 was offered as prizes for each of seven styles of wrestling, open to all, and every available wrestler of any note throughout the Colonies turned out for the occasion.

A big Irishman named Keating came to represent his country in the collar-and-elbow style; Thomas, Blackburn and Hudson for the Cumberland style. Then Miller and Whistler for the Graeco-Roman and catch-as-catch-can styles and Donald Dinnie, all-round champion in all styles.

An extra champion prize was also offered for the best all-round wrestler. The gates were opened at 5.30pm each evening, and when names were called the first night, it was found that Whistler had not turned up, as he had not yet recovered from his match with Prof. Miller at the Theatre Royal on 26th September 1885.

This was a great disappointment as

many countrymen wanted to see the American champion at work.

The different styles were all closely contested[1]. Dinnie won the catch-as-catch-can, after a severe struggle with Prof. Miller in the final, but the professor had again the best of the Graeco-Roman style.

Miller did not compete in any of the other five styles. Dinnie rather easily beat all his opponents at the Cornish style, and also at the American side-hold style; but at the Cumberland he was very closely pushed by Thomas, Blackburn and Hudson, who all hailed from the North of England and were very clever wrestlers.

The collar-and-elbow style, however, turned out to be one of the hardest and perhaps the most interesting contest of the tournament, it being especially important to the big, strong Irishman from Sydney that he win. His first opponent was Hudson, who, though only a middle-weight, brought big Pat to his knees several times. But, being 6st lighter, he did not succeed once in getting him fairly on his back, and after a hard tussle Pat swung his opponent from his feet and laid him flat.

His next opponent was Thomas, who had done a lot of practise in this style with Dinnie during their long tour. Pat very soon realised that he had now found his match. Thomas was some two or three stone lighter but much the quicker, and far more scientific, and after a struggle of over 25 minutes Pat had to succumb to superior science.

Thomas had then to meet Dinnie for the final, and as they had practised together on so many occasions during their long tour through the

[1]There have been a great many wrestling styles over the years and they can be roughly divided into those which are predominantly ground wrestling and those which are standing styles. The sport has been remarkably well documented since the 7th century BC, when the Greeks added a new style of ground wrestling to their Olympic programme in 648BC. In this event, strangling and punching was allowed but biting and gouging were forbidden.

However in the classic Graeco-Roman wrestling the contestants took hold only from the waist upwards. Holding the legs or using them to trip was forbidden. A fall was called when a wrestler had both shoulders pressed to the ground. In the Cornish and Devon styles jackets were worn and there was considerable kicking as well as tripping. The aim was to put the opponents' two shoulders and one hip on the ground, or both hips and one shoulder.

In Cumberland and Westmorland style the wrestlers clasp their hands behind their opponent's back, one arm going over his shoulder and the other going under the other arm. If this grip is lost then it counts against the wrestler who released. The object is to throw your opponent, and a fall is declared if any part of the body other than the feet touches the ground.

The Scottish style promoted by Dinnie involved a good deal of ground wrestling and was probably closer to the catch as catch can or free style wrestling. In this style there was scope for good throws and ground wrestling, without the bone breaking and brutality of all-in wrestling and ultimate fighting, now gaining popularity in America.

Colonies, they were able to give a splendid exhibition at any style.

The three bouts were short and scientific, Dinnie gaining the final by his extra muscular ability. The Scotch style was the last competed for, and after several hard and interesting bouts between Blackburn, Hudson, Keating and Thomas, more especially between the last two, Thomas had the best of it, and had again to meet Dinnie in the final. As usual, this proved a gift for Dinnie, who had thus gained six styles from seven, a feat probably unequalled in the annals of wrestling.

Clarence was unable to show himself at the tournament as after an arduous wrestling bout he had celebrated at a jamboree and then camped out all night in zero conditions. As a result he contracted severe influenza or pneumonia, which in a very short time carried him to the other side.

There is another version of Whistler's death. In an Australian wrestling history book it says that in the celebrations Whistler demonstrated his trick of drinking champagne and then eating the glass. In doing so it pierced his gullet, which proved fatal.

He left at least one record behind him. He drew the largest crowd ever seen in Australia at a funeral. In due course a memorial stone was erected over his grave, we believe by the hotel-keeper with whom he lived, and who probably profited heavily from betting on Whistler's success with the hammer lock v Prof. Miller, at their wrestling match.

On his memorial stone was inscribed the description *'Prince of Wrestlers'*.

> "Only some twelve months later," Dinnie commented, "James Fleming, a famous front-rank, all-round athlete, departed this life, and was buried within a few yards of C. Whistler's resting place. Fleming was a superior athlete to Whistler, yet at his funeral only some two dozen mourners followed his remains to the cemetery!
>
> "During the winter of 1876 James Fleming had suffered from very severe rheumatic fever, from which he never afterwards completely recovered. Consequently, though with great reluctance, he had to retire from the athletic arena, and in 1884 he followed me, his old opponent, to Australia, and travelled as my advance agent."

Jamie travelled ahead advertising in every town the forthcoming appearances. Fleming suffered from asthma and even with the advantage of a fine warm climate his health did not improve. Heart disease set in.

> "Poor Jemmy often got up during the night, gasping for breath and

Dinnie & Fleming – rivals then colleagues, always friends

> putting his head out of the window to get more fresh air," said Dinnie. "It was at times like this that he almost wished the grim spectre with the scythe would knock at the door."

Although good medical care was obtained, Fleming's condition gradually worsened and on the 10th March 1887, at Northcote, a Melbourne suburb, he bid goodbye to his athletic friend and to the world.

The memory haunted Donald Dinnie, who on his return to Scotland told his friends how that night he and his wife Eleanor had gone to see Jamie in his room. Although usually uncomplaining and waving aside his problems, Jamie was different this night. Sitting by the fire Fleming gazed sadly into the embers and complained that his feet were freezing. Eleanor Dinnie wrapped his legs and feet in hot cloth and they both tried to comfort him.

"I doot ye'r worse the nicht, Jem," Dinnie sympathised.

"Aye," replied Fleming, raising his head with difficulty, "I feel much worse."

With this his head slumped sideways and his spirit departed as Donald, devoted friend to the end, came forward to carry him to his bed.

The strong bond between the two athletes was evident throughout their lives and long after the death of his friend Dinnie would speak or write of his pal Jem. Dinnie also had a conscience about this matter of giving his friend a good send-off.

> "In the great land boom that came on about that time, many lost their money, and I among them," related Donald. "Therefor, as no assistance came from Fleming's friends in 'Auld Scotia', I, with great reluctance, had to relinquish the idea of a monument, and my deposit of £5 placed on it was forfeited. So I planted a small tree, which I trust is blooming to this day."

At the Melbourne wrestling tournament prizes were also offered for throwing heavy and light hammers, putting heavy and light balls, throwing 56-lb weight, and tossing the caber. Dinnie, though giving handicaps, easily won all these feats with something to spare. This in itself would be classed as a world record in most people's eyes.

Around 1912 an athlete won nine events at a meeting in Scotland, and the papers next day declared it to be a "world's record". Yet on many occasions Dinnie had won from 12 to 16 events at one meeting, and on at least one occasion he won 20 events. Though this occurred in the mid-1860s, it was a feat remembered until World War I.

Tom Cannon, Harry Dunn and Jack Connor

In 1887 the renowned English champion, Tom Cannon, visited Australia and made much money during his tour. He had already been practising with Whistler and giving exhibitions in America for some time of the catch-as-catch-can and Graeco-Roman styles, but he was a good all-round wrestler, having been successful in England at Cumberland and other styles.

He contracted to wrestle Prof. Miller for a £100 stake in Graeco-Roman style in December 1886. Her Majesty's Opera House was packed for this match, which lasted 40 minutes. But unfortunately the professor had two (some say three) ribs broken during the second fall. He had to retire from the contest, and, of course, Cannon was awarded the match and stakes.

Cannon now wanted to wrestle Dinnie, but though they met at the Sportsman Office to arrange preliminaries, no agreement was reached. Cannon wanted three falls only, and proposed certain styles, but Dinnie preferred others, at which Cannon demurred. Then Dinnie suggested an all-round match as being the best to decide who was the superior wrestler. Cannon admitted this, but thought the time required might prove too long for one entertainment.

Eventually terms were agreed and they met in five styles only. Cannon won in Cumberland, catch-as-catch-can and Graeco-Roman and Dinnie won in Scots style and collar and elbow. At a second meeting, however, an all-round match was agreed on, which embraced all the most popular styles of the day.

This match, being the first on similar terms, created a great sensation among sporting circles, and many bets were laid on each at the different styles as well as the result. Dinnie, having won so many styles at the Melbourne Tournament, was well supported but being over 50 he was at a great disadvantage compared to Cannon, who was just over 30. However, Dinnie had proved his wonderful form for an athlete at that age, so it was generally considered that, bar accident, the one with the most endurance would win.

On the evening of the match, which took place in the Alexandra Theatre, Cannon weighed three pounds heavier. We need not detail each fall here; suffice it to state that the contest commenced within a few minutes of eight o'clock, and though five minutes only was allowed between each fall, they stood still on equal terms at 11.30pm, having won three falls each, and the last, collar-and-elbow, yet to be decided.

In this final fall it was evident to all that the men were exhausted though game to the end. Cannon tried some of his old tricks to down his opponent, but Dinnie seemed to be still clever on his legs. Watching for his opportunity, on two or three occasions he had Cannon almost over. After tugging hard over 25 minutes at this style, the lights were extinguished and the referee left, so that this severe match was left undecided, Cannon swearing that he would rather be pole-axed than again attempt to wrestle a seven-style match.

Dinnie later told his friends that when he and Cannon entered their dressing rooms they were as wet as if taken out of the sea, and their tights were in rags.

Dinnie fully expected to win this match, as he had not once been defeated all-round, but he had to admit that an athlete cannot be as agile in his 50s as he was in his 30s, though he may have a little advantage in experience.

The match was declared a draw. This was the first and last all-round match wrestled in Australia.

Dinnie began to practise all the different styles of wrestling while in America in 1870, and again in 1872. Although he excelled at Highland games, wrestling was always Dinnie's favourite sport and he never missed an opportunity to secure all the information and practise he could.

Harry Dunn, a first-class Cumberland wrestler, visited Australia before Cannon left. It was hard to arrange a match since the

Harry Dunn

latter had most faith in his powers at Graeco-Roman and catch-as-catch-can, while of course Dunn favoured his own Cumberland style. After much wrangling they agreed on five styles, Dunn allowing Cannon the advantage of choosing the fifth style, which he named Cornish; Dunn, in addition to his own, the collar-and-elbow style. Cannon refused to wrestle for less than £100 a side. Dinnie at once came to Dunn's assistance, found the money for him, and also trained him for the match, which duly took place in the Theatre Royal.

However it proved unsatisfactory and disappointing. Cannon guessed that unless he lamed Dunn at the Graeco-Roman or catch-as-catch-can styles, he would run a big risk of being beaten in the other three.

Dunn won the toss and chose the Cumberland first, which he won cleverly. Cannon next chose Graeco-Roman. No sooner was time called than Cannon tried hard for the hammer-lock or strangle. Dunn cleverly resisted for a time; but eventually Cannon got a stranglehold, which he kept so hard that Dunn got black in the face, and would in all likelihood have been choked had not the referee pulled Cannon off. They then went to their dressing-rooms for their five minutes' rest, but Dunn was quite unable to wrestle any more that night. Consequently the stakes had to be awarded to Cannon.

There was much disappointment at this exhibition between Harry Dunn and Tom Cannon. One gentleman, Mr W. P. McGregor from the Loch Lomond district, offered to back Dunn for another £100 against Cannon if Dinnie would agree to act as Dunn's second and bring off a fair trial. Mr McGregor was a direct descendent of the famous Rob Roy, and a great athlete himself – it was he who opened the Broken Hill silver mines and he was the largest shareholder and chairman of directors.

Cannon at once accepted, and some two weeks later they met in the Alexandra Theatre to decide which was the best wrestler at the five styles. Dinnie had been training Dunn regularly and giving him many valuable hints on how to evade the strangle and hammer-lock.

This second meeting also proved unsatisfactory. Dunn won the toss for the first fall and chose Cumberland, which he won in four seconds.

After the five-minute rest, Cannon chose catch-as-catch-can. During the first five minutes, when on their feet, Dunn evaded the strangle, but some two minutes after going on the carpet Cannon secured a firm hold around his opponent's throat, when Dinnie, who was acting as Dunn's second, ordered Dunn to stop defence and give Cannon the fall. The referee announced "Second fall to Cannon," which Cannon refused to accept, insisting that each fall be wrestled to a finish.

Dunn went to his room, but Cannon stayed to dispute the referee's decision. The time being up, Dunn came rushing from his room in a somewhat excited state, saying: "Where is he? I'll wrestle him!" and immediately they caught hold round each other's necks, when, quick as lightning, Dunn gave his opponent the flying mare[1] and landed him flat on the carpet, both shoulders down. The referee gave the third fall to Dunn. Amid much applause Dunn was awarded the match and the stakes held by the Melbourne Sportsman.

These two matches were generally looked on by the public as arranged, or exhibitions, while those more closely connected could testify that no more genuine contests ever took place. However, the public having their doubts, there was poor attendance on both occasions.

Tom Cannon's last opponent in Australia was Jack Connor, a noted catch-as-catch-can wrestler. He had been challenging all comers for some time, including Prof. Miller, at Graeco-Roman. The first match between Cannon and Connor drew a house of close on £600, and Connor lost, as his neck was badly sprained. Another date was agreed on, and the crowd was even bigger than before.

Owing to the way Cannon won at their first meeting, he was again favourite in the betting, but after a very prolonged and severe tussle Connor was declared the winner. This seemed to Cannon a good opening for a third match, so they arranged for a third trial, and engaged the Exhibition Buildings for the occasion. As a result of diminishing interest it has not been possible to find the result of this third match.

Little less than £2,000 was paid to view these three exhibitions. Believing that there was little more left for him in Australia, Cannon sailed on to South Africa and Connor followed later.

Tom Cannon was one of England's greatest wrestlers at the turn of the century. He was born of Irish parents at Tyldesley, near Manchester in 1854 and at 14 years of age became a miner in the same mine as his father. Lancashire was a hotbed of wrestling and he had his first match soon after he started work. The bout was against James Scully at the Royal Oak Rabbit Coursing Grounds and 700-800 spectators were present. They paid sixpence each, but the wrestlers battled only for the £10 prize. Cannon won, taking falls in 12min, 8min and 4min.

[1]To execute a flying mare the wrestler grabs his opponent's arm with both hands and, turning his back, thrusts his shoulder under the armpit of his opponent. Pulling down on the trapped arm, heaving with the legs and bending forward slightly throws the attacked wrestler. A flying mare palm uppermost is against the rules as it could cause serious injury.

Tom left mining after a series of wrestling wins and sailed to New York on 3rd June 1875. He had several notable victories before returning to Britain for more bouts and decided to join the London Metropolitan Police. Although he enjoyed police work, there was such a demand for wrestlers of his calibre he was persuaded to resign and join a troupe at the South London Music Hall for the princely sum of £10 per week.

Following a successful season, he sailed again for America in 1882. On this trip he made a fortune beating greats like Muldoon and Strangler Lewis before embarking on a season with P. T. Barnum's famous show, with which he was undefeated. Three months later he sailed to Australia where he met Miller, Dinnie and the others mentioned here. His successful career continued for many years.

He was 5ft 8in tall and varied between $15^1/_2$ and 17 stones. Cannon wrestled all over the world, including South Africa, France, Belgium and India, and some of his greatest bouts were in America, where on 18th August 1888 he had two sensational matches with Muldoon in Cincinnati.

Duncan C. Ross of America

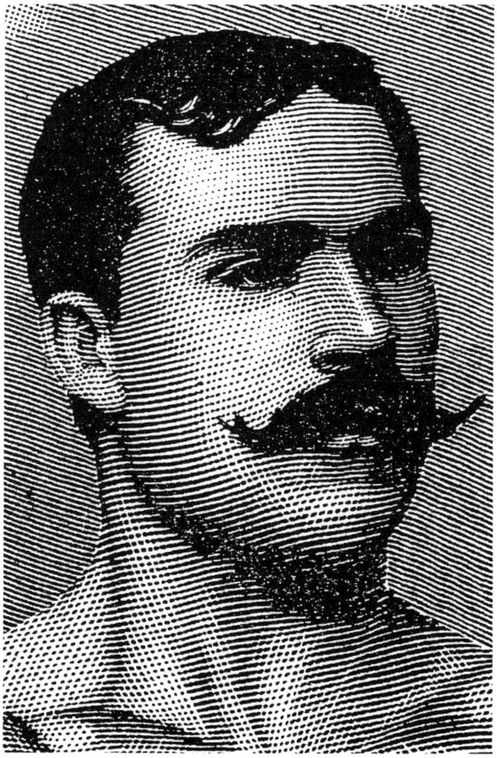
'World Champion' Duncan C. Ross

The next athlete of any note who visited Australia while Dinnie was there was his old opponent, Duncan C. Ross, who arrived from America. Duncan had been Police Chief at Coburg, Canada, but could earn much more as a professional athlete, being one of the best all-rounders in the world.

The noted wrestling and boxing expert Nat Fleischer, editor of The Ring boxing and wrestling magazines, classed Ross as the greatest exponent of mixed wrestling in that era, describing him as World Champion. The title was awarded to him by Richard K. Fox and the Police Gazette, a journal that also gave him many medals for his outstanding achievements. Ross had succeeded Dinnie as Police Gazette Mixed Wrestling Champion.

Although proud of his Scottish heritage, Duncan was born at Scenti, Turkey, on 16th March 1856. In his prime he stood 6ft $1^1/_2$in and weighed around 200-lb, approx 90 kg. One of the best all-rounders in the world, he was as strong as an ox. His biceps measured 16in and his calf was 1in larger, he sported a chest going up to nearly 50in and thighs of $25^1/_2$in.

In 1882 Ross, then of Louisville, Kentucky, had beaten Dinnie in hammer and stone at Yonkers Caledonian Society annual games, much to the surprise of all present. In fairness it should be pointed out that Donald was past 45 at the time and Duncan only 26. They remained in contact and Dinnie later beat Duncan in the same events.

Like Dinnie, Ross failed to reach any agreement with the Caledonian Society of Sydney, but organised an outdoor entertainment on his own account with great success.

He had with him a noted horseback swordsman from the States, and his contest with him, while challenging all comers, drew a huge crowd. Ross, while in Sydney, met the secretary of the Goulburn Caledonian Society, and agreed terms to attend their games and take on all comers at weight-throwing and wrestling.

Later he was matched with Prof. Miller in the Graeco-Roman style. It was a very interesting encounter, Miller eventually gaining the final fall, thus reversing a previous decision.

Ross was much younger than Miller and Miller was then on the down grade. A magazine pointed out that Donald Dinnie was older still and a miracle for his age. However Donald Dinnie knew he could not go on forever and in Australia there was a remarkable Scot, Charles McHardy. Dinnie firmly believed that in McHardy he had a worthy successor.

Charles McHardy

Legends of the bravery and prowess of the McHardy men go back to the 11th century. They were famous as great warriors during the Jacobite rebellions after they and their fellow Jacobites raised the banner at Braemar. This has long been the location of great gatherings and while chieftains conferred, informal and later formal Highland games were held there.

The earliest athletic champions were the McHardys from the Braes of Mar and the Lonach area. Their accomplishments and a fund of anec-

dotes have been well documented and provide evidence of splendid performances long before track and field athletics were inaugurated.

Queen Victoria's love of the area attracted attention to these ancient sporting and cultural traditions and she awarded fine prizes to many of these athletes, including Charles McHardy, father of the man Donald Dinnie visited in Australia.

He was a superb athlete and at the Balmoral Games on 22nd September 1859 Queen Victoria awarded him a fine sword for winning tossing the caber and a silver-mounted dirk for first in hammer throwing. Charles wore the weapons as part of his traditional dress. A portrait of Charles McHardy was painted by Kenneth Macleay RSA (1802-1875) for Queen Victoria and remains in the Royal collection. This rare likeness shows him to be a man of fine physique and posture, with fiery red, bushy chin whiskers but no moustache.

In 1860, his son Charles Forbes McHardy was born at Bellabeg, Strathdon. Great though old Charles was at the games, his son was undoubtedly a much greater athlete. Young Charles won an international reputation in the world of sport. He had brains as well as brawn and graduated from Aberdeen University in 1881.

In 1882 Charles emigrated to Australia, where he joined the police and soon became a sergeant at Gouldburn, New South Wales. His toughness came in handy during the gold rush, when he was appointed mining registrar and warden of Wyalong, New South Wales. Having held this position from 1894 until 1898, he was promoted to inspector at Newcastle and finally Superintendent of Police at Gouldburn.

When Charles was in his prime he was much in demand as an athlete throughout Australia and New Zealand and some idea of his mighty physique can be judged from his physical profile at the age of 29.

He was 6ft 2in and weighed 16 stone (224-lb or 102 kg). His chest measured 46in, his neck 17in, thigh 26in and biceps 16in. He was noted for his extraordinary strength and while in Sydney, for a wager, he lifted 1,964-lb of iron from the ground. This was most likely to be a harness lift or hand and thigh lift with straps. In the heavy events, McHardy threw the 14-lb hammer 139ft 6in. This was done in 1885 with a 4ft 4in stiff-shafted hammer and thrown from a fair stand. He had exceeded this in training, reaching 141ft. On 27th January 1888, in the same standing style, he threw the 16-lb hammer with a 4ft 3in shaft a distance of 129ft 3in. This gives a very good comparison with today's athletes. In those days they were phenomenal throws.

When Donald Dinnie went to Australia the two men, although sporting rivals, became firm friends, sharing mutual respect. While with Dinnie in Auckland, New Zealand, in 1891, Charles put the 16-lb ball 52ft, but not in the standing style. This was an improvement on his previous best of 50ft 3in, which he achieved in 1889. In a practice with Dinnie he threw the 24-lb hammer 89ft 4in. Donald Dinnie was so impressed that he wrote for newspaper publication a statement regarding the all-round heavyweight athletic championships.

He declared that he was handing over his world championship to Charles McHardy of New South Wales, Australia. Dinnie pointed out that McHardy had thrown a 14-lb weight 53ft 11in in the Irish style and he would make many records in the same style with heavier weights.

> "McHardy, I say further, can beat anyone in Scotland in wrestling and in boxing. I believe he could beat any man in the world bar John L. Sullivan. Who in Scotland has a chance against him? In short in summing up all the items it will now be found that Charles McHardy is more entitled to the World Championships than any other man."

McHardy himself was confident of his own abilities, depositing money with the Melbourne Sportsman, challenging any athlete in the world for any amount up to £1,000 on any one or all of the following feats: throwing the hammer, throwing the weight from the shoulder, throwing the 56-lb weight by ring, heavy weightlifting from the ground (now called the dead lift), heavy weightlifting to arms length overhead (clean and jerk), and all-round match, including the above, plus Cumberland style wrestling, Scots wrestling and boxing.

In his earlier years he had been a good sprinter and high jumper, clearing the bar at 5ft 8¼in at Coutermanora, NSW, in 1885. He was a man of exceptional intellect and physique, much admired in academic as well as athletic circles. He seemed to have been quite modest, rarely seeking publicity or speaking of his achievements.

After retiring in 1919 he went to live in Sydney, where he died in 1929. What a man! He was a worthy successor to the great McHardys of earlier years, and a worthy successor to Donald Dinnie.

Donald Dinnie continued to tour in Australia and New Zealand, and as New Year 1894 approached, when 57 years of age, he beat all comers at the Caledonian games in Oamara. Eva, his six-year-old daughter, received eight guineas for her Highland dancing. On 9th June 1895 he defeated Jack Sutherland, the New Zealand Champion in catch as catch can wrestling for a £25-a-side bet, and on 5th July he won again, though this time the stake was only £5.

He continued to compete regularly in all events despite his advancing years, but in Auckland 1896 we see the earliest signs of diminishing involvement. He entered only the stone, hammer and caber events. Eva, now eight, won the entire Highland dancing championships.

From Auckland on 25th October 1896, Donald wrote to the press voicing his displeasure over an article by William McCombie Smith. Smith had

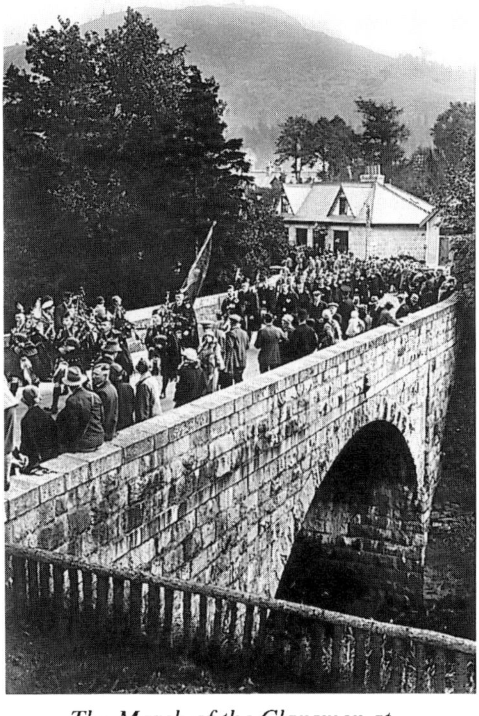

The March of the Clansmen at Braemar Highland Games

written new rules for hammer throwing and Dinnie, in criticising these, concluded caustically: "I suppose he will be writing new rules for Highland dancing next."

Donald got excellent press coverage while in New Zealand and some of the cuttings indicate great versatility in his presentations. L. C. Smith, writing for a Wellington newspaper, described one of Donald's appearances with Harry Woods, a skilled blacksmith. In Manners Street Hall, later the Princess Theatre, Dinnie supported a large rock on his chest while lying on his back, and Woods, the expert farrier, swung the hammer with hefty blows until he split the rock in two. The proceedings were supervised by Jimmy Doyle, Wellington City Council nuisance inspector, a strong man himself and also a popular judge at athletic events.

With advancing years Donald Dinnie increasingly felt the pull of his native land and decided it was time to make his way home to Scotland. Australia had a special place in his heart and it is fitting that Scotland's sporting superstar left behind him a worthwhile, but almost anonymous, reminder of his presence in that land. While at the height of his fame in Australia, Donald was selected to be the sculptor's model for a statue to perpetuate the memory of William Wallace, the great Scottish freedom fighter immortalised by film and television as Braveheart.

The finished work, an 8ft high white marble statue of Wallace, was unveiled on the 24th May 1889, in the Ballarat Botanical Gardens, in the gold fields of Victoria, west of Melbourne. The unveiling ceremony was by the Honourable John Nimmo, another Scot who was then the Minister of Public Works in the Victorian Government. The sculptor Percival Ball, previously of England and then working from Collins Street, Melbourne, saw Donald Dinnie, who was at that time appearing in Victoria. He perceived in the athlete's proud bearing and physique the ideal subject to illustrate Wallace at the age of 27 standing upon Abbey Craig. The statue cost £1,200, the money coming from a bequest by James Russell Thomson, born on 24th May 1818 in Airdrie, Lanarkshire, Scotland, a former Gordon Highlander, who later went to Australia and struck gold while mining in Ballarat.

Each year on the 22nd August, the Ballarat Caledonian Society gathers at the statue to recognise the 'Martyrdom of William Wallace, Scotland's Hero' and no doubt they also keep in mind the other Scottish connections with this tribute.

Dinnie posed as the model for this marble statue of William Wallace, which stands at Ballarat, Australia

Homeward Bound

Stopping in South Africa

After his journeys in the Antipodes Donald sailed for home, leaving Sydney on 1st April 1897 on board the S.S. Aberdeen. On reaching Cape Colony he found the sportsmen there had other ideas, for when they heard the great Dinnie was on board they invaded the ship in port at Cape Town and persuaded Donal' to accept engagements in South Africa as far up as Pretoria.

The tour was an outstanding success. Here he was joined by his son Edwin and Jack Sutherland, the New Zealand Champion wrestler and a good all-round Highland games strength athlete.

On 18th June 1897, they appeared at a games in Durban for the Natal Caledonian Society. Here Dinnie and Sutherland wrestled in an exhibition but did not participate in the heavy events as these were of a local character. Donald demonstrated the finer points of the caber toss, causing quite a stir.

In the evening there was an indoor stage show and there all three demonstrated their strength. Edwin had a good strongman act and Donald did two of his favourite feats. He held a 56-lb weight on the palm of his hand sideways in line with his shoulders, a feat which defied all others who tried it. He then swung Edwin and Sutherland on the ends of a 200-lb barbell round and round the platform until they were dizzy.

Italian strongman Napoli, an inspiration

Dinnie was the first Scot to excel at weightlifting, having been inspired by Napoli, an important Italian strongman born in 1821. Donald saw Napoli (real name Felice Prades) at Kittybrewster, where Aberdeen Highland games were held around a century ago. Donald also said that in autumn 1870 he saw a strong*woman* act in Edinburgh and after admiring her

A photograph of Donald Dinnie taken in Pietermaritzburg during his South Africa tour in 1898

weightlifting feats he decided to train seriously for this sport. He gave credit to George Davidson and G. H. Johnstone as being good lifters who had often appeared in his strongman acts.

For nearly a year they played to capacity audiences at places such as Pietermaritzburg, Ladysmith, Newcastle, Port Elizabeth, Durban, Dundee, Volksrust, Kimberley, Bloemfontein, Johannesburg, Krugersdorp and Pretoria. They took part in numerous Caledonian games, a term more widely used by exiled Scots than Highland games since many organisers were Lowlanders. Often they presented their own stage shows the same evening. It was a very cost-effective arrangement.

On 17th August 1897, while the group was training at Bloemfontein, Donald was placing a marking peg for Sutherland's throw when Edwin threw prematurely. The hammer grazed his father's head and struck his arm with considerable force. A week later the old champion won the light hammer at the Pretoria Games with his arm in a sling.

It was not until the Aberdeen's next round trip that the Dinnies completed their journey at Tilbury Docks, Essex, at the end of October 1898.

A Third Generation Man of Strength

An important part of their stage presentation was the strongman act of Edwin Gellatly Dinnie, who told this story in his own words.

"I was born in Aberdeen, Scotland on the 4th June 1877. I began practising athletics at fourteen years of age and was always stronger than the other boys at school, I could beat any of them. I used to try throwing the hammer, putting the stone and jumping at that time, and even until I was well over sixteen I practised outdoor athletics daily. At that time I was in the employment of D. H. Barry Esq, of Strathglass, Inverness-shire. On many occasions I surprised the ladies and gentlemen of the estate by throwing a 14-lb hammer over 100ft, and putting the stone 36ft. I never had an inclination to become famous in the field sports. I always wished to exhibit my pure strength. When I was about seventeen I was employed by Professor A. R. Simpson in Edinburgh.

Sandow

On Christmas 1893 Sandow, the well-known strongman, was performing in the Waverley Market Edinburgh.

Edwin Gellatly Dinnie, 'The Scottish Hercules'

On several occasions I witnessed his performance and was much struck by the feats he accomplished. Soon after this, knowing I was naturally strong, I determined to go in for weightlifting. I purchased a barbell weighing 150-lb and the very first time I ever handled anything of the kind I lifted it to arms length above my head as if it weighed 56-lb. I had not been practising very long when the late Professor Henry Drummond of Glasgow University heard of my feats and being a great friend of my master they both invited me to give them an exhibition of my powers in the drawing room. Several other well-known medical professors were present. I lifted my 150-lb and swung two of the doctors hanging on it. I next supported the barbell and six ordinary 56-lb weights hanging on it, with both hands upstretched, lying on my back.

My greatest feat at that time was to support on my chest, with my hands and feet on the ground, a small platform on which was placed a piano and six men. The feat was not so severe as one would imagine. The only difficulty lies in the balancing. That night Professor Drummond presented me with a handsome gold medal and an electro-plated dumbbell weighing 70-lb which I loaded to 112-lb and could lift with either hand without putting myself to much trouble.

In July 1894, I was engaged by a concert company to tour around

Scotland and the north of England for twelve months. After finishing this tour I went on the Music Halls and met with greater success than ever. In 1897, I started a company of my own and offered a challenge of £10 to any man who could perform any of my feats. In 1898 I went to South Africa and my very first performance in the Good Hope Hall, Cape Town, was highly spoken of by both press and public.

I next visited Port Elizabeth, Durban, Pietmaritzburg, Ladysmith, Heidelburg, Johannesburg, Krugersdop, Bloemfontein, Kimberley and many other small towns. I challenged anyone to compete with me at genuine feats of strength, but no one came forward. I performed my great feat of fixing a ladder to the ground and with straps around my shoulder I walked along the ladder pulling ten men behind me. At the Highland Society's Sports in Johannesburg I pulled eight men, Boers selected from the police tug of war team.

The strongest man I have ever seen is John Marx. He is German and I have never heard of a man who could accomplish any of his difficult feats. Sandow is a showman, a stage artiste and a strong man as well. I certainly admire Sandow as an effective performer, but as a matter of fact he does not hold a single world record for any feat of strength, and he has never defeated any athlete who holds a world record. Sandow made his name through defeating Samson, a man who was never capable of lifting 160-lb with one hand, and you will get plenty of amateurs who could do that.

Sandow was defeated by Henry McCann in London in 1895 when he failed to lift with both hands a weight of 232-lb, and still he claimed to lift over 300-lb. When on the stage, I am prepared at any time to offer Sandow £20 as a present if he can lift with one hand a dumbbell

A postcard showing poses of John (Marx) Grutin

weighing 200-lb. And that is 120-lb less than he claims at the recent moment. I am also prepared to compete with Sandow at three feats – right hand lift, left hand lift, and a lift with both hands. All weights to be lifted as they ought to be i.e. from the ground to the shoulder, and press or jerk to arms length without touching the body. These three feats are the best test of a man's strength as regards dumbbell lifting.

I can lift over 190-lb with right hand, 170 with the left hand. I have lifted overhead simultaneously 120 in my right hand and 112 in my left hand. With two hands I lift overhead a barbell weighing 250-lb. I can support a 150-lb barbell on the back of my neck, and allow five men to hang upon it as I swing them round. I push with the right hand a ball weighing 180-lb with a 10 st (140-lb) seated on it and lift another 80-lb with my left hand at the same time.

My measurements are as follows: - Chest 45in, waist 32in, neck 17in, biceps $16^{3}/_{4}$in forearm $14^{1}/_{2}$in, thigh $24^{1}/_{2}$in, calf $16^{1}/_{2}$in. Height 5ft $7^{3}/_{4}$in weight 13st 3-lb (185-lb).

I intend to form a School of Physical Culture in Aberdeen at some future date, and I would accept pupils for instruction in physical culture, weightlifting and all forms of wrestling. The town badly needs a proper place of this kind."

Edwin was cast in the same mould as his father and between the ages of 14 and 18 he won over 100 prizes in the light and heavy field events.

Professor Henry Drummond of Glasgow University, for whom Edwin worked for some time, took a great interest in young Dinnie's achievements and would often get him to present his feats of strength before guests at the Drummond residence. Successful at 17, he matured rapidly and at 20 had his own touring concert party, with his own strong-man act at the top of the variety bill.

In South Africa young Dinnie received great press notices. The Cape Times said: "The extraordinary feats of strength accomplished by the famous Scottish athlete, Edwin Dinnie, fairly astonished the large audience, amongst whom was Dr Alfred Milner, who seemed to take a special interest in the performance. We expect to hear more of this young man in the near future, for his feats seem almost incredible, and bear a close approach to those accomplished by Sandow."

The tour was a geography lesson for the young Scot and he benefited greatly from the accumulated experiences of his father, who was a willing teacher. By the time they returned to Britain in October 1898 he was a greatly improved athlete and artiste.

There was unrest in South Africa around this time, between the Boer Wars, and the following year the second Boer War broke out.

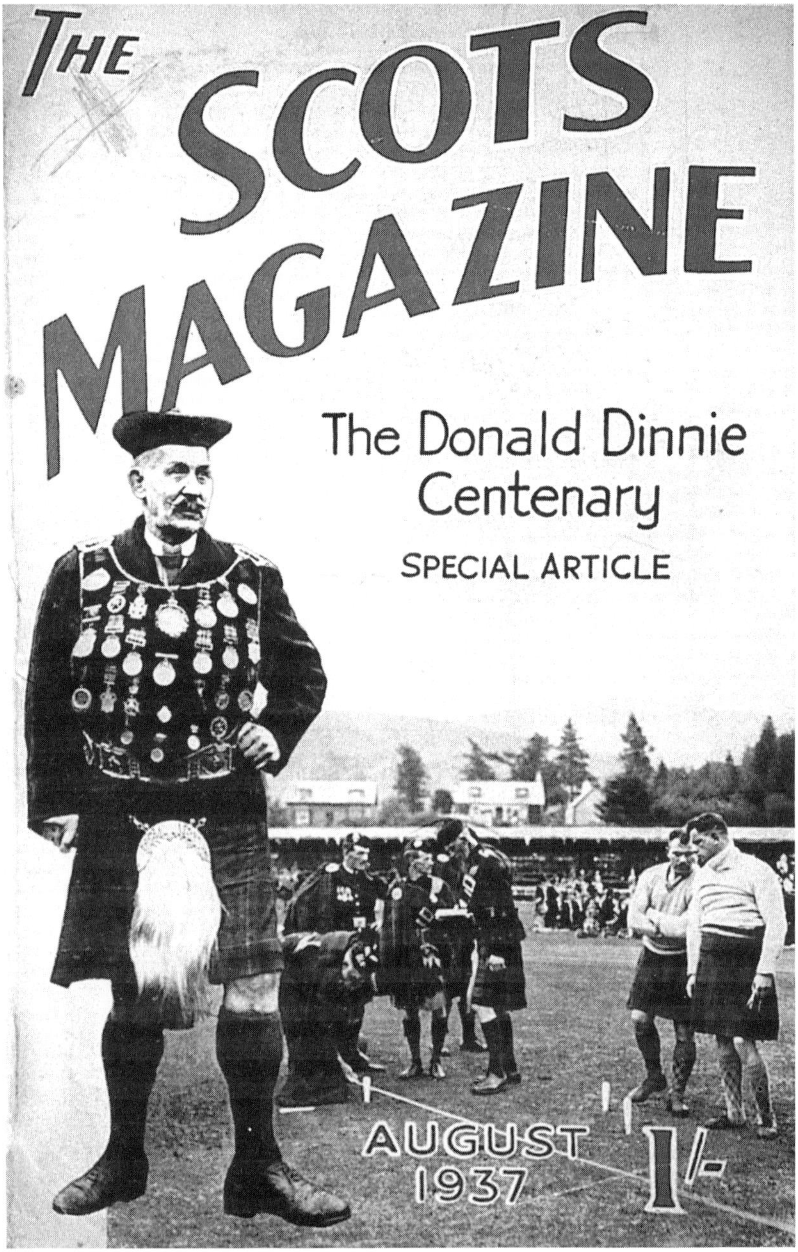

Still a coverman in the 1930s
Courtesy: D. C. Thomson

Back Home

Busk ye, Musie, lauchin' leddy!
Get ye on yer tartan plaidie;
Here am I baith richt and ready,
Come wi' me, my hinny!
Donald's hame, an' a' in fettle,
I maun see him ere I settle,
King he's yet for mak' and mettle,
Scotland's Donald Dinnie.

Northern Scots should a' befrien' him,
Mony a cheer ere this they've gie'n him;
Fifty score o' times they've seen him,
Highest honours win aye.
Throwin', puttin', tossin', shakin',
Rinnin', loupin', naethin' lackin',
A'thing that he liket takin',
Mighty Donald Dinnie.

Finely cou'd he handle ony
Man o'micht an' coup him bonnie;
Stories tru an'grand and mony
'Bout him I cou'd spin ye.
He has trod the earth defiant,
Foremost ever, self reliant;
Scotland's great athletic giant -
Peerless Donald Dinnie.

So wrote John Scorgie of Aberdeenshire, echoing the sentiments of the North-east community.

After a short break, Donald Dinnie resumed his professional stage appearances and soon had bookings in England. He was accorded a rousing reception in St James Hall, London, late in December at a function under the patronage of the Marquis of Huntly, Lord Houpton, who had just been appointed Lord Chamberlain. Other dignitaries included Lord Kinnoull of the Highland Society of London and Col. Mildmay-Wilson, Commander 1st Btn. Scots Guards.

Donald's show strongly featured his sons Edwin and Alfred plus his youngest daughter Eva, but there were many other good performers. The band of the Scots Guards played as Dinnie came on stage to open the show at St James Hall and the whole audience, composed mainly of Scots and their ladies, rose simultaneously. It may have been in London, one journalist wrote, but 'twas a bonny Hielan' welcome.

Edwin and Alfred showed their strength and were not at all worried when they were interrupted by a Sandow pupil in the gallery. Donald had already indicated his willingness to have a match with Sandow, the abdominal showman, by depositing his money with the Sporting Life

Edwin & son Donald - 1901 Courtesy: Ian Edwin Dinnie

and Dinnie seemed to revel in the potential challenge from the gallery.

"Cover my money at the Sporting Life office or come on down to the stage, and you'll have fair play. My boys won't run away."

Edwin raised 168-lb with one hand and Alf, who possessed exceptional arm and chest development, beat this with 170-lb in similar style. After this Alf did one of his favourite feats by sitting on his father's shoulders, then leaning backward to lift and pullover and press the 170-lb weight. This was a version of the Roman Chair feat done by the Italian strongman Napoli, seen by Dinnie in Aberdeen many years earlier.

"The entertainment will long be remembered," praised the London press.

After several bookings in England it was only fitting that after an absence of 17 years his first appearance in Scotland should be in Aberdeen. He sailed for the Granite City and booked a one-week stint in the Trades Hall, opening on 26th January 1899.

The memories of his former triumphs had lingered in the Granite City to such an extent that there were unruly scenes as the audience struggled to get the best view regardless of the seating arrangements, and the start had to be delayed. Finally, Dinnie went on stage and restored order, sternly stating that this conduct was uncharacteristic of Aberdeen.

The varied entertainment then proceeded and among the musical items were some by Eva (billed as Evie) Dinnie, who, according to the Aberdeen Journal critic, "acquitted herself with excellent taste and skill for her years with several violin solos". In another part of the programme she displayed ease and grace in the sword dance and Highland fling. It was not generally known that her father was a fine violinist and prize-winning Highland dancer.

There were many accomplished artistes, but the majority were there to see heavier fare and an enthusiastic reception was accorded to Donald Dinnie and George Davidson of Bucksburn, his erstwhile athletic rival in many a Highland games. It pleased the crowd greatly when it was clear that Donald had not lost his Aberdeen accent and still spoke the Doric; they noted that despite the passing of the years he was "not so bulky of yore but still well knit and upright".

Appearing with them was Alf Dinnie, who elevated two half hundredweight for several repetitions with the greatest of ease. He then proceeded to lift a 140-lb dumbbell and pressed it overhead without the slightest semblance of a jerk. Next he hoisted a 160-lb dumbbell with almost equal ease and then raised a 224-lb (over 100 kg) overhead in the standing position. Lying down he did a press on back with the same weight and on completion of the press he also supported Donald Dinnie on the barbell, probably around 200 kilos or 440-lb.

The Roman Chair type feat completed Alf's turn. Here he pulled over and pressed the 2 x 57-lb dumbbells several times in succession.

At subsequent shows in the Trades Hall, Aberdeen, George Davidson was successful in breaking the record for pressing two 56-lb weights simultaneously, one in each hand, for maximum repetitions. After weighing the weights and other preliminaries, George increased the record to 52 repetitions. The previous best had been 41.

Alf attempted to beat Sandow's record of 180-lb in a single hand lift to the shoulder. The weight being attempted by Alf was 190¼-lb, properly weighed and witnessed. The hall was cold but eventually he did succeed in lifting the bar to his chest. During the process, Alf steadied the weight with his left hand, which infringed the rules and the lift was disallowed. Nevertheless it was a fine feat which drew considerable applause.

George Davidson

Although he was billed as Alf Dinnie, there is no evidence that this was Dinnie's son, indeed Eva Dinnie denied it.

An old cutting in the family archives mentions Alf Dinnie and the surname has been scored out. It is most likely that billing a Dinnie trio was simply following a showbusiness custom of the time by having a family act. The Saxons, Rassos and many others did this at that time. Alf was almost certainly Alf Stone of Glasgow, described around 1902 by Glasgow Evening Times correspondent Charles Donald as being "as good as any perhaps in the whole world".

At this Trades Hall show Donald Dinnie did what must still be a world record for a man of his age. He held a 56-lb weight horizontally at arm's length for six seconds. At his best he had held such a weight for an extraordinary 45sec, but considering his age, those six seconds were just as impressive. Even today this feat would beat many professional strongmen, regardless of age. Dinnie's performance concluded with him cutting a block of lead with a slash of sword.

Other feats scheduled for later in the week were wrestling by George Davidson and Donald Dinnie.

Although he lost £12 on the Aberdeen venture, Donald used his South African earnings to fund a tour including Cults, Banchory, Lumphanan, Peterhead, Fraserburgh, Inverurie, Keith, Elgin, Nairn, Golspie and Dundee, to name but a few.

This biography so far has dealt almost entirely with Donald Dinnie as a sporting superstar, but he was a man of many parts. He had unbounded energy and this, combined with his canny disposition, prompted him to fill every waking hour with activity of one sort or another. It started when he was very young and serving his time as a granite stone mason; at that time the Highland games proved a good money-earning sideline.

When he finished his apprenticeship the games assumed more importance, but in addition he struck out in business for more than 15 years on his own account. In 1869 he took over a hotel in Kincardine O'Neil and stayed three or four years before seeking to buy a hotel in Dundee. A deal was almost concluded when he found the hotel yard was a few feet too short for him to practise hammer throwing, so instead he bought the lease to the Royal Ury Hotel, Stonehaven. Donald's version was the magistrates would only give him a pub licence and not a hotel licence.

At Stonehaven, with the aid of his fellow athlete James Fleming, he did great additional business in carriage hiring and funeral undertaking. He thought it could be even more lucrative if he moved to a more remote place where there was no hearse for miles around, so when his lease expired he bought the Kintore Arms, Auchenblae (now called the Drumtochy Arms). Charles Donaldson told the following sad story with a mischievous gleam in his eye.

"Here he set up a pretty large establishment, prepared to bury the whole population at short notice, and on most reasonable terms. But business hung fire, as it were. The people were in no hurry to die and when they were finally compelled to leave the vale of tears, they preferred to be carried as their forebears had been, and Donal's hearse and horses stood idle."

When in the Southern Hemisphere, Dinnie resumed the combination of hotel and carriage business at the Croxton Park Hotel, mentioned earlier, and he still pursued his sporting activities. There he had some of the fastest trotting horses in Australia and they won several important races. He had a restaurant at Auckland, New Zealand.

On returning home, after finding that there was not a great interest in his sporting shows in the north of Scotland, he moved to Glasgow's South Side. There he lived at 17 Portland Crescent, Kinning Park, Glasgow, and had a dining room on Crookston Street[1]. In 1900 he moved to a similar facility in Old Govan Road. It was this year, on 21st March, that his son Hector was born. Donald became a well-known personality in Govan. He was still a fine figure of a man, always in the kilt and fiercely independent in spite of his advancing years. Serving fish suppers was not much of a job for such a superstar.

Only a stone's throw from Donald's premises in Old Govan Road, he had earned more in one day than he was now getting in a week at his dining room. That was in 1876 when he was competing at the Vale of Clyde running track, which later became Cessnock Dock, and latterly part of the site of the Glasgow Garden Festival.

For a while Donald was in charge of a billiard saloon in Glasgow. This was situated a few doors from a junction of Sauchiehall Street and Parliamentary Road or Buchanan Street. The proud old Scot still wore his kilt when engaged in his supervisory activities.

In 1901 Donald, his wife Eleanor, daughter Eva and son Hector moved South before finally settling at 144 Portland Road, Nottinghill, London, but he still maintained his Scottish links and activities. His reputation had a tremendous boost in 1903 when Barr's Iron Brew, introduced to the market in 1901, used Donald's name and image to endorse and promote their new drink.

"I can recommend Barr's Iron Brew to all who wish to aspire to athletic fame," signed Donald Dinnie, All-round Champion Athlete of the world.

Such endorsements appeared in everything from theatre and sports programmes to the Catholic Herald and other newspapers. For a great many years a little label at the top of the bottle carried a picture of Dinnie, a variation of the original where he lifted a big old-fashioned iron dumbbell above his head and had his left foot resting on a crate of

[1]Crookston Street originally ran from the junction of Morrison Street and Paisley Road West to Scotland Street, but most of it disappeared during the construction and development of the Kingston Bridge in the 1970s. The remaining section of the street, which still joins Scotland Street, was renamed Carnoustie Street.

THE

ATHLETES' BEVERAGE.

Opinions of the World's Champions.

BARR'S IRON BREW is a strengthening and invigorating beverage. I have used it for years to my utmost satisfaction. A splendid tonic while training, and a grand PICK-ME-UP after a tussle.

ALEX. MUNRO,
Undisputed Champion Wrestler of Great Britain.
Champion Caber Tosser of the World.

I can recommend **BARR'S IRON BREW** to all who wish to aspire to athletic fame.

DONALD DINNIE,
All-round Champion Athlete of the World.

Iron Brew advert of 1906
Courtesy: A. G. Barr

Iron Brew. In a later label, in track athletics costume, the athlete's raised right arm and left leg made it look as if he was doing a Highland Fling. Now known as Irn Bru, the refreshing beverage still has a macho and trendy image and is hailed as Scotland's other national drink.

Donald Dinnie moved to Newcastle, where he owned the Scotia Hotel. He had forged strong links with the good people of that city who had long since shown their admiration of the world's greatest all-round athlete, although this was not widely known until quite recently.

On 25th June 1996 a 22¾in high mid-Victorian stained pine and gilt-embellished figure of Donald Dinnie was auctioned by Christie's in Glasgow. Its appearance was a complete surprise, as to the best of our knowledge its existence had not been reported or publicised in any way. The value was estimated at £1,200 - £1,800 with a reserve price of £1,500. After brisk bidding it went to Aberdeen District Council Art Gallery and Museum for the sum of £3000.

Statuette of Donald
Courtesy: Christies Scotland

The statuette depicts Donald standing in kilt and sporran and a sash type belt decorated with medallions. It has a silvered plaque inscribed "Presented to Donald Dinnie, Champion Athlete, In Appreciation Of His Athletic Prowess, By His Scotch Friends, In Newcastle 1870." Roughly carved into the underside of the naturalistic octagonal base is G. Robinson, Carver, Newcastle.

The figure was sent to auction by Mr Ronnie Bourne of Falkirk, whose family had the statuette for 60 years. Mr Bourne's great uncle, William Howie, a lay preacher, Master Painter & Sign Writer in Falkirk, received it in 1935 as part payment for work done in the Clachan, a public house which still exists at 15 Main Street, Shieldhill, near Falkirk.

The pine wood statuette had stood on the bar and Mr Howie, recognising the subject, asked the landlord if it was for sale, and if so, at what price. He was due £27 for his labours at the Clachan and settled for £22 plus the statuette. William Howie didn't like the sporran, part of which hung well below the level of the kilt, as they often did in Victorian times. So when he had the statuette refurbished to its present condition he had the offending *sporan molach* (hairy purse) trimmed to be in line with the kilt.

How the statue came to be in the hands of the pub landlord is a mystery. There are some possible links in that Donald had a similar trade in Newcastle, where the statuette originated, and was very friendly with Robert Barr of Barr's Iron Brew, who lived in Falkirk.

On Mr Howie's death in 1940 the statuette passed to his sister Mary Howie, then to her daughter Maisie Howie (Mrs John McDonald) and finally to her nephew Ronnie Bourne, who is thanked for this background information.

This work of art made its appearance in the newcomer's section at the Aberdeen Art Gallery & Museum on the 2nd December 1996. Gordon Dinnie travelled from East Kilbride to view the 125-year-old figure and helped publicise it in the Scotsman, the Herald, Aberdeen Press & Journal, the Bon Accord and on Grampian Television.

Dinnie and the Saxons

When he moved to the Scotia Hotel in Newcastle, Dinnie kept in close touch with the strength scene and was surprised when, in 1904, he read of the weightlifting feats of the great Arthur Saxon (Artur Hennig of Leipzig 1878-1921).

He responded to an article in VIM, a physical culture journal, expressing his disbelief and, coming from such a well-known personality, this was a blow to the Saxon brothers' pride. They decided to visit him at his hostelry in October of that year and Dinnie, being a very fair man, immediately wrote to the magazine telling them what had happened. Of Arthur Saxon he wrote:

Dinnie, left, watches as Sandow performs his feats of strength. Drawing by David Webster

As a one-handed lifter I have not seen his equal, and do not think there is another in the world now who could equal him at the 'slow press'. He called on me last week, and seeing a large dumbbell lying inside the bar, asked the weight of it. I told him 230-lbs.

His younger brother carried it outside and put it up with both hands easily. Then Arthur Saxon stood it on end, pulled it to his shoulder with one hand and pressed it up easily and also tossed it from hand to hand – an extraordinary feat. He then tied a 56-lb dumbbell to one end and at third attempt put it to arm stretch overhead, in all 286-lbs, and this without taking off his coat. The 56-lb weight at one end made the feat all the more wonderful.

I have no doubt now, but that he can exceed 300-lbs at any time, he having style as well as strength. Louis Cyr has no doubt more brute strength, as several of his feats denote, but at the one-handed slow push Arthur Saxon tops all. Then Cyr had so much advantage in weight and measurements which places Saxon as the most wonderful weightlifter living. I believe in a few years his younger brother will be another wonder .... Your favour of a place in your magazine for this will oblige,

Yours respectfully, D. DINNIE, Scotia Hotel, Newcastle-on-Tyne.

A month later Saxon appeared at the Pavilion in Newcastle, where Dinnie and Adam Teviotdale, a noted Scottish weightlifter, watched the lifts and checked the weight of the barbells after they had been lifted. On this occasion Saxon lifted 230-lb in his right hand and 150 in his left while still supporting the other – a two-hands anyhow with 380-lb. Afterwards Dinnie wrote: "His young brother (only 20) lifted a barbell of 302-lb to stretch of arms overhead. This is a wonderful feat for his age and weight (168-lb)."

Apart from showing Dinnie's sense of justice in becoming one of the Saxons' staunchest supporters, the correspondence provides important information about the Saxons and a first-hand comparison with Cyr, a topic of discussion for decades.

Although he was well into his 60s, there were demands from Scotland to see Donald Dinnie compete again in open competition in

Scottish Highland games. One of his supporters reported that "His countrymen expected him to compete against all comers of any age, and many were disappointed when he refused to do so. He was quite ready to give ten years to all comers, which was a very great advantage." This enthusiast went on to say that Donald Dinnie at his best would not have to take off his jacket to win all the heavy events, and in wrestling at least he would win with as great ease as he had done in his own day.

Dinnie compromised and made several appearances at games such as those at Crieff, Rothienorman and Nairn. At a Partick Police gathering at the turn of the century, Dinnie appeared along with Kenneth McRae, George Davidson and James (Clogger) Currie of Alexandria. Their wrestling exhibition was much appreciated. In his series of articles in the Glasgow Evening Times, Charles Donaldson wrote: "The veterans were very well received by the spectators, and many were the flattering remarks passed upon their manly proportions as, in the garb of old Gaul, they appeared on the field.

Dinnie age 69 wrestling J.M.Gray of Glasgow at Rothienorman Games 1905

At the Crieff Highland games in 1905, in a competition for the over 60s, he threw the hammer 101ft 10in, a remarkable feat for a man in his 68th year. Indeed many amateurs today, in spite of modern training, would be proud of such a throw. The following year at Rothienorman, near Aberdeen, he did some fine hammer throwing and wrestled with J. M. Gray of Glasgow. We had a first hand account of this from former athlete Allan Jamieson, who as a young fellow had found it an inspiring occasion. The memory remained throughout his long life.

The 1906 Skye Games were particularly exciting for the younger generation as well as the old-timers. There were two major attractions, and the first of these centred around a flotilla of naval torpedo boats anchored in Portree Bay. The crews integrated well with the community and the sailors entered teams for the tug of war competitions. Tug of war had long been a naval tradition, dating back to the time when the Jack Tars trained to pull heavy cannons from one side of the ship to the other.

The other great attraction was Donald Dinnie, who appeared as a guest of honour and judged the heavy events. Two years later, in 1908, Donald went over the seas to Skye, again to judge the traditional events. Resplendent in his beautiful Championship Belt, the distinguished septuagenarian issued a challenge to anyone ten years younger than himself to compete in an all-round contest. Not surprisingly, there were no takers.

These were not Dinnie's first appearances at the event. In the programme for the 121st year of the Skye Games Roger Hutchinson wrote of: "...Donald Dinnie, the Stonehaven athlete whose presence had so elevated the first years of the Games, and who had helped more than anybody from outside the district to get them under way".

Donald won the heavy events at the inaugural games of 1877 and, as often happened, provided some controversy by querying a decision. Second in the sprint, Dinnie protested that the winner, the Portree excise officer M. Macaulay, had overtaken him unfairly at one of the first bends. Frank Blair, a great runner of the late 1920s and 1930s, used to tell us the tricks of the trade and we believe it most likely that Dinnie made a fast start to take the lead and then ran a little wide at the corner to make Macaulay run round him. The winner's 'unfair' tactic was most likely to run inside Dinnie, perhaps slightly cutting the corner.

The committee ordered a repeat run, for which Dinnie won the £2 prize. Macaulay declined to run again but took his revenge in the high jump, beating Dinnie by 2in. Dinnie earned £11 19s 6d that day, the equivalent of about £600 today.

He went back the following year with his friend George Davidson and the two North-east athletes shared all the prizes for heavy events. These early appearances helped lay a firm foundation for the Skye games, so 30 years on the committee and crowd of 1908 gave him a very warm welcome.

On 13th August 1910 Donald competed at Nairn, where the veterans handicap hammer throwing prizes were 40s, 30s and 20s.

Before the event Dinnie wrote to Kenneth McRae complaining: "My leg is still very weak – and I fear it will never be right again, yet I must do something for a living." But Donald won in spite of having the biggest handicap.

The letter to McRae was written from 240 Buchanan Street, Glasgow. He was then 73 years of age and this may have been his final major competitive appearance at Highland games. He did some exhibition work, including throwing the hammer at Stamford Bridge Highland Games, although he had past his three score years and ten. He was a marvel even then, but not so sure-footed as before. He slipped and fell, badly injuring his thigh.

Dinnie continued to appear at Highland gatherings and there are several stories of his verbal clashes with John J. Miller, an athlete journalist who often judged. Strangely, Miller did not feature Donald Dinnie in his book on Scottish sports.

On one occasion when Miller was judging a games in London, the famous high jumper and record holder J. A. Speedie cleared 6ft to win first prize. Miller commented to Dinnie: "Here are four lads who have only an inch and a half between all four. The first is 6ft and the fourth 5ft 10$^{1}/_{2}$in. How does that compare with the ancients, Donald?"

Donald Dinnie circa 1901

"Hoots!" replied Donald, "I was niver muckle o' a jumper, but mony a time I traiveled throu' aneth the stick efter I cleared it."

Dinnie was 6ft 1in and he is credited with a record high jump of that height in 1868 at Turriff. He did 5ft 11in on more than one occasion and this is generally the height credited to him.

Donald was a very outspoken character, sometimes clashing with Highland games officials and amateurish committees. Usually local games committees organised, and still organise, only one games a year; with changing, well-intentioned volunteers. The level of expertise could often have been improved. If equipment or conditions were not good for athletes, Dinnie was the spokesman.

He hated to be ripped off on the field or in daily life, and his associates relished stories about this aspect of his character. Dinnie arrived in

London about 2am one morning for an 8am meeting with a colleague. London's horse drawn cab owners were as notorious for overcharging then as some taxi drivers are today, but that did not trouble Donald Dinnie. He asked the cabby to take him to his destination, Euston Station, and settled down comfortably in the coach. He was soon sound asleep. Noting the snoring the cabby thought he could put one over on this hick from the sticks and he too had a cat-nap before continuing on his journey.

As dawn broke the journey was resumed and he eventually awoke Donald at Euston, asking for a fare to cover the several hours taken. Donald did not flinch, he simply called to a nearby policeman and asked how much it should cost for a cab between the two railway stations. On being informed, he carefully handed over the exact amount plus a tip. The gloomy-faced cabby took in Dinnie's athletic appearance and the nearby police presence and realised that on this occasion he had come off worst.

A journalist, whose byline reads only S. G., had seen Donald Dinnie on an Aberdeen tram and recalled his impressions. "This legendary figure was arrayed precisely as in the family album, and little older save for a tinge of grey at the temples. There was no mistaking this man. His entry was like a piece of history coming to life. I felt much as one would feel if the traditional figures of Wallace, Bruce or Burns were suddenly to revisit and seat himself in a tram car. ... I could scrutinise Dinnie at my leisure. I noticed particularly his eyes which were dark like his hair, and he had a sort of keen but forbidding look, indicating that he was the sort of man to whom you would not speak first or employ any idle remark. Then I took stock of his physique... He was of beautiful proportions with a round tournure of limb such as one associates with Greek statuary. He was not excessively broad of shoulder but immensely deep-chested. There was a sort of close-coupled economy about him, which gave him a splendidly-knit figure. And when he walked, with what an easy, graceful carriage he bore himself.

"There he excelled any man I have ever seen in Highland dress, despite the fact that he was then in his sixties. His kilt seemed to swirl and fizz as he walked, and this was due to no swinging of the arms or anything of that kind. He carried some papers in one hand and a cane in the other, and he did not take long steps; yet his perfect figure gave the kilt that motion which many may aim at but few achieve ...I have never seen one who looked so clearly a part of Scotland's story."

Donald Dinnie and his contemporaries

As a young man Donald Dinnie was a noted stone mason as well as being a great athlete and we should not overlook this part of his life. He also encountered many great athletes in a very important era for traditional sports. He mentions a number in his writings earlier in this book and we have been able to find further details on some of them and the feats they performed. The research for this book has revealed a variety of fascinating facts not included in his own memoirs, but inserting these along with Donald's own perspective would have interrupted the flow of his personal account. The following information fleshes out some aspects not covered elsewhere.

Locals remembered that Dinnie as a small boy displayed a great interest in all the Highland games in the neighbourhood. They would tell of him climbing trees to look over the head of spectators. At ten years of age Donald Dinnie was one of two boys who could keep pace with the Deeside coach in a two-mile stretch between Kincardine O'Neil and the Bridge of Potarch.

He played with stones and hammers and wrestled in fun with his friends until he was a youth and ready for serious competition.

In his younger days Donald would often compete in two events at the same time, throwing and jumping alternately. At Luss Games one year Dinnie had two consecutive failures in the high leap and a third would have meant elimination from the competition. He whipped off his kilt and cleared the bar with ease. There was a mixture of cheers and laughter, many being amused at the briefness of his tartan underpants.

He was one of the few competitors who played a part in organising and administration of the games.

On the 27th July 1867 Donald and Lubin Dinnie were amongst the many businessmen and farmers who attended a public meeting in the Huntly Arms Hotel. At that meeting they were elected to the committee, becoming founder members of the Aboyne Games. The games were held at the Market Stance that year and Donald, with nine firsts and a second, carried off the chief honours.

The hotel lounge bar now features a large stained glass window, depicting Donald Dinnie competing on a games day.

Lubin Dinnie, Donald's brother, was 6ft 4in and 18st. He achieved

This stained glass window depicting Dinnie is in the Huntly Arms Hotel, Aboyne

considerable fame when he built the walls of his own four-roomed house in one day. Constructed of stone and lime, Lubin did all the building himself while two labourers carried stones and kept the lime tub filled. It was his home for many years.

Donald Dinnie worked as a mason until he was over 30 years of age and he too set a record as a stone mason. At one time he issued a challenge to any mason in the world to compete against him in dressing and building granite, the hard stone for which Aberdeen is famous. At Crossroads, Lumphanan, Aberdeenshire, with his colleague William Gilbert acting as labourer, the pair set a record. The amount one carried and the other built in a given time has probably never been equalled.

Strangely, Willie Gilbert came from a small, rather remote estate known as Leochel-Cushnie, where 100 years later Henry Gray farmed. He was the 6ft 4in, 240-lb heavy athlete who did some fine lifting of the Dinnie stones.

When Donald Dinnie was a stone mason he did a lot of heavy lifting. Once, using shoulder straps, he supported 1,904-lb and one old book states that when building the Union Bank at Ballater, Dinnie, completely unassisted, carried the huge lintel stone up the scaffolding.

Around and after 1853, Dinnie was considered a big mason lad with athletic potential who enjoyed the games at weekends. From 1858 to 1868 he downed tools during the summer only in order to compete in as many games as possible. An exception was 1867, when he was very ill with influenza early in the season and was hardly into his stride by the time the season was over.

Dinnie made great improvements in his athletic career after he ceased hard daily toil as a stone mason.

At that time a railway was being built in the north of Scotland and on pay days or Saturday nights the navvies would sometimes descend on the villages looking for trouble. They certainly met their match when they encountered the Dinnie brothers and after that first experience the railroad workers gave Aboyne and district a wide berth.

There were a number of setbacks for Donald Dinnie during this period, but he does not dwell on them. As a youth he fractured his left arm. It was badly set and he felt he never developed his full power potential with this arm. The accident probably occurred during his work as a stone mason, there being a separate reference indicating an accident but not stating the nature of the injury. The illness just before the 1867 season took a heavy toll and considerably cut down his activities at that time. In the winter of 1867/68 a serious knee injury was sustained in a horse-riding incident, when his leg was smashed against a gatepost.

He took many hard knocks while jumping and vaulting, including a severe straining of the left hand and arm while in North America in 1872, which badly affected his throwing for the rest of the season. There was little in the way of soft landings at Highland games; very often there was no sand at all, even for the pole vault. When there was some sand it would be about as much as there is in a back yard sand pit for children. Little wonder he broke his ankle in the long jump at Rothesay Games in 1871. This injury probably prevented him going to the USA that year with James Fleming, and became a permanent handicap.

Dinnie appears to have had at least four fairly serious injuries of this nature. Professional athletes like Dinnie usually returned to training and competition before full recovery and the cumulative effects were seen and felt years later, as Donald sometimes mentioned

Among many noted athletes mentioned by Dinnie were champions John Tait, James Fleming, Kenneth McRae and high ranking William Stewart and Owen Duffy. Here are a few pen pictures of these worthies.

William Stewart was born near Pitlochry, Perthshire, in 1829 and died in Liverpool in 1900 aged 71. He was particularly good at the stone put and the heavier the stone the better he liked it, being seldom beaten with the 28-lb rock. He was also excellent in throwing the 56-lb weight.

He grew in physical stature beyond the early stage mentioned by Donald, developing to 168-lb (approximately 12 stone or 76 kg) at 5ft 7¾in. Away from the games field he was an exceptional quoiter and golfer. He went to Liverpool in 1869 and became prosperous as a game dealer in St John's Market.

John Tait was born in 1829, one of seven brothers, several of whom were outstanding athletes. Their father was a shepherd at Glendoch in Crawfordjohn, Lanarkshire. John and William (1836-1900) were champion all-round heavies.

John Tait

John was capable of a 48ft putt with a 16-lb shot and he won many overall championships at Scottish games, including Inverness and also at Glasgow, when the games were held at College Green, just off the High Street. He was 6ft and weighed 15 stone (210-lb or approx 95 kg). He was a gamekeeper, employed for 30 years by the Duke of Hamilton. After retiring from this post he had a farm in the north of England and died about 1896.

Owen Duffy was born in County Monaghan, Ireland around 1847 and as a young man came to join Edinburgh Police Force. He served with the police for many years, then opened a little hardware shop at Abbey Hill, Edinburgh, which is between Holyrood Palace and Meadowbank, the national sports centre. A happy, witty man, he was popular among the athletes. Duffy was at his best between 1869 and 1876 and did not compete at Aboyne until 1883. This is probably because he much preferred an iron ball to the stones that were used at the Deeside games and most of those in the Highlands.

Kenneth McRae was born at Windwell, Beauly, on the Moray Firth in 1850. He worked on a farm from 12 until 18, when he got a job in a distillery producing Scotch whisky. At 31, with increasing industrialisation in Scotland and movement to the cities, he went to work in Edinburgh Gasworks – a typical tale of the times. He began training for the games at the age of 14 and was at his best around 1880-1890, becoming Scottish Champion in 1887 when George Davidson went to the USA.

By then he was 6ft 3in and weighed 217-lb (almost 100kg). His best hammer throws were done in 1882 at Kingussie, when he did 125ft 5in with the light hammer and 99ft 9in with a 21-lb hammer. His best putting was probably at the Edinburgh Exhibition of 1886 when, after torrential rain, he did 40ft 3in with the accurate Inverness heavy stone to beat the hotly fancied Owen Duffy and George Davidson. He also won the light stone, hammer and caber to take the overall prize.

At the great Paris Exhibition where the Scottish heavies provided a highlight for the event, Kenny McRae won the hammers and cabers while Duffy won the puts. These competitions were open to the world so the Scot was justly proud. McRae was also a good wrestler and at his best could clear 5ft 8in in primitive high jumping conditions. He finished his days managing a small farm in Nairn.

George Davidson of Drumoak was born in Kincardine O'Neil, virtually making him Donald's neighbour. Born the year Dinnie began his athletic career. Davidson was a good weightlifter as well as being very competent in the traditional throwing events. In the mid 1870s he began to take over Fleming's position as second only to Dinnie in Highland games. He also appeared in circuses and on stage as a professional strongman, often with Donald. He was particularly good at repetition pressing with two 56-lb weights and by contrast in the single arm bent press, having succeeded with 200-lb.

Davidson became Dinnie's successor as champion in Scotland. He went to America to compete in 1879 and was the leading athlete there that year, beating all the best, including Duncan C. Ross. As well as being considered Scotland's best weightlifter of that time, George Davidson was a good sprinter, high jumper and vaulter.

In the mid-1890s he was the landlord of the Station Hotel, Bucksburn, Aberdeen.

Donald Dinnie and George Davidson appeared in Myers Circus at the Bingley Hall, Birmingham, giving exhibitions of weightlifting and wrestling. The Scots were seen by a young gymnast, Lawrence Levy, who was inspired by the performances. In the autobiography he wrote many years later, Levy said:

> "The demonstrations of feats of strength by these two men appealed to me very strongly and I said to Professor Hubbard (Chief Instructor at the Birmingham Athletic Club) 'I am going in for weightlifting.' He strongly dissuaded me, told me that I should get 'muscle bound', cart-horsey and lose all elasticity; but my mind was made up, and my next move was to buy a pair of 56-lb dumbbells for private practise at home in the School-room or my parlour."

E. Lawrence Levy, born in 1851, was a teacher at Birmingham Hebrew School and Jewish Collegiate School. He became the first World Amateur Weightlifting Champion. Over the years Donald Dinnie inspired many young persons to take up sports and adopt a healthy lifestyle.

When over 40 Donald Dinnie appeared at the Royal Aquarium with George Davidson. This was long before Samson, Sandow and Cyr appeared at this famous venue. The Aquarium became the Mecca for strongmen because of the traditions established by people such as Dinnie and Davidson. There was a strong weight-lifting content in the Scottish act as that

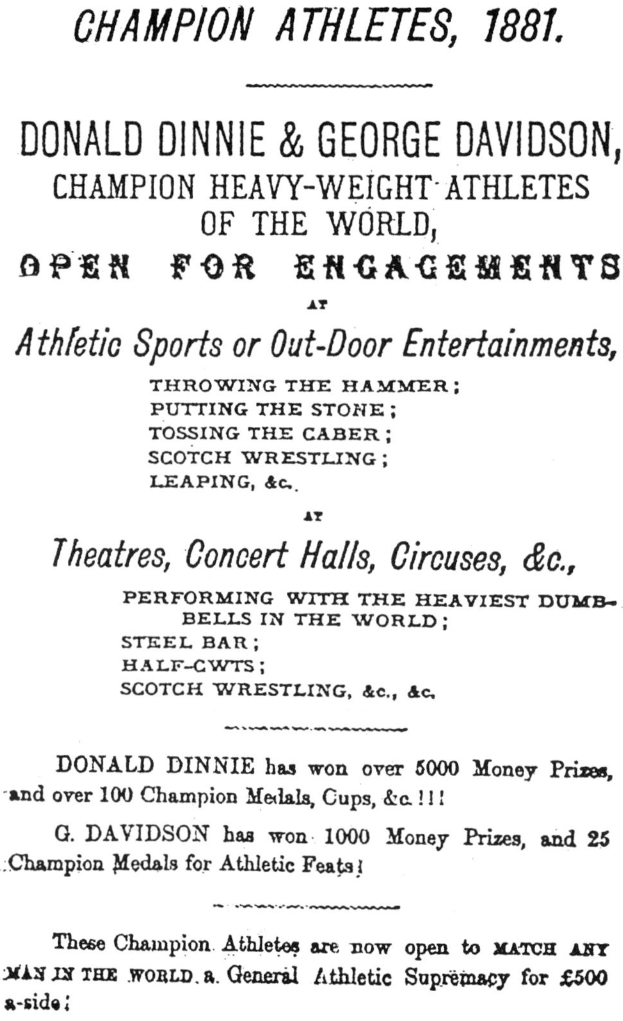

CHAMPION ATHLETES, 1881.

DONALD DINNIE & GEORGE DAVIDSON,
CHAMPION HEAVY-WEIGHT ATHLETES
OF THE WORLD,
OPEN FOR ENGAGEMENTS
AT
Athletic Sports or Out-Door Entertainments,
THROWING THE HAMMER;
PUTTING THE STONE;
TOSSING THE CABER;
SCOTCH WRESTLING;
LEAPING, &c.
AT
Theatres, Concert Halls, Circuses, &c.,
PERFORMING WITH THE HEAVIEST DUMB-BELLS IN THE WORLD;
STEEL BAR;
HALF-CWTS;
SCOTCH WRESTLING, &c., &c.

DONALD DINNIE has won over 5000 Money Prizes, and over 100 Champion Medals, Cups, &c.!!!

G. DAVIDSON has won 1000 Money Prizes, and 25 Champion Medals for Athletic Feats!

These Champion Athletes are now open to MATCH ANY MAN IN THE WORLD a General Athletic Supremacy for £500 a-side;

An advertising flier for Davidson and Dinnie, from 1881

Louis Cyr, who appeared at the Aquarium

was the fashion of the time because of the growing invasion of foreign strongmen. The Highlanders' lifts were outstanding for the late 1870s and early 1880s. Dinnie would one-hand-snatch 168-lb and also did a two-hands clean and jerk/press with dumbbells of 128-lb (right hand) and 112-lb (left hand) simultaneously. He also did the same lift with 132-lb and 102-lb. Davidson did a one-hand clean and jerk with 180-lb, which was a record at that time. When it was eventually said to be broken by Richard Pennell (USA) it should be noted that the American used two hands to take the weight to the shoulder and bent pressed it. While this was a one-hand lift it was one where much greater weights were possible.

George Davidson, Dinnie's successor as champion in Scotland

Donald McDonald was one of a trio of Titans from the remote Lairg in Sutherland; G. M. Ross and Alex Munro being the other two outstanding strength athletes from there. The three were better at putting than at hammer throwing, saying that although there were stones a-plenty, in that exposed locality there was little wood for hammer shafts. Donald was one of many Highland athletes who joined Partick Police to enhance his quality of life and gain opportunities to train and compete.

James Fleming, born at Ballinluig in Perthshire in 1840, was one of the greatest athletes of Victorian times. At his best around 90 kg to 200-lb, he was a handsome figure with a fair, well trimmed moustache. James Fleming was a very popular man in the area, with the polished manners of a gentleman, gained from his experience as the favourite butler and brewer of his Grace the Duke of Athol. This area still has important links

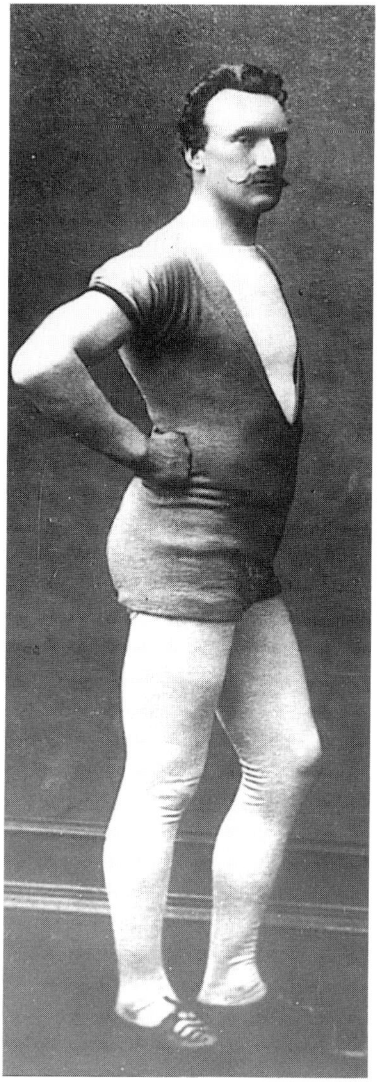
James Fleming, a close friend

with Highland games, with the Dukes of Athol being Patrons of the International Federation of Heavy Event Athletes. In the 1980s and '90s we have had the opening international Highland games of each season in front of the castle, by the mound surmounted by a larger-than-life statue of Hercules, the god of strength. The links with past gatherings do not end there; the Swanston/Robertson family of Ballinluig is prominent at the games (in dancing and sprinting) and the Athol Highlanders are the last private army in Europe.

Fleming was at his very best when in this environment and he pushed Dinnie very hard at this time, especially with the stones and caber. Fleming put a genuine 22-lb stone 38ft on level ground at Perth in 1867 and 41ft at Dundee, slightly downhill. When Dinnie was in America in 1870 Fleming took over the championship, winning nearly every games he entered.

The following year he had a very successful North American tour, a highlight being his defeat of the McLennan brothers of Glengarry, Canada. The following year he returned to the USA with Dinnie and they became close friends, for three years travelling from games to games taking most of the first and second places and not worrying very much about the detailed results.

Fleming went into partnership with Dinnie at Stonehaven and until 1881 looked after the management of the carriage hiring business when Dinnie was otherwise engaged.

Rory of the Hammer

There were four athletic McLennan brothers in Glengarry, Canada, an area as Highland as any place outwith Scotland with the exception of Nova Scotia. Until a century ago there was more Gaelic spoken in

Glengarry than there was in Cape Breton. The athletic McLennans became famous in their own area but never really got the credit they were due.

There was Angus R. McLennan (1839-1912), Farquhar R. McLennan (1849-1917), Alexander R. McLennan (1852-1911), and best of all, Roderick R. McLennan (1842-1907), the famed 'Rory of the Hammer'. They were pioneers in throwing the wire-handled hammer in the turning style, which eventually became the accepted amateur method. The throws made by Roderick, with various sizes of hammers, were undoubtedly international records, probably world records, at that time.

Their grandfather, Farquhar MacLennan, emigrated from Kintail in 1802 and their father, Roderick (1803-1893), was a veteran of the 1837 rebellion. They were all big men, over 6ft in height and the men on the side of their mother Hannah (nee McDonald) were equally genetically gifted. Her father Calum Mor (Big Malcolm) was 6ft 6in and 250-lb, and her brothers, Col. Big Jim of Gleninore and Finnan the Buffalo, were also well known for their physiques and abilities to use their muscles.

Rory was an exceptionally fine figure of a man, who continued to grow in height after Dinnie had seen him, reaching 6ft 4in and weighing 17st. According to David G. Anderson, former president of the Glengarry Historical Society, Rory's athletic prowess won him a gold medal in 1870. Turning to railway construction above Lake Superior, he earned a fortune from these efforts and for a time operated a private bank (McLennan & Brown) in Alexandria. After this he merged two newspapers in Cornwall and created the Cornwall Standard. Next he introduced The Glengarian newspaper to Alexandria. His lovely mansion of that era still stands in Dominion Street, Alexandria, opposite the post office.

A poet, sadly unnamed, was inspired to write about 'Roderick of the hammer' and the last part of a five verse rhyme tells of his mighty throw.

"For Roderick's feat it is a treat
That's worth a long day's going
Words cannot ring his mighty swing
It's the sublime of throwing!
Transformed into a living wheel,
The demon of the centre,
He gathers power, yet guides the steel
Where mortal dare not enter."

R. R. McLennan
Courtesy: Doug Fales

Unfortunately one sad day a mortal did dare enter the throwing arena when the hammer throwing event was in progress. The dire consequences of this changed the course of Canada's athletic history.

This tragic accident happened during Queen Victoria's birthday celebrations of 1877 and finished Big Rory's athletic career. Ellen Kavanagh, a young textile worker, met her death when she wandered into the throwing arena during the hammer throwing competitions and Rory never threw a hammer again.

Turning to politics, Rory defeated the local Liberal candidate to represent Glengarry in Ottawa and later, in 1896, Big Rory again trounced the opposition. He was elected an MP for Winnipeg and in 1897 became Lt. Col. Officer Commanding the Glengary militia, a post he held until 1900. He departed this life seven years later.

Here are some of the performances credited to R. R. McLennan in North America, using the terminology given.

May 1860 at Cornwall	*12-lb hammer, run and swing*	216ft
1864 Gold Medal	*24-lb hammer, run and swing*	106ft 9in
	14-lb hammer, run and swing	162ft 4in
July 11 1865 at Buffalo, New York	*10-lb hammer, run and swing*	285ft
Aug 1872 at Charlottentown R.E.I.	*16-lb hammer, run and swing*	180ft
	23-lb hammer, standing at mark	91ft 7in
	23-lb hammer, run and swing	130ft 4in
	56-lb hammer, run and swing	37ft

Awards

Cornwall 1865	*Champion of World. Match with Thomas Jarney. $1,000 cash 12, 14 and 16-lb hammers.*
Toronto 8 Aug 1870,	*12-lb hammer for American Championship.*
11 Aug 1872	*Montreal Hammer Championship Medal.*
20 Aug 1872	*Heavy hammer, standing style. Longest throw on record. (Distance not mentioned.)*
Aug 1872	*World Championship in throwing 56-lb. Gold Medal presented by Hon. George Brown.*

Throwing rules and techniques in the days of Donald Dinnie were so different that distances cannot be accurately compared with those of modern times. For example throws with the 56-lb weight for distance were usually done in standing style with right foot to the stance. The weight would be swung pendulum fashion a few times with the right hand and then thrown sideways from the body. This was the technique used mainly by Dinnie and Davidson.

Dinnie topped 29ft 7in and Davidson 28ft from this standing position without foot movement. Where the rules were a little more lenient, allowing the competitors to move their rear foot to the stopboard, the competitors would stand with their left foot to the trig and after preliminary swings would bring the right foot forward as they released, much as was done in stone putting.

Block 56-lb weights and standard ring weights for scales were invariably used in Scottish games.

In Canada Rory McLellan had developed wire handles for hammer throwing and in weight throwing used a ring weight and chain, achieving a tremendous throw of 37ft in Toronto in 1872, while Dinnie did 40ft 6in with an 18in chain weight.

Canada and America provided rich pickings for top Scottish athletes willing to travel and Dinnie had great support from Caledonian Clubs.

At a meeting of the New York Caledonian Club, on 2nd February 1869, Chieftain G. Mitchell proposed that the club pay the passage of Donald Dinnie, the great Scottish athlete to attend and compete at their annual games.

The Finance Committee Report of 1870 shows that they agreed to pay Donald Dinnie's passage, his ticket costing $130. While the trip was financed by the club, whose games attracted around 20,000 people, this appears to have been a seven-week tour covering around 12 major venues. One of Dinnie's greatest achievements was beating George Goldie, the Caledonian Club's golden boy.

George Goldie (1841-1920) was born and educated in Edinburgh until he went to New York and started work at the age of 13. He became the Caledonian Club's gymnastic instructor in 1861 and did a stint as a circus performer in and around 1867. Goldie was a very influential figure in sport and physical education and in her fine book Ann Donaldson says that as a Highland games athlete, Goldie was as well known in America as Donald Dinnie. Our own research shows that in the 1860s and 1870s Goldie won many prizes in heavy events as well as in jumping and pole vaulting.

In Canada George Goldie became the country's first great pole vaulter and while he was living in Montreal in 1869 he was headhunted to become the first Head of Physical Education at Princeton University. He established Caledonian games at Princeton in 1873, pioneering university competitive track and field athletics. Princeton continued to call their annual event the Caledonian Games until 1947. In an article published in The Highlander in May 1987 Richard D. Smith wrote: '...the face of American and world athletics had been changed forever, thanks to George Goldie'.

George Goldie
Courtesy: Dr Gerry Redmond

From 1885 until 1893 he was a popular director and the first coach of the New York Athletic Club. Then he returned to Princeton, where he remained until he retired in 1911. At the age of 65 George could still do 'grand circles' on the horizontal bar. Vigorous in his 79th year, he died after a heart attack on 23rd February 1920.

The fact that Dinnie soundly defeated the great George Goldie in nearly every event on his first two visits to the States speaks volumes for Donald's abilities. On his second visit, in 1872, Dinnie threw at the New York Caledonian Club Games and also acted as a judge. The Scottish games inspired American strongmen and led to the formation of the New York Athletic Club in 1868, the first such organisation in the USA.

The very first Cowal Highland Games was held on a Friday in September 1871, in a field at Auchamore Farm, where cottages and bungalows were later erected at the top of Mary Street and Alexander Street. "There was a large and respectable gathering of spectators from all parts of the district to witness the feats of the champions. The day was fine and everything passed off well," stated a reporter in the Argyllshire Standard. The champions referred to were Donald Dinnie, McCombie Smith and Tom Carruthers. The very junior reporter was Robert Ingles, a mere 11 years old. From these small beginnings grew one of the greatest gatherings.

The charisma of Dinnie attracted to the games many people from all walks of life. Nearly 100 years ago Charles Donaldson wrote in the Glasgow Evening Times that when Donald was in his prime an old woman from Deeside tramped many miles to get a glimpse of the man about whom she had heard so much.

The Cowal Trophy

Worming her way through the crowd, with more than a little jostling and elbowing, she finally got to a ringside position from which the athletes could be seen. Eagerly she enquired which of the sturdy lads was Donal' Dinnie.

"That's him with the sun-tanned skin."

"Aye; he's a braw chiel; a real braw chiel. A'weel, I'll awa' hame again; I'll dee happy noo I've seen Donal' Dinnie."

Donald Dinnie took this story as a deep compliment. To him she was one of many who had paid from meagre earnings to see the games. He took a slightly different view on another occasion at the Braemar games when they were held at Mar Lodge.

'I Dinnie Gie a Damn!'

The heavy gang was about to leave the field, their events over for the day, when the call went out that the Prince of Wales was arriving. He had been expected much earlier but was far behind schedule. Flustered committee members debated on what to do and naturally their discussion immediately centred on the champion. Dinnie was approached to exhibit the hammer and toss the caber, a suggestion to which he readily agreed.

"Aye, I'll gang oot," said Dinnie "But I want twa pound."

"But Donal', it's the Prince of Wales. It's an honour, ye ken, tae throw afore the Prince."

"I dinna gie a damn," stormed Dinnie; "I pay my taxes, an' I'll no' tak less."

He refused to be persuaded so the other athletes went out without him. The hammer went quite well but when it came to the caber there was failure after failure. Not one of the athletes succeeded in turning the long tree trunk; it was a total anti-climax. Suddenly there was a stirring in the crowd, Dinnie rushed to the centre of the field and, confidently picking up the caber, tossed it with ease.

Dinnie later said he asked for the £2 as an extra prize for which all the athletes could compete, but really the end result would have been the same.

A good deal about Donald Dinnie was written by William McCombie Smith, a schoolmaster who was also Dinnie's brother-in-law. Far from being sympathethetic to his relative by marriage, he was one of his severest critics.

McCombie Smith appeared at Highland games for the first time in 1871 and was coached by Donald Dinnie. Like many teachers he liked learning but did not enjoy being taught and was often critical of Dinnie. He was always quick publicly to point out any anomalies. For example, one of Dinnie's best recorded hammer throws achieved a

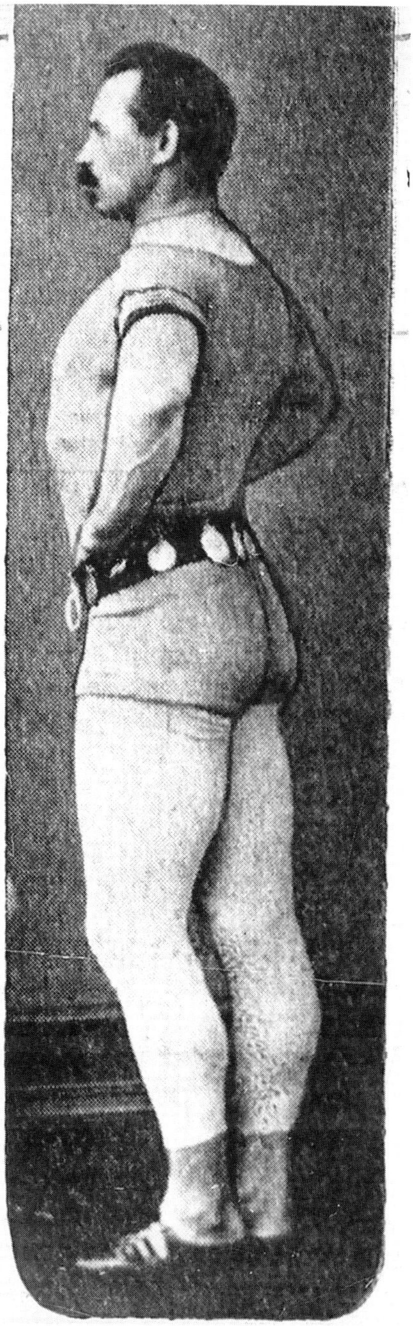

Donald Dinnie in the style of outfit used for field athletics and wrestling. There was a lengthy period in late Victorian and Edwardian times when kilts were optional in the heavy events.

distance of 138ft 7in, but this was not validated because the shaft was 4ft 6in and a short trench was dug in front of the thrower so the hammer would not hit the ground at the lowest part of the swing.

A book of the Braemar Royal Highland Society described McCombie Smith as a great authority on Highland sports. He was only a second class performer in the heavies, but ran a good race in his younger days. He married Donald Dinnie's sister Nory Celia in Glasgow in 1878 but Dinnie and McCombie Smith continued to argue about throws and throwers.

The Big Issue, a magazine produced for and sold by the homeless in Scotland, regularly used a photo of Donald Dinnie in a sportswear advertisement. The photo above was featured, in colour, in the 1994 Christmas edition.

Changing Fortunes

As the years went on Donald Dinnie, through no fault of his own, found himself in difficult circumstances. While overseas and earning large sums he had sent much of his money to his relatives in Scotland. The savings of a lifetime had been lost in building and railway investments in Australia's land and property crisis of 1893. A year earlier Dinnie had 12 blocks of land to sell and was offered £1400 for them. After the crash he received only £30, from which he had to pay £6 for the transfer of deeds.

Donald regained some of his wealth through hard work long after the age at which many would have retired. By the time he was 75 he had been driven to the verge of poverty by a series of misfortunes.

Always willing to work hard, Dinnie obtained bookings in London

Donald Dinnie in 1912

music halls with a strongman act. Still tremendously strong for his age, in part of his act he supported a platform made from a large table while two Highlanders danced a fling on it.

Another of his favourite feats was to hold a 56-lb weight sideways at arm's length. London County Councillors in 1912, noting that Donald was now in his 76th year, were concerned about the potential damage to the sturdy veteran's health and refused further permission to appear on stage with his act. This ruling, albeit humane, put an end to Donald Dinnie's working life.

T. C. Barbour, an enthusiastic strength fan, approached Stewart Smith, Editor of Health & Strength Magazine[1], with a view to assisting Donald. A meeting was held at the Clachan, Mitre Court, Fleet Street, London, and a very influential committee was formed to establish a Donald Dinnie Testimonial Fund. The British Olympic Treasurer, James Blair, and Stewart Smith (Hon. Sec.) were among those elected and London Scottish associations were very active in the project, which aimed at purchasing an annuity to take him out of penury and give him a better quality of life in his declining years.

An appeal through the press and Scottish athletic associations quickly raised over £100, but much more was needed. Stewart Smith decided to promote a great rally of champion athletes and star artistes which would not only raise money but would give physical culturists a chance to show the high regard in which Donald Dinnie was held throughout the fraternity.

On Saturday 12th April 1913, the London Scottish Drill Hall, Buckingham Gate, Westminster, London was packed to capacity "by brither Scots and Sassanachs too" for a triumphant galaxy of star performers, including some of the greatest names in sport.

It was not simply an athletic display: there was pipes and drums, the London Scottish Band, bonny Highland dancers and Hungarian dancers. The famous boxers Jim Driscoll and Spike Robson, who had fought so

[1]Over the years the owners, editors and writers of Health & Strength Magazine have played a major role in promoting the subjects of their title. It has greatly influenced their lives and benefited many thousands, not least those producing this current publication. From the time it was founded in 1900 by Hopton Hadley until the present day, when the title is owned by Roy Edwards, the magazine has been much more than a mere periodical, thanks to the entrepreneurial flair of its owners and their associates. They have encouraged and promoted great men with potential and they have supported and honoured others who have contributed to physical culture in all its forms. Donald Dinnie's last years were made easier by this fine journal, which provided the inspiration and Dinnie's personal input for this book.

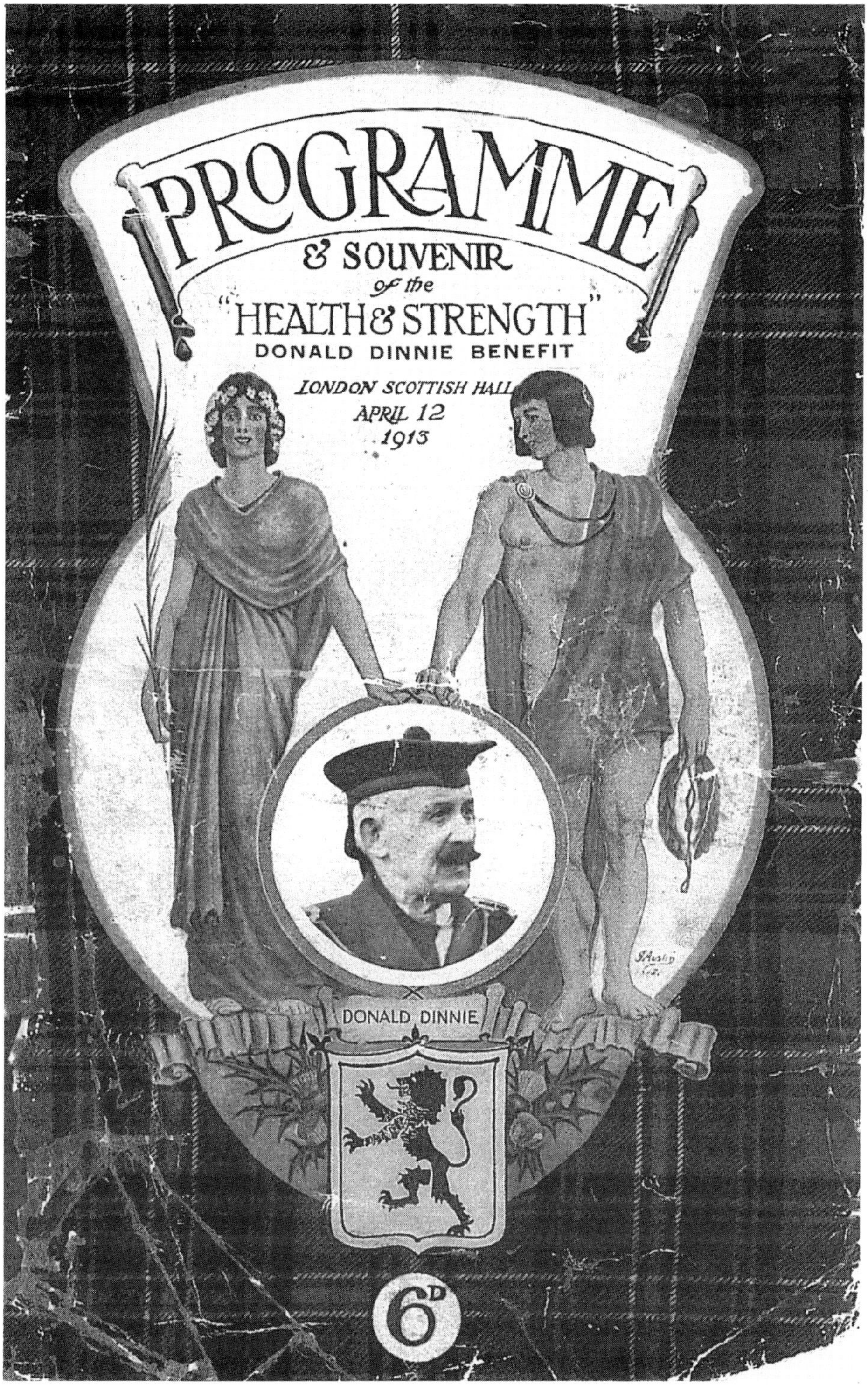

A programme from the Dinnie benefit of 1913. Courtesy: Ian Edwin Dinnie

fiercely in past battles, put on the gloves again for old Donald. There was exciting fencing, not just in modern sporting style but also including a stirring bout with sword and dagger. Edward Aston and Thomas Inch, genuinely Britain's Strongest Men, gave separate superb displays, Aston bringing the audience to their feet when he lifted three men at once. Inch had a near miss with a 300-lb single hand bent press, and the fact that he failed proves that the strong men were not just putting on a show but trying to break records in honour of the beneficiary.

Tom Burrows, the 'King of Clubs', was in scintillating form in his Indian club-swinging act, and so the night went on. The whole entertainment was expertly stage-managed by William Bankier, or 'Apollo', the great Scottish strongman and wrestler who was master of ceremonies. After his strongman career he became Britain's leading professional wrestling promoter.

At the end Dinnie, his breast and back

Jimmy Esson - Aberdeen

William Bankier, of Banff, whose stage name was Apollo

ablaze with medals, was ushered on to the stage to the accompaniment of the bagpipes and introduced to the excited crowd by Apollo. At this time Dinnie was still able to perform a one-hand holdout with a 56-lb weight. In a voice quivering with emotion, Donald thanked all who had espoused his cause. A journalist reporting the show described the moment.

> "There stood the man who in years gone by had carried all before him in the field. He is an old man now but he still bears the marks of the greatness that was his, and the memory which will be Scotland's forever."

After the show one spectator wrote: "I ventured rather timidly amongst the boxers and wrestlers (Jimmy Esson, the Scottish Champion was one of those billed) and was surprised at the goodwill with which they spoke about Dinnie. Several of them had given up engagements in order to give him a helping hand by giving a free turn. I felt proud to be amongst them."

The Testimonial Fund rose to well over £220, the benefit show raising over £80 after all expenses had been paid. Arrangements were then made to provide Donald with an annuity.

Dinnie holds the caber at the Braemar Gathering, Braemar Castle on 1st Sept 1864

Dinnie's Many Awards

Donald was always proud to wear some of his medals on such occasions and many of his numerous awards are still in existence. The best collection of Dinnie memorabilia is in Aberdeen Art Gallery and Museums which, in addition to the pine statuette of Dinnie (see page 90), also acquired 56 of Dinnie's medals and a magnificent silver belt. The belt was made by Walker & Hall and assayed in Sheffield in 1899-1900. It was presented by Dinnie's admirers in Scotland on his return to Scotland at the end of the 19th century after many years abroad. Dinnie's feats and abilities were endorsed by some of Scotland's greatest athletes, named on the belt.

The collection of awards had been feared lost, for they had been passed to a financial backer in Margate, East Kent, when some debts accrued. But the medals and belt returned to the North-east about a quarter of a century later through the combined efforts of John Frost and Cliff Jordan of Aberdeen's Marcliffe Hotel. Cliff tracked down the medals when visiting his mother in Kent during the wartime blitz.

John Frost, host of the Criterion Bar, next to the Tivoli in Guild Street, Aberdeen, had long coveted the medals and was delighted when the debonaire Cliff Jordon, musical director at the Tivoli, passed them on to him. They were displayed behind the Criterion bar for many years and John Frost resisted all efforts by Alex Thomson and David Webster, who wanted them to adorn the walls of the Aberdeen Spartan Club, now Scotland's oldest physical culture club. The club was also represented at the two auctions when other Dinnie items went under the hammer, but the costs were well beyond the means of this amateur organisation.

The medals were sold again in 1963 to MacDonald Ewen of the Banks of Ury Hotel at Inverurie and he subsequently put them up for auction at the Kittybrewster mart, Aberdeen, in 1972, along with Donald's walking stick and two large framed photographs. Bidding did not go as high as he expected, stopping at £1,300 instead of the £20,000 Mr Ewen had hoped for, and were withdrawn. However the large but light medals, while very interesting and valued for their connection with the great athlete, have little other monetary worth.

On 3rd September 1981, at Aberdeen's Belmont Street auction rooms, the medals and presentation belt were once more put under the hammer and were purchased by John MacMillan, a Perthshire art dealer. He immediately re-sold them to Aberdeen City Council for the purchase price of £6,600. The whereabouts of the two framed photographs and the walking stick remain unknown.

The silver belt is something quite different from the medals and by far surpasses in beauty and value other similar sporting awards[1]. Whereas many championship belts have medallions mounted on a leather strap, this one links together ten lovely moulded and engraved plaques depicting Donald Dinnie's greatest achievements. The combining of the mouldings in relief and informative summaries provides a most illuminating testimony to this wonderful athlete.

An extremely important aspect of this award is that Dinnie's best efforts quoted on the plaques were recognised by his contemporaries. The award was endorsed by first class professional athletes including George Davidson and Charles McHardy, as well as by the 'gentlemen amateurs'.

This is significant, as some Scottish athletes resented Dinnie's successes and the press adulation he received. This is easy to understand when one reads papers such as the Aberdeen Herald reporting on the Speyside Gathering in 1878.

"The most popular athletes of the day were present, topped by the redoubtable Donald Dinnie, with whom all competitors at feats of strength appeared as pigmies."

Can you imagine how a strongman more than six feet tall would feel being described as a pigmy?

While Dinnie was appearing at the Folly, Manchester, in 1881, the Manchester Echo enthused:

"Donald Dinnie's performance is certainly wonderful and bonnie Scotland can pride herself on having produced the Man of the Century. Compared with other strongmen, the Lion Athlete for instance at Mayer's circus, Donald Dinnie is as a mastiff contrasted to a half starved terrier."

Any records claimed for or by Dinnie which could not have been substantiated would rapidly have been denounced by his competitors, yet the authenticity of distances and weights detailed on the champion's belt does not seem to have been a source of controversy.

Although we are aware, from correspondence from Eva Bulle, that many of her father's medals were stolen in America, all that are known to us remain in Scotland.

---

[1]Details from the plaques on this belt are given in Appendix 2, page 154

Many of Dinnie's early Highland games medals (1859-1871) are held in the fine collection in Aberdeen City Council's Art Gallery and Museums[1].

There is another excellent, although lesser known, collection of Donald Dinnie's medals on one of the original cloth breastplates once worn by Donald[2]. Edwin Dinnie displayed this breastplate in the Commercial Hotel for many years and we first saw these in a glass case at a weightlifting competition in a Brechin sports club in 1952.

Charlie Allan was able to acquire the medals in the 1970s, and when we went to photograph them he told of his reaction when he first saw them.

"They were being kept in a dusty old bowling bag placed in a storage cupboard, where they seldom saw the light of day. I thought that this great man's wonderful prizes deserved something much better, but guess what..."

Smiling wryly, Charlie opened his cupboard and produced the same old bowling bag with the superb medals.

The Dublin award and the Perth Highland Society medal, top centre of the breastplate, are particularly good medals.

In the course of writing this book the medals were acquired by Gordon Dinnie. He will bequeath the collection to the museum in Aberdeen – where all will be able to see them.

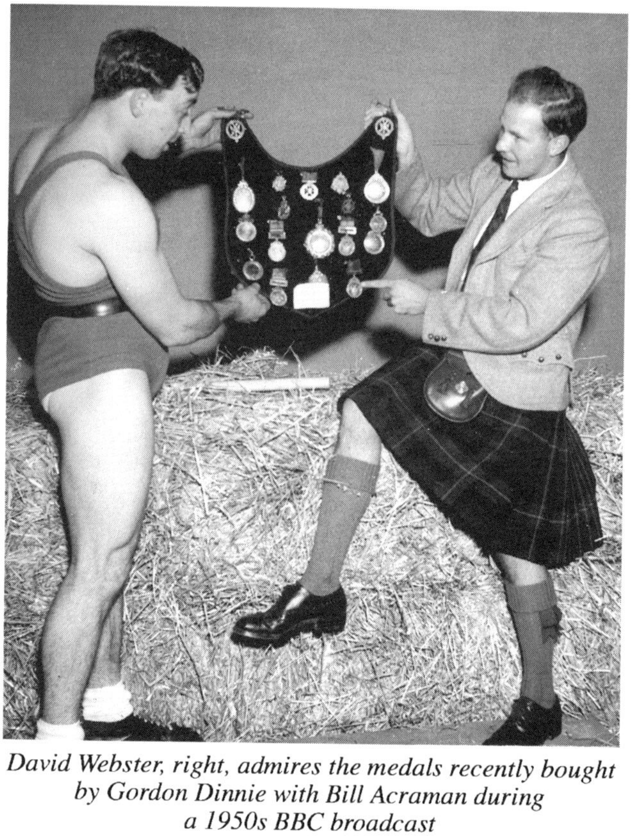

David Webster, right, admires the medals recently bought by Gordon Dinnie with Bill Acraman during a 1950s BBC broadcast

[1]Details of this collection are given in Appendix 3, page 155

[2]Details of this collection are given in Appendix 4, page 156

Famous Aboyne Trophies

The Aboyne Games were originally held on the first Wednesday of September but are now held on the first Saturday of August. Each year at these games three magnificent trophies are awarded to commemorate Donald Dinnie and encourage competitors to follow in his footsteps. The beauty of these prizes, given in addition to cash, makes them very coveted awards.

Mrs Edwin G. Dinnie, Brechin, presented the main Dinnie Challenge Trophy in 1931. It is about 18in high and surmounted by a small statuette of Donald in a stone-putting pose. A fine likeness of Dinnie stands out boldly on the front of the trophy and other aspects show him in athletic events. At each side, rising from the base, are two silver cabers. This is presented specifically for the open heavy events.

Lt. Col. William Lilburn of Coull, then chairman of the games, presented the other trophy to the games, the Dinnie Stone Trophy. This incorporates a putting stone which was used by Dinnie from 1867 to 1881. It sits in a silver ring that accommodates many medallions giving

Dinnie Challenge Trophy & Dinnie Stone Trophy

Marquis of Huntly presents the Dinnie Stone Trophy to Jack Hunter
Courtesy: Aberdeen Journals

the names of past winners; it is a memorable record of the greats of yesteryear. The stone was broken, said to be by one winner who removed it for practice. We were told that prior to becoming part of the trophy, the historic putting stone had been lost and was eventually recovered from some travelling people. This is now presented to winner of the open competition in the light (11-lb) stone.

The Chief's Challenge Trophy is presented to the best all-round athlete, for versatility in Highland games is still seen as an outstanding quality[1]. To win this competitors must score points in light events as well as heavy events.

Jay Scott

During the 1950s there appeared at Highland games in Scotland and abroad a man who truly followed in the Donald Dinnie tradition by competing in the widest possible range of events.

Jay Scott of Inchmurrin was, like his predecessor, a very colourful, larger than life, character. Jay competed with distinction in all the heavy

[1]Recent winners are given in Appendix 5, page 157

events, all the jumping events and the sprints. He was also known to have danced at Highland games.

Such an all-rounder naturally won Aboyne's famous trophies on several occasions and he was one of the most popular athletes ever to appear on the circuit.

Born in Ayrshire in 1930, he and his brother Tom were nephews of Bryce Scott, a famous light event competitor whose name appears on many record lists. Tom and Jay were rugby players before taking up Highland games in 1947. Tom concentrated more on light events, declining the throws if the top heavies were present. During his first season Jay did the jumps and the sprints and the following year entered as many events as possible, running from one to another, sometimes jumping while still wearing his kilt.

The athletic ability of this man can be judged from the performances he did under normal games conditions – remembering that these conditions fall far short of those at amateur international meets. His high jump of 6ft 3½in at Tobermory was recognised as a record. The amazing thing is that he did it in the old-fashioned scissors style, which was the sensible way to avoid injury when there was little or no sand on which to land. He pole vaulted around 11ft 6in at many games, using a stiff pole with a small spike on the end to stop it slipping, as there were no boxes in which the pole could be planted. Once again the style had to be modified to allow him to land feet first in view of the poor landing conditions.

His best time for the 100 yards was 9.8sec, on an undulating grass surface. He was proud of being third in the Powderhall Sprint and of the

Jay Scott competing at Aboyne Games

Bill Anderson, the greatest heavy since Dinnie, with the Dinnie Trophy and Bob Aitken with the Chief's Trophy

fact that he was back marker in this famous handicap race. Jay was remarkably light for a successful heavy, never reaching 200-lb bodyweight as a competitor, otherwise he would have increased his distances considerably. As it was, he threw the hammer 110ft at the end of his first season of heavy events, could putt 16-lb 47ft 3in and in a training putt once approached 50ft, which was a long-held ambition. He threw the 28-lb 73ft and did 14ft 1in with the 56-lb for height. These were very good distances indeed in the days before Bill Anderson shattered all the barriers and opened the flood gates to better performances.

Growing up on the island of Inchmurrin on Loch Lomond, Jay habitually wore shorts all the year round and when he went on business trips or to social events he invariably wore the kilt. I have many great memories of this happy-go-lucky daredevil, who was the greatest practical joker ever seen among the heavies. His pranks would fill a book.

When a group of us toured America in 1972 with The Wonderful World of Sport, one of our heavies remarked several times on an attractive little shrub which we saw each day on our way to the arena. There was great merriment at his reaction one morning when he woke to find this shrub growing in the middle of his bedroom floor, courtesy of Mr Scott.

Jay married a lovely show business personality, Fay Lenore, and they settled down happily together, running a small hotel. Sadly his career was brought to a premature end by a brain tumour, which he managed to overcome. Jay died in 1997 at 67 years of age.

Bob Aitken and sons

The most successful winner of the Chief's Quaich, as it is often called, was Robert Aitken of Auchenblae, a village roughly half way between Stonehaven and Laurencekirk. Bob won the trophy nine times; an amazing achievement. Born on 17 February 1935, he began taking part in professional Highland games in the early 1950s and he quickly rose to the top, being outstanding in the high jump and the light hammer, which he could throw up to 135ft 4in. He took many first prizes in these events but the arrival on the scene of Bill Anderson robbed him of many top places in the hammer.

Stephen Aitken, a versatile and popular athlete

Aboyne was his favourite games, and he competed there as often as possible until he retired from competition in 1972 at the age of 37. His sons Bruce and Stephen have followed in his footsteps and have risen right to the top, both winning the Scottish Championship. Stephen Aitken won the Chief's Trophy at Aboyne and also the Dinnie Trophy. This athlete displayed all the versatility of his father and his outgoing personality made him a very popular competitor. We recall with pleasure that as one of a group of Scottish heavies selected to appear in Highland games events in Wilhemshaven, Germany's 'Sports City of the North', Stephen not only won the competition but was one of the leading spirits in all the entertainment presented during that memorable week in 1989.

Charlie Allan, World Caber Tossing Champion in 1972

Alistair Gunn

Born in 1963, this most northerly thrower in Scotland is also one of the country's finest traditional athletes. He and his brothers are the Gunn family's third generation of Scottish heavies and Alistair's record is the most outstanding. In addition to Aboyne's Chief's Challenge Trophy and Dinnie Challenge Trophy, he has won many titles since he turned professional, and he won the Scottish Junior Championships in 1982.

His victories include the World Heavy Events Championship in 1995, World Caber Tossing Championships of 1992 and 1993, World Hammer Throwing Championships of 1994, 1995 and 1996 and five Scottish Championships. At 5ft 10in and 105kg he is one of the smaller heavies, and this has earned him the nickname of the Giant Killer.

Charlie Allan

Brought up in Aberdeenshire, Charlie won the boys' race at Gight Games in 1947 and quickly established the nickname Charles the Third because he was so often third to Bill Anderson and Arthur Rowe.

Charlie was among the first of the post-war Scots to follow Dinnie's footsteps overseas, competing in four continents in a career that lasted until the mid 1970s. His most important wins were the World Caber Championship in 1972 and the Scottish in the following year.

Charlie also won the Chieftain's Trophy at Aboyne in 1968. He considered that his best achievement as he had a first equal prize in the caber tossing and the high jump in that win. He tells a fine story about it in his book the Scottish Highland Games, published by Famedram in 1973.

"When you are successful in the Highland games you are not expected to run around kissing people or punching the air. But the emotion is strong. When I got back to the anonymity of the train I could control myself no longer. I cried and cried and cried. The trophy comes in a large wooden box. I sat it on the table in front of me. I must have made a pathetic figure for a kind old lady asked if the box held the remains of a dear one, and if it would help to talk about it. I hadn't the heart to tell her."

A true all-rounder, Allan played senior football, was a touring cricketer, captain of his university basketball team and led the Aberdeen pack which beat a full London Scottish team in London in 1960. His weight training enabled him to set a Scottish super-heavyweight record in the dead lift in 1971. Always competitive, when he hung up his hammer-throwing boots Charlie took up jogging, completing several marathons, and at 60 was improving fast in Scottish cycling competitions.

James McBeath

James McBeath, from the little clachan of Dunbeath in the most northerly part of Scotland, was the youngest, lightest and least experienced of our globe-trotting group of the late 1960s and early '70s. He was also the fastest improving athlete and competed with great success, chalking up notable victories over much better known opponents. He and his identical twin brother Tom had promoted positions in the famous Caithness Glass factory and Tom competed in every running event from 100 yards to a mile. He won the British Professional Light Field Events Championship and was declared Sportsman of the Year by the Scottish Games Association. Jim devoted more time to the heavy events and, while he did not take most first prizes in these, his overall scores in light and heavy events were very hard to beat when he was at his peak.

These men are just some of the great athletes who have followed in the tradition of Donald Dinnie by competing in a wide variety of events, both heavy and light, track and field.

Although traditionally the Highland heavies have competed for cash awards, the trophies and medals competed for at games such as those at Aboyne are very important because they help shape tradition by encouraging a versatile approach.

James McBeath throws the hammer

Then and Now

Interesting Comparisons

Dinnie's many medals continue to inspire today's athletes and the wealth of such fascinating memorabilia will continue to commemorate the grand old man of Scottish sport. Yet Donald was a professional in sports where cash was almost always given rather than prizes.

Frank Zarnowski, an American writer, used private and public consumer price indices from 1890-1998 to calculate that Dinnie's total winnings were the equivalent of more than $2.5 million (£1.5m) today.

There should be enough information here to convince even the most sceptical that Donald Dinnie was the first superstar of sport, but just in case there are a few doubters, it's worth considering how Donald Dinnie would have fared at the Olympic Games.

Dinnie's recorded, and widely accepted, performances were well ahead of several gold medallists in the 1896 Olympics at Athens. They show that in good form he could easily have beaten winner Thomas Burke in sprinting. Dinnie did 100yd in under 10.7sec and on one occasion there is a reported 10.25sec. Burke's time for the 100m was 12sec.

Although Dinnie never boasted about his sprinting abilities, he had competed with the best in the world in 1870 at the major pedestrian meeting in Scotland, the forerunner of the famous Powderhall Sprint. Donald could have taken the high jump gold and the long jump silver against Ellery Clark. He would have taken another silver in the triple jump, his best being a reported 44ft. He could have had one or two golds in weightlifting, against the Scot Launceston Elliot, who won the gold medal in two-hand lifting, and Jensen of Denmark, who won in the one-hand lift.

In putting the shot he could have given the winner, Robert Garrett, a good start and still beaten him with ease. And since he had beaten the best professional wrestlers in the world, all the bets would have been on Dinnie to take another gold in this event. He would undoubtedly have won a medal in pole vaulting and given a decent light pole to take his weight, the gold would have been his. He had a habit of breaking poles and having sustained severe injuries in this sport gave it up for fear of further broken bones. His recorded heights in the pole vault easily exceeded Damaskos of Greece's height for the bronze.

This gives a good comparison with the best athletes of last century;

he would have been an Olympic great, a multi-medal winner. Alas, there were no Olympics until Dinnie was in his 60th year and in any case, like all the best Scottish sportsmen where Highland games flourish, he became a professional at an early age.

In Victorian times there were snobbish distinctions between 'gentleman amateurs' and professionals who received payment. These attitudes were rampant in university-based track and field circles and had things been otherwise the fame of Donald Dinnie would have been more lasting. However it is gratifying to note that in a 1996-1997 Internet vote on the world's best ever track and field athletes, Dinnie's name was included along with Carl Lewis, Jesse Owens, Michael Johnson, Linford Christie and a host of other household names.

Strangely enough this snobbishness does not exist at the highest levels. Since Victorian times the Royal Family have always taken a great interest in Highland heavies. One of David Webster's proud recollections of 1986 was introducing Her Majesty the Queen Elizabeth and Prince Phillip to the heavies who were to compete before Prince Edward the following evening at the Commonwealth Games Highland Games at Meadowbank, Edinburgh. Her Majesty and Prince Phillip had a brief but witty conversation with them.

About a century earlier, one of the officials at Braemar gave the Prince Edward of that era, His Royal Highness the Prince of Wales, a similar invitation, asking: "Would you like to meet some of the mighty men of Deeside?"

"Dee-side-edly!" replied the man who became King Edward.

The Final Fall

On 2nd April 1916 Donald Dinnie, in his 79th year, died of valvular disease of the heart at his home, 144 Portland Road, Notting Hill, London, where his wife Eleanor Bagley was present at his death. He was laid to rest in Lair No.9, Section 36, Kensington Cemetery, Hanwell, London on 6th April 1916, Rev. W. L Gibbs presiding. Contrary to information given elsewhere he was not buried in a pauper's grave. His wife bought him a larger than usual plot and spared no expense. Many years later, in 1961, his daughter Eva and son Hector provided a white marble stone. On it is the following inscription: -

HERE RESTS
DONALD DINNIE
1837-1916
CHAMPION ALL ROUND ATHLETE
OF THE WORLD FOR 30 YEARS
also his wife
ELEANOR
DIED 1943

The last resting place of Donald Dinnie
Courtesy: Eva Bulle (nee Dinnie)

There was a touching tribute to Donald from the First World War trenches, written by Corporal Joseph Lee, 1/4 Battalion The Black Watch, who had met Dinnie some 12 years or more earlier.

"I had just stepped ashore in South Shields after a considerable absence from this country, and here was this tenacious old fibre of Scotland to be greeted and gripped by the hand. Out here, amidst a familiarity with death, we have not heard of his death unmoved. He is gone on the mountain, he is lost to the forest."

Here is Corporal Lee's poem.

DONALD DINNIE'S DEAD!

Donald of the dance,
Donald of the song,
In flight swift as a lance.
Strongest among the strong:
Thy fleetness hath forsaken thee,
Grim Death has overtaken thee.
Donald Dinnie's dead!

Donald of the stone,
Donald of the caber,
Achieving all unblown
Each Herculean labour:
Staunch Scottish Pine, at last
Uprooted by the blast!
Donald Dinnie's dead!

Donald tough of thew
Donald great of muscle,
Donald who o'erthrew
A giant in each tussle:
Defeat has never known thee-
But Wrestler Death hath thrown thee!
Donald Dinnie's dead!

Donald left a trail of glory and a name that became a legend. At times he was quite mercenary and uncompromising, but he was also very generous to those who needed and deserved financial help. The brawny, highly intelligent Scot had a soft-hearted streak which would sometimes show through an extremely tough exterior. Donald Dinnie had a knack of always doing something sensational.

What the Papers Said

April 1916
GREAT SCOTTISH ATHLETE DEAD
Donald Dinnie's World-wide Fame
TRIUMPHS RECALLED

Donald Dinnie, Scotland's famous athlete, who was hailed as the greatest athlete of all time, has died in East Croydon, London. How often at the Highland Games did the mighty shout go up as the great "Donal" beat all comers in every contest in which strength, skill and training counted towards victory.

Dinnie was undoubtedly the greatest all-round athlete the country has ever produced. (This is the start of a lengthy article which goes on to detail his victories, travels, measurements etc. as contained in this book.)

New York Times, April 1916
Scotland's Greatest Athlete Dead

LONDON - Wednesday, April 5. - The death has occurred in London of Donald Dinnie, who was regarded by many as the greatest athlete Scotland ever produced. He was 79 years of age. During his career he won contests which included wrestling, hammer-throwing, running and jumping. Several of his victories were won on American soil.

From Gordon Dinnie's cuttings book, source unknown
DONALD DINNIE

The death of Donald Dinnie will excite far-away memories in many readers in Scotland. Dinnie was undoubtedly the greatest all-round athlete that Scotland, and probably the United Kingdom, has ever produced. .... His triumphs numbered in thousands, and it would have taxed even his strength to carry all the medals he won in athletic contests. The country will cherish a kindly memory of the man whose prowess and fine figure excited its unstinted admiration.

During his eventful life Dinnie received strong support from newspapers and magazines throughout the English-speaking world. The media might have wished to support their own local or national representatives competing against the mighty Scot, but they very rarely published even the slightest derogatory remarks. The snide comments by his brother-in-law McCombie Smith seem to be the only negative voice in the many press cuttings collections we have reviewed. The respect, awe and affection in which Donald Dinnie was held are reflected in the following extracts from his native heath to the farthest points on the globe.

Daily Telegraph, July 1873.

Alexandria Palace Sports, London, England. "There was amongst the competitors one Scottish Giant, Donald Dinnie, whose performance was worth all the money to witness. It seemed almost child's play to Donald to do things the others strove so hard at."

The Sheffield Daily Telegraph, June 1874.

"A great display of athletic sports and pastimes took place in Sheffield on Monday, at which Donald Dinnie and James Fleming seemed quite to have astonished the natives. These two men are splendid specimens of muscular development; their thews and sinews being something wonderful to behold, and their brawny chests and thighs a spectacle for the gods to admire."

Land and Water, October 2nd 1875.

Oban Games. "Now there was at Oban this day, a man Donald Dinnie by name, as fine a specimen of the 'Genus homo' as anyone would wish to see. He stands 6ft and weighs 15st 10-lb. Dinnie's name has been a household word in Scotland for many years; he has been the champion of all these athletic feats and wherever he goes no one can come near him at stone, hammer or caber. He is also a fast runner and a splendid wrestler and the best all-round athlete we have extant in the professional world. Dinnie has a *fidus Achate* when he contends at these Scotch games, in James Fleming, a big burly fellow who, in other company than Dinnie's, can hold his own against the best of all comers."

City Lantern, August 1876.

Manchester Athletic Games, England. "As usual Donald Dinnie carried all before him, in every contest in which he engaged. He is a dark complexioned Scot of a quiet and unassuming manner. Looking at him from a distance there is nothing particularly striking in his appearance indicative of his immense strength and muscular power, but when he strikes his jackets, and his enormous dorsal and pectoral muscles are displayed, one ceases to wonder at his prowess. As they say of horse "he is all there." His shoulders, back, loins and limbs are so well adjusted that he has much greater physical powers than bigger and heavier men."

Galloway Herald, July 1877

Dumfries Sports. N.B. - "Donald Dinnie was undoubtedly the observed of observers in the field. With a muscular frame and supporting about 100 gold and silver medals on his breast, he certainly looked a man that would be ill to beat, in the events where sheer strength and muscle, combined with a wiry constitution are most required – and in these not one of his opponents stood a ghost of a chance."

The Bailie, March 6th 1878

"The country which can number among its sons the names of a Wallace, a Burns and a Donald Dinnie, must be in every sense of the word a remarkable one."

Figaro, April 1878

Lilliebridge. London, England. "Antellus himself might think twice before throwing down the gauntlet to Donald Dinnie, whose feats with stone and hammer would have won deafening applause from the spectators in the palmiest days of the Olympian Games."

Boston Herald, August 1882

Boston Games. "Donald Dinnie is the champion of the world in throwing weights, wrestling &c &c. He is a man of splendid physique, and although all the noted athletes of America were present, they became diminutive when compared with him."

The Australasian, 1892

Melbourne, Australia. "Donald Dinnie is the greatest all-round Athletic who has ever visited this country."

Egmont Settler, April 11th 1894

Taranki, New Zealand. "Of Donald Dinnie's part of the entertainment we need only say he was magnificent, as he stands without a rival as an all-round athlete throughout the wide world."

Health & Strength Magazine, 1907

"At no period in the history of the age has there lived a man who for such a long series of years has accomplished so much in all the hardy, vigorous and daring contests with the most gigantic and muscular specimens of athletic perfection in every part of the world. This much and a great deal more does one glean in conversations with this greatest of great Scottish gladiators.

And the other day I asked the deep-chested and lion-hearted athlete to give me his signature, which he did, and here it is:-

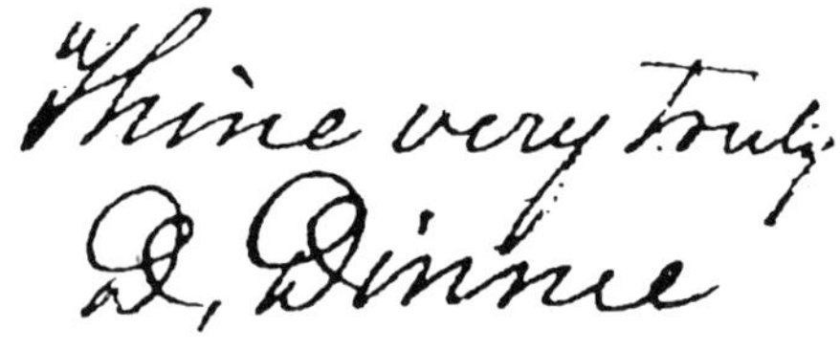

Health & Strength Magazine, December 1906

"Dinnie, the greatest athlete of the nineteenth century. Though well nigh three score years and ten, he is still a great athlete, of whom his fellow-countrymen are so proud that he might very well be described as the Athletic Robert Burns. Less than a year ago we saw him at a Highland Games, away yonder in the Far North, perform feats of strength and skill that put to shame many a young athlete upon the field. As Nester was to the Greeks encamped around the Walls of Troy, so is Donald Dinnie to those who seek distinction in "all that makes a man." He rests upon his laurels now, a noble example and a never failing source of inspiration to the age, and a living exponent of the text, "Quit ye like men; be strong."

"His pristine vigour age has overthrown,
But left the glory of the past his own."

From Gordon Dinnie's cuttings book, circa 1897.

"To readers who remember seeing him compete in Scotland in 1881 or in 1882, just before leaving, there seems nothing very wonderful in hearing of him competing in South Africa at hammer throwing and caber tossing in 1898. But if these readers recall that he was past his best then, and had been competing every year for over 25 years before his last appearance in Scotland, and that many first class athletes have risen to fame, past their best and are now practically forgotten who were not yet born when Donald Dinnie was first competing, they will begin to open their eyes to the extraordinary position he holds in the athletic world."

Era, February 26th 1881

New Star Music Hall. "Quite a sensation was caused at this centre of amusement on Monday evening by the appearance and extraordinary performances of the two Scottish Champions, Donald Dinnie and

THE GRAPHIC

AN ILLUSTRATED WEEKLY NEWSPAPER

No. 1,282—Vol. XLIX. *Registered as a Newspaper*

SATURDAY, JUNE 23, 1894

WITH EXTRA COLOURED SUPPLEMENT "*Lord Salisbury*"

PRICE SIXPENCE *By Post 6½d.*

George Davidson, whose fame is known not only in England, but throughout the world. Dinnie's extraordinary manipulation of the enormous dumbbells, and Davidson's feats with huge weights, were conspicuous features of an entertainment which throughout elicited most enthusiastic applause."

Aberdeen Journal, February 1879

"Theatre Royal, Aberdeen.–The great attraction of the evening was the performance of some extraordinary feats by the Champion Athletes – Donald Dinnie and G. Davidson – with heavy Dumbbells weighing from 60-lb! – we believe the heaviest in the world. The way in the Athletes handled these ponderous implements rather astonished the audience."

Era, October 24, 1880

"Scotia Music Hall, Glasgow[1].–The bill at the Scotia this week is headed by our Great Scotch Athletes – Messrs Donald Dinnie and G. Davidson – whose extraordinary feats of strength elicit vociferous applause!"

Manchester Echo, January 1881

"Donald Dinnie and George Davidson are drawing the 'Canny Scots' to the Folly like flies to a treacle pot – or like Manchester accountants around a fat bankruptcy case. Their performance is certainly wonderful, and 'Bonnie Scotland' may pride herself on having produced the man of the century. Compared with other 'strong men', Donald Dinnie is as a mastiff contrasted to a half-starved terrier."

Edinburgh Courant, 18th May 1880

"Donald Dinnie recalls to us the labour of Hercules, and the feats of Samson."

And in an elderly lady's writing desk in the 1950s, an old Valentine Card appeared with the following verse:

"Run, postman, like Donald Dinnie,
And take this card to Bella Binnie
Ye'll ken her by her bonnie face,
At number 7 Carlton Place."

[1]The Scotia Music Hall was at 116 Stockwell Street, adjacent to today's Scotia Bar (Est. 1792). When Queen Victoria's death was announced on the 22nd January 1901 the Music Hall had been renamed the Metropole, and was playing Bo-peep.

Like Father, Like Son

When Donald Dinnie went into semi-retirement from sports, his son Edwin continued touring with his own shows. As strongman acts phased out in favour of professional wrestling, young Dinnie moved into that sphere. Among the top liners he met in the ring was the most famous of all, George Hackenschmidt, the Russian Lion. He also encountered many other legendary wrestlers whose names are still recalled in awe.

One of these was Jack Carkeek, a famous opponent of the mighty Hackenschmidt. Edwin's tussle with Carkeek earned him £12, a mighty fine purse in 1902. He also fought Paul Belling of Germany, who became a British citizen, Emil Krohn, Charlie Green, one of the most skilful grapplers of that era, and a great Scottish favourite, Willie Withers Bain, who never really got the publicity he deserved.

In our collection the authors have a cutting which advertises Edwin representing Scotland in a match for The International Championships of the World against Gunner Nicol of America. The event took place at Port Glasgow Town Hall and proudly proclaimed E. G. Dinnie as the son of the renowned Donald Dinnie.

When he appeared in London, Edwin's performance was praised by the Lord Chamberlain and the Marquis of Huntly, amongst many others. From the stage there, Dinnie issued a challenge to Sandow to duplicate any of his feats for a £50 wager, but the titanic Teuton completely ignored the offer. By this time, Edwin Dinnie could do a one-hand lift with nearly 200-lb and 165-lbs with his left hand. With two hands he

The Royal carriage arrives at the Braemar Gathering

could jerk 256-lb overhead and snatch 165-lb. In the finale of his act Edwin would support, on his chest, a platform on which was placed a small piano, all the weights used during his performance, then six big men. The total weight was generally estimated to be over a ton.

Standing only 5ft $7^3/_4$in, he weighed $13^1/_2$ stone of solid muscle. His chest was 45in normal, he had a 32in waist and $16^3/_4$in biceps. Thighs like tree trunks measured 24in and his $16^1/_2$in calves looked great in the kilt. He was the beau ideal of the strength athlete of the period.

Edwin achieved his long-held ambition when he opened a school of physical culture in Aberdeen, but for a while he still worked part-time in show business. He finally left the stage to learn the hotel trade, first taking a job at the Grand Hotel, Aberdeen. The way he handled heavy baggage was a source of wonder to all who saw him lift and carry massive travelling trunks with the greatest of ease. After this he was employed as head boots at the Salutation Hotel, Perth.

About 1915 Edwin achieved a long-held ambition when he became the proprietor of the Commercial Hotel, Brechin, and successfully upheld the traditions of this old established hostelry. True to his roots, he prominently displayed his father's wonderful breastplate of medals. They were much admired for many years and later they were moved to a display cabinet at the Brechin Boxing Club.

One morning in April 1930, Edwin Dinnie appeared in his usual good health. But towards lunch-time he complained of being unwell and asked his wife to send for a doctor. Before the doctor arrived Edwin Dinnie had collapsed and died. He was buried in Brechin and his fine gravestone carries the following inscription: -

In loving memory of
EDWIN GELLATLY DINNIE
Who died 30th April 1930
Aged 53 years
Beloved husband of Mamie Collinson
This memorial is dedicated to him
By his devoted wife
and to perpetuate the memory of his father
DONALD DINNIE
The world renowned Scottish athlete
Whom he ever held in affectionate honour
who died 2nd April 1916 aged 79 years
and who is buried at Croydon.

People sometimes wonder what happened to Donald's other children[1]. Cuthbert died in 23rd September 1879. Royaln emigrated to the USA. Hector dropped out of sight completely but, as he was living in London he was responsible for maintaining the grave of his mother and father. Eva married Mexican Vice Consulate Adolfo Cayetano Bulle, and was last heard of when she contacted David Webster after the publication of his Scottish Highland Games book in 1959.

Close relatives of Donald still live in Deeside, and quite recently some met with Gordon Dinnie and David Webster to see attempts to lift the Dinnie Stones at Potarch Hotel. Robert Dinnie, tenant farmer of Birsebeg, after many years on the committee, was elected Chairman of the Aboyne Games Committee in 1997, maintaining a family tradition with this long-established gathering.

Robert Dinnie

While there is an abundance of biographical sketches of Donald Dinnie, little has been said on the remainder of this remarkable family. This will be rectified by Gordon Dinnie's publication of the Dinnie family tree[2], with its many fascinating associated notes. However some information about his remarkable father will help readers put the whole Donald Dinnie story into context.

Robert Dinnie was born at Alancreich, Birse, near Aboyne, in 1808. From the age of seven until he was 14, he went to the Parish School of Birse, where he was educated by James Smith. Robert was academically inclined but was singled out for rough treatment by the dominie (headmaster) and so packed up his books and left school for good. At 14 he was half a head taller than his tormenting teacher. The Reverend Joseph Smith, minister of the parish, tried to effect a reconciliation between Dinnie and his oppressor, to no avail. Robert went to his father's trade and served seven years as an apprentice stonemason.

Soon after leaving school, Dinnie met his old enemy and, blind with passion and no longer having to fear the dominie, he forced an apology from James Smith. Smith dropped to his knees, apologised profusely and beseeched Dinnie not to kill him. Nobody knew of this incident until years later and by that time folks found it hard to believe that Robert Dinnie, the poet, naturalist and antiquarian, could have been so fierce in his youth.

[1]Information on Donald Dinnie's children is given in Appendix 6, page 157

[2]For more information on the family tree, see page 149

Throughout his working life he was a calm and assured, law-abiding citizen who loved a joke and was not scared of hard work. He was well known for feats of strength and was a fine stonemason and master builder, leaving many bridges, churches and monuments as a tribute to his energy and skill.

The Earl of Dalhousie was quick to perceive Dinnie's gifts of head and hand and awarded him many local contracts, including the Maule Memorial Church at Invermark, the shooting lodge there, and the memorial Gothic crown which commemorates the visit of Queen Victoria and Albert, the Prince Consort. At Lochlee he built the huge cairn on the summit of the Rowan, in memory of the first Baron Panmure, and another church and many stone bridges over the River Dee, the last one being the Effock Bridge, which cost him £600.

This contract shows another side of Dinnie's character. It was late on a Saturday evening and with the work on the bridge all but finished, his colleagues urged him to work on and complete the job. The Dee was rising fast but Robert refused to remove the wooden coom beneath the arch for fear his task might encroach on the Sabbath. The spate increased and swept away the coom and the bridge. So Robert had to rebuild the whole bridge at his own cost. Many bridges were swept away in the flooding of 1829 so for many years there was plenty work for the Dinnies. Robert Dinnie wrote a poem about the great spate and converted the story into a bothy ballad.

Robert and Celia Hay. Courtesy: Robert Dinnie

Robert's routine over the years hardly varied. He would rise at 4am and have for breakfast a wooden bowl of brose, made with meal and water with milk or cream poured copiously over it. By 5am he had left the house and usually had a six-mile walk to work. If the job was more distant, he would leave earlier, as it was his rule that he would be working at six throughout the year except for the darkest days of winter, when he would start as soon as it was light. For his midday meal he carried a hunk of cheese, oatcakes and a pint of milk to wash the lot down. Tools would be downed at 6pm, when he would walk home in time for an evening meal. This could again be a bowl of brose, the staple diet of the country at that time. This was the lifestyle that Donald Dinnie left in 1867 when he became a full-time professional athlete.

In 1833 Robert Dinnie married Celia Hay, a woman strong in mind as well as body. Well-known locally as an intellectual, she was an ideal mate for him and they shared a long and happy life. The pair celebrated their Golden Wedding at Wood Cottage, Birse, with their friends and family and many a bottle of 'mountain dew' that never saw the exciseman's seal. The whisky was served in beautiful antique glasses, some of which are now in an Edinburgh museum with other parts of his collection, for antiques were a lifelong interest. Robert had a fine collection of old Scottish coins, and was particularly protective of six prized Ferrera swords. There were axe and arrowheads from bygone battles, coins going back to William the Lion, mahogany furniture later acquired for Edinburgh Museum, a slipper from Mary Queen of Scots and a whole lot more. The upper part of his home was turned into a museum and visitors included nobility and the gentry of the district.

Robert Dinnie was so fast at his trade that he needed two labourers to keep up with him. He trained his eldest son Donald to work on the same lines, but Donald could never quite match his father's skill. An old Deeside legend surrounds Robert, with implications for his famous son.

A big islander from Skye, working at the Carmyllie stone quarries in Angus, frequently delighted his fellow quarrymen with exhibitions of his strength. Inevitably the call of the isles urged his return, so he gathered his belongings and began the long journey home.

His route took him over the Grampian Mountains, eventually reaching what we now believe to be Inver or Potarch, and stopping to rest at an old inn, he was invited to join some Deeside men enjoying a drink outdoors on that pleasant evening. Noting the stranger's physique, the conversation turned to feats of physical strength and one of the locals rose from the bench, walked over to a big boulder lying there and with tremendous effort raised it chest high. " I never met a man who could do that," he said, returning to his seat.

Without uttering a sound the big islander rose, picked up the boulder and, changing his hand positions, quickly raised it above his head, lowered it, and went back to his seat without speaking. For a few minutes the company sat in silent admiration, and at length the big Deesider asked the man his name.

"Donald Macdonald of Skye," answered the stranger.

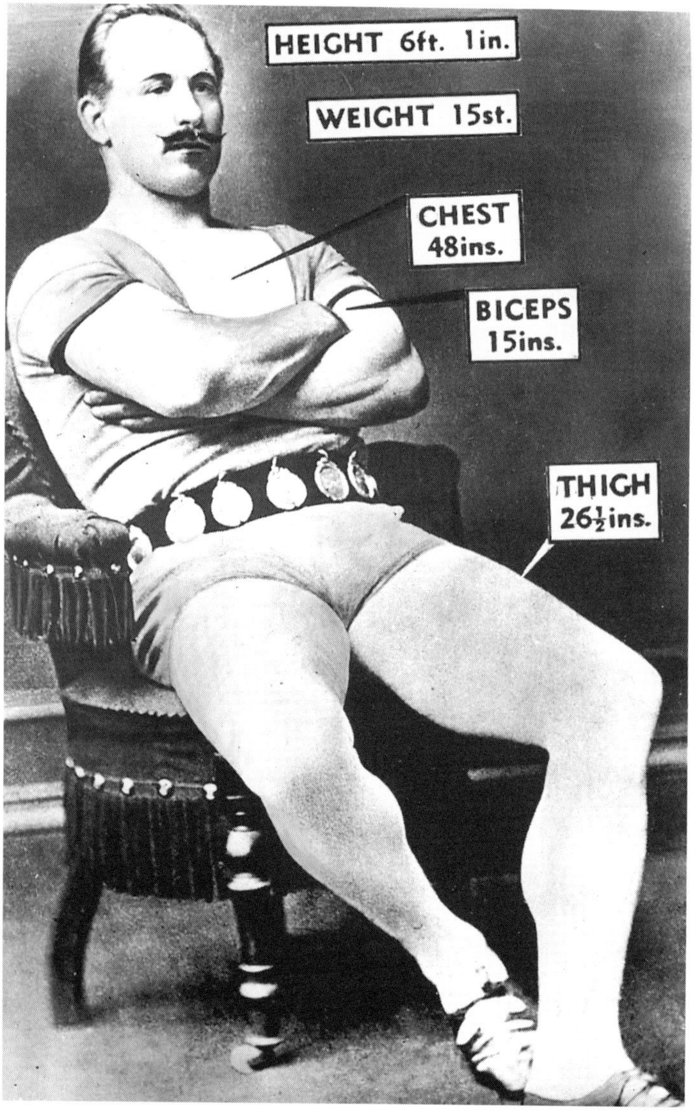

The vital statistics of Donald Dinnie

"Well friend," replied the native, "If I ever have a son I shall call him after you, for you are the strongest man I've ever met."

Years later, in the parish of Aboyne, in Aberdeenshire, a son was born to the big Deesider, and, mindful of his promise, the proud father called the boy Donald after the giant from Skye. And that's how Donald Dinnie got his name.

Old journals have said that Robert Dinnie could lift the 'Stones of Dee' at Potarch, but these reports in themselves cannot be considered reliable. However, there is no doubt that he was an exceedingly strong man for, although he was not an athlete of the calibre of his famous son, he could certainly beat everybody in the locality in pulling the swingle-tree. It is a simple test of power and Dinnie was never beaten in his many contests on Potarch Green, the Green of Charleston at Aboyne or at Ballater. His strength was well known and twice Mr Ord, a well-known circus proprietor, approached Robert with a view to recruiting him for his circus. Dinnie refused, for he said: "They cheer today and hiss tomorrow and tomorrow comes to all."

When Dinnie was recounting this story to a reporter his wife chimed in: "You are a clown enough without joining Ordie's Circus."

"Aye," joked Robert in response to his wife's good-natured tease: "That was plain enough when I took you."

In 1888 well-known Aberdeen newspaper the Press & Journal wrote of Robert Dinnie's abilities and particularly mentioned his incredibly muscular legs. They were compared and measured alongside those of another famous local worthy, big Andrew Davidson. Davidson had tremendous powers of endurance and, unusual for long distance runners, a huge frame and very large calves. Those of Robert Dinnie, however, were even larger, each measuring 18in. Donald was proud of his father's strength and often spoke of his abilites on the swee tree.

Robert Dinnie was a great character, always a centre of interest. He admitted that one of the daftest things he ever did for a wager was to play cards for three days. One Sunday at the kirk gate he struck this silly wager and next morning he began the marathon. One by one the other players dropped out but Dinnie played all day and night for three days, then went to bed for three days. It was the most severe test he ever had. His speech was slightly affected for a long time and ever afterwards he advised strongly against such tests of endurance.

A man of remarkable individuality, Robert Dinnie was brainy as well as brawny and between 1865 and 1885 wrote at least five books of historical, anecdotal poetry and song, all of which are still to be found in Aberdeen Central Library.

The Aberdeen Press published a series of articles on Robert in 1888, and the journalist described how Robert and his wife Celia, though they did not approve of some of his earlier idiosyncrasies, were always proud to hear about their son Donald. A splendid photograph of Donald by an Aberdeen artist had a conspicuous place on the parlour wall among other favoured treasures.

The portrait below of Donald Dinnie, by Aberdeen artist C. J. Beattie, was presented to the Scottish National Portrait Gallery in October 1961 by Donald's niece, Mrs Elsie Montague Lynas F.S.A. Scotland. She was the daughter of Nory Celia Dinnie, Donald's youngest sister, and Elsie's father was schoolteacher William McCombie Smith, well-known athlete and author.

After a long and painful fight, Robert died in 1891 at the age of 83.

Portrait of Donald Dinnie
Courtesy: Scottish National Portrait Gallery

Even his illness and death were extraordinary and reported in the Lancet. He suffered from chronic dropsy, and the medical world marvelled that the human frame could stand so much, for it was calculated that Dr McHardy of Banchory had, over five years, 'tapped' more than four tons of water off Robert Dinnie. Truly a Hercules to the very end.

The last resting place
Courtesy: Robert Dinnie

Close to the west wall of the Birse Kirk in Aboyne stands a monument to the Dinnies of Deeside. Hewn and dressed by sons and a son-in-law of Robert Dinnie, it first stood for many years in the grounds of Wood Cottage, where Robert and his wife Celia spent most of their married life. The 6ft grey granite monument has a copper plate mounted on it bearing the names, birth year, and full date of death of the entire family, The plate reads: -

In memory of Robert Dinnie Born Allancrigh – 1808
Died at Wood Cottage in the Parish of Aboyne – 1891
Also his spouse Celia Hay Born at Kirktown of Echt – 1810
Died at Wood Cottage in the Parish of Aboyne – 1891
Married in 1833 and had a family as follows

Sarah	Born 1834	Died 11th May 1919
Barbara	Born 1835	Died 23rd July 1920
Donald	Born 1837	Died 2nd April 1916
Edmund	Bòrn 1840	Died 4th January 1900
Montague	Born 1842	Died 20th January 1925
Lubin	Born 1844	Died 6th May 1922
Clarinda	Born 1846	Died 4th March 1927
Digby	Born 1849	Died 22nd December 1928
Walter	Born 1852	Died 7th May 1923
Nory Celia	Born 1855	Died 17th May 1941

Shortly before this book was written photos of Donald Dinnie's sister Sarah, and his brother Walter and his family, were bought in a car boot sale in Aberdeen. Walter became well known as a detective inspector at Scotland Yard and later as Police Commissioner of New Zealand.

Acknowledgments

By David P. Webster

While it would be impossible to thank all who have helped over the years it is essential to gratefully acknowledge those who have played key roles in the production of this publication.

As a strength historian I have long wished to go into more detail regarding the participants in Highland games. It is difficult to do this when your subject is the whole range of activities seen at the gatherings.

The involvement of Gordon Dinnie in helping me achieve this ambition was so coincidental it seemed almost pre-ordained. He had been researching his family tree at the Glasgow Genealogy Centre looking for details of his illustrious relative Donald Dinnie and was comparing notes with a lady who was making a similar study of her roots. When Gordon mentioned Highland games she told him that a next door neighbour was a games enthusiast, and when he heard my name he lost no time in getting in touch. He had been seeking my address for years. That chance encounter at the registrars led to the volume now in your hands.

The final postcard of Dinnie
Courtesy: Health & Strength Magazine

Gordon's input, family contacts and interest in the topic have been invaluable. Our discussions may have slowed down the writing process, but they sparked off many enquiries and investigations which might otherwise have been neglected. Much of the information and some of the photos came via Gordon from the Dinnie families, and to all of them we are greatly indebted.

The inclusion of anecdotes and experiences in Donald Dinnie's own words and his son Edwin's personal writings are of major importance. In this regard I must thank the owners and staff of Health and Strength Magazine over the years. Back in the 1950s, editor David Johnstone gave me my first opportunity to become a writer by inviting me to become a regular contributor. With his assistant editors

George Kirkley and George Greenwood, we all became lifelong friends. The owners, Link House Publications, and later Gordon Grose, W. A. Pullum and W. S. Pullum, gave me unstinted support and I was able to purchase from Oscar Heidenstam the volumes I needed for the Dinnie recollections. Later Malcolm Whyatt and Roy Edwards have carried on the high standards and helpful philosophies long associated with this magazine.

It should be becoming clear that sporting and family associations have played their part in shaping and producing this book and this becomes even more evident in the actual publishing. Charlie Allan of Ardo Publishing, that great Highland games all-rounder, is probably the only one who rivals Gordon and me in our enthusiasm for (or obsession with) Donald Dinnie. I sat with Charlie by the auction ring in Kittybrewster, frustrated with the knowledge that there was no use bidding against him for the Dinnie medals as he had more bawbees than me. I hoped he would get them as we had become firm friends travelling around the world together with a pioneering team of Highland games athletes, including greats such as Bill Anderson and Jay Scott. Charlie's personal interest made it possible to go well beyond the normal limitations which a publisher might inflict, by restricting the number of illustrations for example, and other such economic factors.

To these and all the others, such as librarians and historians, who have contributed to this publication in various ways, we give our sincere thanks.

Further Reading

Gordon Dinnie has compiled and published a Dinnie Family Tree with many notes of great interest to those who wish further detailed information.

He can be contacted at: 4 Berriedale, Gardenhall, East Kilbride, Glasgow G75 8ST, Scotland, UK. Telephone - 01355 235233

Internet address: GDinnie@aol.com

David Webster's books include:

Scottish Highland Games, Sons of Samson Vol. 1 & 2.

Barbells & Beefcake, Sandow, Mighty Monarch of Muscle.

He can be contacted at: STRENGTH GAMES '90 Ltd.,

43 West Rd., Irvine, KA12 8RE, Scotland, UK

INDEX

Appendix 1

The Dinnie Steens

Donald Dinnie's most impressive feat took place around 1860 while he was helping his father repair the Bridge of Potarch which crosses the River Dee near Kincardine O'Neil. Donald lifted these enormous stones – one weighing 340-lb and the other 435-lb, totalling some 775-lb. He carried both across the bridge, a distance of five yards. The stones had served as anchors at either side of the wooden structure while the work was carried out.

It became common for attempts on the Dinnie Steens to be made at the feeing market at Potarch. In days gone by, before labour exchanges, these regular gatherings were very similar to the 'mop fairs' in England. Farmhands, labourers, servants and others seeking employment gathered on specific days to offer their services. Shepherds would carry crooks, housemaids a mop, woodsmen an axe, carters would have a whipcord round their hat and some perhaps woven horsehair – all to indicate their calling. Farmers and other masters-to-be would circulate, questioning those looking for jobs. Having settled the fees, they would seal the deal with a handshake and a small cash advance, often a shilling. Markets were very important to the local economy and until the early 19th century Marywell was the main focus of the parish where the Dinnies lived. The three Birse markets were held there in May, October and November. In 1814 the markets went to Potarch, after the bridge was built, and the old hamlet of Marywell disappeared.

The stones were originally given as approximately 340 and 435-lb. The most recent weighing, in 1998, showed the stones are now 321 and 413-lb. This weighing was to ensure accuracy for granite replicas commissioned by Gordon Dinnie. Lost from sight after two world wars, the handle of the larger stone had broken off before the boulders were brought to public notice at our Spartan Club shows in Aberdeen during the early 1950s. We had a new, larger ring made to replace it. Since then the stones have had an enormous amount of use, being lifted, dropped, and dragged across stony ground. It will be interesting to see what the stones weigh in ten years' time.

A letter in Aberdeen Press & Journal of 3 December 1956 vouches for Robert Dinnie lifting the two stones.

The Glasgow Herald of 9th May 1972, said Donald Dinnie lifted the Stones in 1860. At present the stones lie at the entrance of the 18th century Potarch Hotel, which sits beside the Potarch Bridge, just off the A93 near Kincardine O'Neil in Aberdeenshire. Magnificent framed photographs of Donald are displayed at each side of the open stone fireplace of the hotel. Guests are offered a hearty breakfast described as The Dinnie Platter.

The stones now lie outside the Inn at the Bridge of Potarch, where travellers on horseback previously used the rings to tether their horses. Despite many attempts, only one person has managed to emulate Donald's feat, when in 1973 Jack Shanks, a 37-year-old Belfast policeman, carried the stones a few inches at a time and covered a distance of 17 feet, the equivalent of the width of the bridge at Potarch, using the platform section of a flat bed lorry brought in for the benefit of the large crowd of spectators that turned out to watch the proceedings.

The event was also witnessed by Deeside man Syd Strachan, a Banchory slaughterman, who lifted the stones but could not move them, Aberdeen weightlifter Mike Crawford, at the time Scottish lightweight champion, and Aberdeen bodybuilder Stan Main.

Jack was assisted in his pre-lift training in Ireland by author David Webster and Banchory police constable Jim Dawson, who sent a diagram to Jack, who had concrete blocks made up.

At the time of writing, the most recent attempts of significance were on Sunday 5th April 1998 when David Horne, British Grip Strength Champion, and several colleagues took up the challenge. David and Nick McKinless, a film stunt man, succeeded in correctly lifting both stones. Nick did a lift and drag of around four yards and David did a two-finger lift of the smaller stone. It was an impressive performance.

The Dinnie Stones of Strength continue to attract strongmen from all around the world like moths to a flame.

Henry Gray carrying one of the Dinnie Stones at the Spartan Club Show in the Music Hall, Aberdeen in 1954. The popular North-east Highland games athlete outlifted several well-known strong men to win the £20 prize. This competition was an important first step in developing unusual tests of strength which are now seen in the World's Strongest Man contests on television.

Appendix 2

Dinnie's Silver Championship Belt

The following information is given on the various plaques on the belt. which was bought by Aberdeen City Council in 1981 and is held in their collection.

Wrestling: Won over 2,000 contests. Won Police Gazette Champion Medal for Mixed Wrestling, 1882. All round Wrestling Championships of World. Melbourne Tournament, 1885.

Hammer Throwing: Won over 2000 contests. Best efforts on level ground from a 'fair stand', no turning:-

16-lb 4ft 2in stiff handle	132ft.
16-lb 4ft 8in stiff handle	138ft 8in
22-lb 4ft 2in stiff handle	104ft 6in
44-lb 4ft stiff handle	56ft 6in

Stone Putting: Won over 1800 contests.

16-lb 7ft 6in approach	49ft 6in
22-lb 7ft approach	39ft 9in
24-lb 7ft approach	37ft 9in
28-lb Fair Stand	32ft 10in
56-lb Fair Stand	20ft 6in

Weight Throwing: 56-lb. Won over 300 contests. Best throw on level ground. Overall Length including ring:-

14in Fair Stand	28ft 4in
24in Fair Stand	40ft 6in
56-lb weight for height	13ft 11in

Tossing Caber: Won over 1400 contests. Unbeaten for over 40 years[1].

Weightlifting:

Single hand to overhead 168-lb.

Two hands to overhead 132-lb in right and 102-lb in left (two motions)

Single hand hold-out on palm of hand, arm and hand horizontal. 56-lb for 45 seconds at Wagga Wagga, New South Wales in 1884[2].

Running: Won over 800 contests for flat racing and hurdles[3].

100 yards $10^{2}/_{3}$ secs.

Won Champions silver medal for hurdles at Philadelphia and gold Medal at Lucknow, Canada in 1882, on the same day winning the heavy athletic championship in America. Won Scottish All-Round Championships at Coatbridge, Scotland in 1864.

Miscellaneous All-Round Champion of the World: Won over 1800 contests for leaping (high and long jumping and triple jump). During 1860 cleared 5ft 11in on several occasions and record of 6ft 1in at Turriff, Aberdeenshire.

Best long jump 20ft 1in.

Hop, Step & jump 44ft.

Hundreds of prizes for dancing, rifle shooting, quoiting, etc.

---

[1] It is on record elsewhere that he once tossed a 20ft caber.

[2] This is probably his most outstanding single feat. He used this as a regular challenge to all weightlifters and strong men and although this is his best, many other exceptional times were recorded

[3] Dinnie also won some road racing events

Appendix 3

Aberdeen City Council's Medal Collection

The following Dinnie medals are held in Aberdeen City Council's Art Gallery and Museums. It should be noted that the distances must be treated with caution since there are no indications of ground levels or equipment. In particular, many of the hammer throws would be with short, thick, inflexible handles. When Dinnie had won a competition he would usually stop at that height or distance and not take further attempts unless there was a separate prize for records. When he improved a record he would do it by just a little to allow another record the following year.

Glenisla	**1859**	Caber Champion Medal
Glenisla	**1859**	Hammer Champion Medal
Glenisla	**1859**	Stone Champion Medal
Perth	**1859**	Hammer Champion Medal
Angus & Mearns	**1860**	Stone
Camphill	**1862**	Champions Medal
Clova	**1862**	Light Hammer
Kincardine O'Neil	**1862**	Hammer Champion Medal
Kincardine O'Neil	**1862**	28-lb Stone Champion Medal
Perth Highland Society	**1862**	Caber Champion Medal
	1864	Caber First Prize
	1864	Hammer First Prize
	1864	High Leap First Prize
	1865	Caber First Prize
	1865	High Leap 5ft 9in First Prize
	1865	Hurdle Race First Prize
	1865	22-lb Stone 37ft Champion Medal
Braemar	**1865**	27-lb Hammer
Braemar	**Undated**	Caber
Dundee Highland Society	**Undated**	No medal details
	1866	Caber First Prize
	1866	Stone
	1866	Hammer
Glenisla	**1866**	Stone Champion Medal
Dundee	**1867**	Wrestling Champion Medal of Scotland
Perth Highland Society	**1867**	Hammer First Prize
	1867	Stone First Prize
	1867	Stone First Prize
	1867	Caber First Prize
	Undated	Hammer First Prize
	Undated	Stone First Prize
	Undated	Caber First Prize
	Undated	Hammer First Prize
	Undated	Stone First Prize
	1868	22-lb Stone 41ft 3in First Prize
	1868	22-lb Stone 41ft 2in First Prize
Not Recorded	**Undated**	Caber Champion Medal
Ballater	**1868**	Champion Athlete

Culter	**1869**	Heavy Hammer First Prize
Perth Highland		
Society	**1869**	High Leap 5ft 11in Champion Medal
	1869	High Leaping Champion Medal
	1869	22-lb Stone 39ft 8in Champion Medal
	1869	22-lb Hammer 100ft 8in Champion Medal
	1871	22-lb Stone 39ft 7in Champion Medal
	1871	19-lb Hammer 103ft Champion Medal
	1871	High Leaping 5ft $10^{1}/_{2}$in Champion Medal
Probably Perth	**Undated**	Caber Champion Medal
Braes of Gight	**1873**	16-lb Hammer
Aberdeen Games	**1873**	Wrestling Champions Medal
	1874	20-lb Stone 41ft 4in Champions Medal
	1874	56-lb Weight. fair stand 29ft 3in Champion Medal
Brisbane, Aust.	**1884**	Club Swinging[1]
Probably Perth	**Undated**	17-lb Hammer 112ft Champion Medal
Probably Perth	**Undated**	28-lb Stone Champion medal 30ft 7in Fair Stand
Probably Perth	**Undated**	Caber Champion medal
Caledonian Club		
of Sacramento	**Undated**	Heavy Hammer First Prize

The Perth Medals and similar were made by Whytock & Sons.

[1]For swinging 50-lb club 109 times round the head with the right hand and 75 times round the head with the left hand.

Appendix 4

Gordon Dinnie's Medal Collection

The collection kept in East Kilbride includes the following: -

Perth Highland	**1860**	1st – Dancing Highland Fling
Society	**1862**	Champion Medal for Stone
	1864	Champion Medal for Stone
Highland	**1864**	Champion Medal for Hammer
Society	**1865**	Champion Medal for Hammer – 19-lb 90ft 9in
	1866	Champion Medal for Throwing Hammer Putting Stone and Turning Caber.
	1867	1st – Dancing Highland Fling
Dublin	**1863**	1st Prize – Putting 28-lb 32ft 9in
Dublin	**1863**	Champion Medal for most successful athlete
Alyth Merchants Medal,		
Glenisla	**1867**	Champion Medal - High Leap - Three years
Royal Patent Commission		
Championship	**1868**	Putting 18-lb ball 43ft
Philadelphia	**1872**	23rd August 150 Hurdles. Front initials CAAA
Buffalo Caledonian		
Society	**1872**	Most successful competitor at the Games

Toronto C.C.	**1872**	Putting 28-lb 37ft 9in
Saline Games, Fife	**1877**	Champion Stone & Hammer. Hercules on front
SAS	**1884**	Wrestling. Farnese Hercules on front.
Queensland Caledonian Society		
Brisbane	**1884**	Hurdle Race. Has Caledonian Club initials
	1892	Putting the Stone 28-lb 31ft 4in
	1896	Wrestling

Appendix 5

Recent winners of Challenge Trophy, Aboyne Games

1961 - 1968	Robert Aitken	1991 - 1993	Stephen Aitken
1969	Charlie Allan	1994	No award
1970 - 1986	James McBeath	1995	Alistair Gunn
1987 - 1988	Stephen Aitken	1996 - 1998	No award
1989 - 1990	No award		

Dinnie Trophy heavy event winners

1961 - 1962	Bill Anderson	1983 - 1984	Bill Anderson
1963 - 1964	Arthur Rowe		Geoffrey Capes
	Bill Anderson	1986 - 1987	Bill Anderson
	Arthur Rowe		Alistair Gunn
1967 - 1970	Bill Anderson		George Patience
1971	Arthur Rowe		Alistair Gunn
1972 - 1978	Bill Anderson		Gordon Martin
1979	Grant Anderson		Stephen Aitken
	Bill Anderson	1993 - 1995	Alistair Gunn
	Grant Anderson	1996	Francis Brebner
	Hamish Davidson	1997 - 1998	Alistair Gunn

Appendix 6

Donald Dinnie's Children

1858	21 Nov.	Emily	Died 8 March 1935
1860	5 April	Cuthbert	Died 23 Sept. 1879
1862	8 May	Royaln	Emigrated to USA
1863	9 Nov.	Mary	Details unknown
1877	4 June	Edwin Gellatly	Died 30 April 1930
1879	8 Aug.	Amy Gellatly	Died 15 March 1966
1887	24 June	Eva Lena Ida	Died 14 Jan. 1969
1900	21 March	Hector	Died 7 Nov. 1969

Appendix 7

Scottish Champions of Heavy Events

(an extract, with permission, from SCOTTISH HIGHLAND GAMES, Updated by David Webster)

The Act of Proscription of 1746 put an end to the gatherings which had long been held in the Highlands and particularly those which had been held at Braemar, where the standard of the 'Old Pretender', James Stuart (1688-1766) had been raised to start the Jacobite rebellion against the throne in England. After the repeal of the Act, from the late 1700s the North-east of Scotland again became the centre of traditional heavy events. The MacHardy family took most prizes.

Only when transport improved and the population became more mobile did it seem appropriate to recognise a national champion. Even then it took some time before Alistair MacHardy became the first widely accepted Scottish Champion. Although there were challenges and competitions claimed as championships, it was not until 1955 that the winner at Crieff became the official SGA Scottish Champion.

The following list has been compiled after extensive research of all available information.

1840s	Thomas Menzies was top prize winner along with A. MacHardy.
1844 - 1850	Alistair MacHardy (1825-1897)
1850 - 1854	John Tait (1829-1896).
1854 - 1855	William Tait (Born 1836)
1856 - 1869	Donald Dinnie (1837-1916)
1870	James Fleming (1840-1887)
1871 - 1876	Donald Dinnie
1877	George Davidson (b. 1853)
1887	Kenneth McRae (b. 1850)
1890 - 1900	George H.Johnstone (b. 1864)
1901	James Morrison (b. 1874)
1902	George H.Johnstone
1903 - 1914	A.A. Cameron (1877-1951)

A whole generation of Scots were killed in the Great War.

1920s	James (Jim) Maitland & Sgt.Major Robert (Bob) Starkey
1927	R. Starkey (1890-1956)
1929	Edward Anderson
Mid-30s	George Clark (1908-1987)
1937	Robert Shaw

Until after World War ll Clark and Shaw shared honours.

1950 - 1952	Jack Hunter
1953	Ewen Cameron (1927-1995)
1954	Henry.A.(Sandy)Gray
1955	J.L. McLellan (b.1914)
1956 - 1957	A. (Sandy) Sutherland (b.1930)
1958	Jay Scott (1930-1997)
1959 - 1962	William (Bill) Anderson (b.1937)
1963	Arthur Rowe (b.1935)
1964	W.Anderson/A.Rowe
1965 - 1966	Arthur Rowe
1967 - 1968	W.Anderson
1969	W.Anderson/A.Rowe
1970	W.Anderson
1971	Arthur Rowe
1972 - 1978	W.Anderson MBE
1979	Hamish Davidson
1980	W. Anderson MBE
1981	Geoff Capes (b.1949)
1982	Geoff Capes/Grant Anderson
1983 - 1985	Grant Anderson
1986	Grant Anderson/Geoff Capes
1987	Bill Anderson MBE
1988	Geoff Capes
1989	Eric Irvine (b. 1961)
1990	Francis Brebner (b.1965)
1991 - 1993	Alistair Gunn (b.1963)
1994	George Patience (b. 1959)
1995 - 1996	Alistair Gunn
1997	Bruce Aitken (b.1970)
1998	Stephen Aitken (b.1967)

Contents

Left: *Celebrating the Birth*, 1664, Jan Steen (1625/26–79)

Foreword

The scope of subject matter in Dutch Golden Age painting is such that it is easier to enumerate what is not represented – from gods disguised as elements of nature to martyrs receiving their palm fronds, among other elements invisible and immaterial. That is because artists in the Dutch Republic focused on what could be seen and touched (and smelled, heard and tasted) in daily life, down to seemingly the most granular detail.

This apparent obsession with mundane materiality was what the culture of the time permitted, and what Netherlandish men and women wanted to buy and have in their daily lives. Connoisseurs in other nations might dismiss this preoccupation with the quotidian as vulgar and uninspiring, but the Dutch understood the importance of the real.

Today, close attention to the elements of daily life is what renders these pictures relatable. Domestic order, but also disorder, noisy gatherings, the pleasures of solitude, playing and working under humid skies, the poignancy of old age or a sick child, these are things that art lovers know in their own lives. Some truths found in the familiar, however, are apparent only in retrospect – most tellingly, Gerrit Dou's portrait of a young African man, who wears a gold padlock and chain around his neck. What ironically might be interpreted as 'bling' today was then, the text reminds us, casual evidence of the slave trade that helped support the tidiness of Dutch lives.

Such connections between pictorial content and historical context are made throughout *Vermeer & The Dutch Masters*. Closely attended detail, which makes Dutch Golden Age art compelling today, is examined in thematic chapters. Pictures and text interact to indicate why this art looks the way it does. Generous but not gratuitous, the selection of images inspires discussion of the wider world reflected in Vermeer's private interiors, of the scientific disinterest captured by Rembrandt in his paintings of cadavers and the Calvinist morality echoed in still life paintings and ribald tavern scenes, alike. Painted some five hundred years ago, these pictures remain as relevant as ever.

Janet Tyson, MA, MFA

Above: *Still Life of Cherries and Peaches*, c. 1620s, Balthasar van der Ast (1593–1657)

Right: *View of Houses in Delft, Known as 'The Little Street'*, c. 1658, Johannes Vermeer (1632–75)

I·VMeer

The Ordinary Made Extraordinary

THE HISTORICAL ERA celebrated as the 'Golden Age of Dutch Art' summarizes a plethora of illustrious artists associated with Dutch painting, c. 1585–1680 in the Republic of the Seven United Netherlands. It was a richly cultured period during the seventeenth century, from which emerged a sublime wealth of artistic talent within the Dutch territories.

Leo Belgicus

In the sixteenth century, until the divergence of the northern and southern Netherlands, the collective term for the Low Countries, including the Netherlands, Luxembourg and Belgium, was Belgae. Austrian nobleman, historian and diplomat Michaël von Eytzinger (*c.* 1530–98) published the first cartographic map of the Low Countries in *Novus de Leone Belgico* in 1583, with the figure of a lion (*Leo Belgicus*) containing all the territories, illustrating its collective size. The Belgae lion motif was taken from the heraldic coats of arms of William, Prince of Orange, and heraldic symbols of the Dutch territories. Eytzinger's symbolic lion, in a fold-out map in his book, was widely emulated by other cartographers, such as the Austrian School *Leo Belgicus*, showing the Low Countries in the shape of a lion, from *De Leone Belgico* (after Michaël von Eytzinger), 1586 (*see* right).

The Dutch lion roared a representational challenge toward Austria and the rest of Europe during the Eighty Years' War. Eytzinger wrote an account of the war in serial volumes from the viewpoint of Spain, ruler of Hapsburg Netherlands. Soon after the first publication, the capitulation of Antwerp in 1585 back to Spanish control saw the migration of countless southern Netherlanders to the North, thus dividing the *Leo Belgicus*.

From War to Peace

Today the Netherlands are united territories with separate identities, collectively known as the Netherlands and to many outsiders as Holland. In the sixteenth century Protestant aversion to Spanish-Catholic rule led to revolt by the northern Netherlandish provinces against Spain.

Above: *Leo Belgicus*, 1586, from *De Leone Belgico* (after Michaël von Eytzinger)

Their success and breakaway from Spain left the southern Netherlands under Spanish-Catholic rule. The battle for Antwerp in 1585 led to its surrender to Spanish rule and a mass movement of its Protestant citizens to the northern Netherlands. One can identify from this date the rise of the Dutch arts' Golden Age in the northern territories, where many artists – at least 200 are known to have moved for religious and socio-economic reasons – and craftsmen, publishers, architects and art and book dealers were amongst the many artisans who chose to resettle.

Art and Protestantism

In northern Europe from the mid-sixteenth century, the rise of Protestantism pushed debate on religious doctrine towards the outbreak of rebellious wars across European countries, particularly between Catholic Spain and the Protestant northern Netherlands. The Augustinian monk and professor of theology Martin Luther (1483–1546) had sparked the religious rebellion in Wittenberg, in Saxony-Anhalt, Germany, in 1517. On a visit to Rome in 1510–11, on behalf of the Augustinian monastery, he found a lack of morals and spirituality at the heart of the Church of Rome. At its head was an astute, quite fearless warrior-pope, Julius II (1443–1513), Giuliano della Rovere. During his reign, from 1503 to 1513, his aggrandizing materialism was visible to all who visited the Vatican. Luther found the church in Rome raising funds to build a new Basilica of St Peter.

A Catholic Indulgence

Julius II's favoured method for raising funds was through the sale of indulgences, an earthly entitlement to be released from mortal, material sins in Heaven, in return for monetary payment to the Catholic Church.

Priests were sent out across Europe to sell indulgences, to raise money for the Roman Catholic Church's coffers in Rome, to glorify the Vatican, not the people of Rome, or wider community.

Above: *Battle Between Carnival and Lent*, 1633–34, Jan Miense Molenaer (1610–68)

In Rome, the building of the new Vatican and Basilica created a lucrative period for artists, which saw the artist's status rise in Italy, from skilled manual guild tradesman to highly prized, sought-after painter. Michelangelo (1475–1564) and Raphael (1483–1520) were two of Pope Julius II's favoured artists, and they were commissioned to decorate the private rooms of the pope, the Stanze in the Vatican (Raphael) and the ceiling of the Sistine Chapel (Michelangelo). This decorative extravagance was taking place during the period of Martin Luther's visit. On the death of Julius II, the practice continued under the Medici pope, Leo X, Giovanni di Lorenzo de' Medici (1475–1521).

Above: *Interior of the Church of St Bavo in Haarlem*, 1636, Pieter Jansz Saenredam (1597–1665)

Wittenberg 1517

On his return to Germany, to Wittenberg, Luther began to write his theses on the state of the Catholic Church and how it should change. The texts containing his arguments and debate, a total of 95 theses, were nailed by him to the castle church door in Wittenberg, on 31 October 1517.

Luther's phenomenal success in changing public opinion, turning it away from the Catholic Church, its dogma and materialism, towards Lutheranism and religious reform, was fuelled by the publication of Lutheran pamphlets and texts, published and distributed across the Netherlands and Europe. Luther was not alone, others followed his beliefs. His Protestant reforms were debated across countries in northern Europe, most positively by the theologian and pastor John Calvin (1509–64) in France, as well as followers in Germany, Belgium, Scandinavia and the Netherlands. Soon Protestant reform would be known as Calvinism in the Dutch Republic.

Luther's 95 theses were distributed to official legates of the church. His theses argued for a less materialistic church and adherence to the Biblical scriptures. His actions resulted in his excommunication from the Catholic Church and he was pronounced a heretic. Luther responded to the Holy Roman Emperor, Charles V, at the Diet of Worms: 'Unless I am convinced by Scripture and plain reason – I do not accept the authority of the popes and councils'.

The result of Lutheran reform was to drastically alter the lives of Netherlanders and also the working lives of artists. The most dramatic, visual effect was the removal of excessive displays of paintings and frescoes in churches that did not explicitly adhere to the Biblical scriptures. In addition, the placement in churches of devotional chapels, aggrandized with paintings of private patrons, was frowned upon and eventually ceased. Luther's belief that only the Biblical text should be illustrated left the donors at the church door, and the artists without lucrative commissions.

From Excess to Austerity

Interior of the Church of St Bavo in Haarlem, 1636 (*see* left), by Assendelft-born Dutch artist Pieter Jansz Saenredam (1597–1665), noted for his architectural paintings of churches, revealed the extent to which Luther's reforms were carried out. The bare, whitewashed plaster walls of the interior of the Grote Kerk (also called St Bavo), a Protestant church and a requisitioned Catholic cathedral in Haarlem's central market square, are a visual metaphor for the cleansing of overt materialism by the Reformers.

Iconoclasm

The reaction to Luther's reforms prompted iconoclasm, defined as the destruction or rejection of religious images or objects as heretical. It resulted in the eradication of many churches' interior adornment and ornamentation, and the toppling of statues, the destruction of sacred vessels, altars, rood screens and even priests' vestments – any object associated with the Catholic Mass. It related to the people of the Netherlands wanting separation from Spanish rule and linked to the arrest of Protestant 'heretics'. Tens of thousands fled to

Above: *Fishing for Souls*, 1614, Adriaen Pietersz van de Venne (1589–1662)

safer refuges in London, southern England, and Cologne, Wesel and Emden in Germany. In Emden, northwest Germany, the fleeing exiles formed a group creating the Dutch Reformed Church, espousing a Calvinist Presbyterian doctrine. After failing to receive a response to petitions to Philip II in August 1566, fanatical Protestant followers, beginning in Antwerp and spreading throughout churches in the Netherlands, went on a rampage of destruction. Precious early Dutch paintings, stained-glass windows, vestments, sculptures and statues were torn down and destroyed.

A Spanish Backlash

The outcome of Luther's protestations at Roman Catholic materialism and the corruption of Holy Orders resulted in the breakaway of northern Netherlands. Philip II's dispatch of highly trained soldiers, under the leadership of the fearsome 'Iron Duke', the Duke of Alba, in August 1567 to crush the 'heretic' protestors, led William of Orange to openly side with the Netherlanders against the Hapsburg king. It encouraged Protestant reformers in southern Netherlandish states to migrate to the northern territories. Included in this vast migration were artists, craftsman, potters, book publishers and others, looking to join and expand the artistic community in the north, triggering the cultural flowering since known as the 'Dutch Golden Age'.

William I, Prince of Orange

Prince William I of Orange (Willem van Oranje), Count of Nassau and Stadtholder (1533–84) – also spoken of as the 'father of the fatherland' (*Vader des Vaderlands*) – is renowned as the leader of the revolt in 1566 against the Spanish Hapsburg dynasty. This kick-started a rebellion, leading to the Eighty Years' War and formal independence

Above: *A Winter Landscape with Figures Skating on a Frozen River, Prince Maurits of Orange-Nassau with a Hunting Party in the Foreground*, 1620, Adriaen Pietersz van de Venne (1589–1662)

of the United Provinces (the military confederation of the northern provinces, Holland, Zeeland, Utrecht, Friesland, Overjissel, Gelderland and Groningen) from Spain in 1581, although hostilities between the two countries did not cease.

A New Era

After twelve years of continuous fighting with little result for either country a truce was agreed in 1609. A symbolical history painting by Adriaen Pietersz van de Venne (1589–1662) *Fishing for Souls*, 1614 (*see* page 11) highlights the fragile 'Twelve-Year-Truce' between Protestants, standing on left bank, and Catholics on the right bank of a river, seeking to 'catch' souls. De Venne makes a play on the words of Christ to his disciples 'I will make you 'fishers' of men.' (Matthew 4:19). During the periods of war artists caught the mood, as in *Battle Between Carnival and Lent*, 1633–34 (*see* page 9), a piece of religious theatricality and allegory – in the tradition of Hieronymus Bosch (1450–1516), and Peter Bruegel the Elder (1525-69) – by Jan Miense Molenaer (1610–68), where peasants engage in a raucous fight with monks.

Assassination of William I

The assassination on 10 July 1584 of Stadtholder William I, Prince of Orange, had been instigated by Philip II, who offered a sizeable reward to any man who killed the prince. A first attempt had failed, but a second attempt succeeded. The assassin was a French Catholic, Balthazar Gérard, a supporter of Philip II, who shot the prince dead from close range. Far from unsettling the Republic, the murder strengthened people's determination to remain independent. The role of Stadtholder remained with the royal House of Orange-Nassau, until the death of William II (1626–50), when the hereditary role of Stadtholder was eliminated.

The Regents

From the fifteenth to eighteenth centuries the Dutch Stadtholder was the title given to executive officers with civic and military powers, originally chosen from the nobility, to oversee provinces and provincial armies and appoint civic officers in the Netherlands. From 1650 to 1672 the Dutch Republic allowed citizens in the north freedom to choose leaders (Regents) from their own people. These Regents were businessmen, financiers and merchants, a wider

Above: *Interior of the Council Chamber of Amsterstam Town Hall*, c. 1663–65, Pieter de Hooch (1629–84)

Top: *Regents of the Lepers' Asylum*, c. 1668, Ferdinand Bol (1616–80)
Bottom: *Three Regentesses of the Lepers' Asylum*, c. 1668, Ferdinand Bol (1616–80)

democratic division of society than nobility but with similar responsibility. Each town and city had a burgomaster (mayor), a prestigious position with a powerful role in the community. *Interior of the Council Chamber of Amsterdam Town Hall*, c. 1663–65 (*see* page 13), by Pieter de Hooch, painted soon after he moved from Delft to Amsterdam, reveals the architectural features and decoration within the newly built Amsterdam Town Hall designed by Jacob van Campen (1596–1657), a grand setting for the burgomaster meetings. The population of the city in 1650 was 30,000 inhabitants.

Ruling the Cities

Wealthier citizens were expected to help the less fortunate in their communities. The Regents (*regenten*) became the rulers of the Dutch Republic and sat on an extensive variety of committees to control standards covering commerce, education and correction. The men were portrayed together officially in their associated roles in *Regents of the Old Men's Almshouse of Haarlem*, 1664, by Frans Hals (1582/83–1666). Its companion painting, *The Regentesses of the Old Men's Almshouse, Haarlem*, 1664, depicts the ladies, often the Regents' wives, who gave their service to oversee poorer members of the community. Individual portraits were commissioned too.

The Regentess's Role

Regentesses, as already stated often the wives of Regents, held the same role as Regents, sitting on charitable committees overseeing education, correction and provision for the poor, orphaned and sick. Ferdinand Bol (1616–80) of Dordrecht portrayed three of these women in *Three Regentesses of the Lepers' Asylum*, c. 1668, (*see* bottom left). On the left the woman holds a goose quill pen. On the table before them is a ledger

book and coins. Bol illustrates not only the Regentesses' wealthy status through their fashionable dress but also denotes their role in keeping the asylum's accounts in good order. Bol painted a companion piece, *Regents of the Lepers' Asylum*, c. 1668, (*see* top left). The pair of paintings would have been hung in the asylum entrance, or in the Regents' headquarters.

The Treaty of Münster 1648

Disturbances continued between Spain and the Netherlands, resulting in the Treaty of Münster in 1648, ending the Thirty Years' War (23 May 1618–15 May 1648), a religious war that had erupted across Europe between Protestants and Catholics for dominion. All United Provinces of the Netherlands joined together without Spanish interference, domination or control. Haarlem-born Bartholomeus van der Helst (1613–70) was one of several artists who commemorated the occasion. His vast group-portrait painting *Banquet at the Crossbowmen's Guild in Celebration of the Treaty of Münster*, 1648 (*see* above), features 25 individual persons, including servants. In art, Netherlandish painters made ordinary scenes of everyday life extraordinary, and created a boom market in Dutch paintings, of all types, from portraits and group-portraits to still life.

The Academic Tradition

Genres of art, originally based on ancient academies of classical art and learning, were reintroduced by the Italian artist and architect Giorgio Vasari (1511–74) in 1563. Emerging from the medieval guilds, such as the Guild of Saint Luke for painters and engravers, the Accademia del Disegno was established in Florence, Italy. It served as a formal arena for the study of art, design, architecture and sculpture, with honorary

Above: *Banquet at the Crossbowmen's Guild in Celebration of the Treaty of Münster*, 1648, Bartholomeus van der Helst (1613–70)

Capi (presidents) Duke Cosimo I de' Medici, Grand Duke of Tuscany (1519–74) and celebrated Florentine artist Michelangelo Buonarroti. In other countries, Giorgio Vasari, the 'father of art history' (a title gained from his publication of *The Lives of the Most Celebrated Painters, Sculptors, and Architects* (1550; 1568)), set the aesthetic for art academies.

The Netherlands' Academies Emerge

In the Netherlands the earliest art 'academy' was founded in Haarlem in 1583 by painters Cornelis Cornelisz. van Haarlem (1562–1638), Hendrick Goltzius (1558–1617) and Karel van Mander (1548–1606). In France, the Académie de peinture et de sculpture (Academy of Painting and Sculpture) was founded in 1648 by Cardinal Mazarin. Later, in the Netherlands, the Royal Academy of Art in The Hague, evolved from the Haagsche Teeken-Academie (Hague Drawing Academy), was established in 1682. In England, the Royal Academy of Arts was established in 1768.

The Dutch Tradition

In step with other countries across Europe, the medieval system of guilds for trades – art was considered a manual trade – prospered in the Netherlands. The Guild of St Luke, patron saint of the arts, included painters, sculptors, goldsmiths, engravers and glaziers. Apprenticeship took place in the workshops and studios of guild members. This led from workshop trainee – learning to crush and grind paint pigments – to initiation into the guild, which was essential to work as a professional artist. Foreign artists could work with guild approval, thus establishing a strong network of Netherlandish painters controlling work within the Republic. This system was in line with other countries' guilds' monopoly.

From Guild to Academy

In 1656, dissatisfied with the outmoded system of the guilds, 48 painters from The Hague formed the Confrerie Pictura, a fraternity primarily founded to protect and promote local artists, all of whom had to be members. In 1682, five founding members of the Confrerie Pictura – Willem Doudijns (1630–97), Robbert Duval (1639–1732), Daniël Mijtens the Younger (1644–88), Theodor van der Schuer (1634–1707) and Augustinus Terwesten (1649–1711) – furthered the promotion of their art practice with the establishment of Haagsche Teeken-Academie, The Hague Drawing Academy, to provide artistic training for students with the aim of promoting local artists.

Above: *A Still Life of Flowers in a Vase on a Ledge*, Rachel Ruysch (1664–1750)

Hoogstraten's Art Theories

Samuel van Hoogstraten (1627–78), born in Dordrecht, was a pupil of Dutch Master Rembrandt van Rijn. A Dutch realist artist, he was a remarkable painter of architectural perspective paintings and *trompe l'oeil* still life, such as *A Trompe L'Oeil of Objects Attached to a Letter Rack*, 1664. In addition, he was a poet and art theorist. Hoogstraten continued the Dutch theoretical approach to art begun by van Mander. He was one of the first to use the word 'theory' in relation to art. His outstanding treatise *Inleyding tot de Hooge Schoole der Schilderkonst* ('Introduction to the Academy of Painting: The Visible World'), published in 1678 just before his death, debated the theory of the theory of art (which was a new subject in his time), equating art with philosophy and realist painting as a 'sister of reflective philosophy'. He considered many theories, such as whether nature or teaching produced the better painter, and explored various painters' methods, including the approach to art and teaching of Venetian master Titian and that of his own tutor, Rembrandt.

Forms of Painting

Whereas Vasari's prototype art academy encouraged freedom of expression and encouragement of the arts rather than highly formal training of the artist (retained by the guilds), later academies were schools of art with a teaching curriculum based on a hierarchy of art, from 'high' art to 'lower' forms. The lowest was still life. The highest involved the human figure in significant historical, legendary, or allegorical representation, the concept originating from Leon Battista Alberti's treatise *On Painting*, published in the 1430s. An example would be Rembrandt's *The Night Watch*, 1642 (*see* page 100), also known as *Militia Company of District II under the Command of Captain Frans Banninck Cocq*, or *The Shooting Company of Frans Banning Cocq and Willem van Ruytenburch*. From this component of art theory – developed further by the French (from 1648) and English (from 1768) art academies and institutions of art – categories of art were introduced and recognized by the arts establishment. There were the four major forms, starting from the highest: history painting on a grand scale with figures actual or mythological; single and group portraiture; landscape and animal painting; and then still life. The fifth, scenes of everyday life, was known as genre art. Beginning as the lowest form of art, it was promoted to between landscape and still life in the middle of the seventeenth century, when its popularity rose across Europe, particularly in the Dutch Republic.

Above: *Grace Before Meat*, c. 1665, Jan Steen (1626–79)

Form Equals Artistic Status

The hierarchy of forms indicated to academicians the skill required by the painter. The higher the form, the greater the skill. Architect and biographer André Félibien des Avaux (1619–95), court historian to Louis XIV of France, as an honorary consultant to the French Royal Academy of Painting and Sculpture, addressed the subject of hierarchy in a 1669 conference address to members, students and tutors. Félibien stated:

> *'... the artist who does perfect landscapes is superior to another who paints only fruit, flowers or shells. The artist who paints living animals deserves more respect than those who represent only still, lifeless subjects ... as the human figure is God's most perfect work... the artist who imitates God by painting human figures is more outstanding by far than all the others.'*

The orator reserved his finest praise for the allegorical and historical painter, who worked in a form above that of all other artists.

Above: *A Peasant Holding a Jug and a Pipe*, c. 1650–55, Adriaen van Ostade (1610–85)

The Legacy of the Golden Age of Dutch Art

Today, Dutch painting of the sixteenth and seventeenth centuries is recognized as superlative, and more than equal to art of the Italian Renaissance of the same period. It was not always so. Although Dutch paintings, such as landscapes by Cuyp or Ruisdael, or genre paintings by Jan Steen (1626–79), were in demand in the eighteenth and nineteenth centuries, the subject matter was considered 'low' art. One such was *The Farmyard*, 1649 (*see* page 133), by Paulus Potter (1625–54). A rural scene, mirroring aspects of realism, it featured many farmyard animals, including a cow urinating. Potter created popular genre animal paintings, such as *The Bull*, 1647 (*see* right), with animals and farmer set against the backdrop of an enormous sky that fills two-thirds of the picture plane. His painting *A Young Bull and Two Cows in a Meadow*, 1649, another 'low' art subject, entered the collection of George IV in 1819, valued at 2,000 guineas, a seven-figure sum today. 'Low' art fetched a high price.

End of a Golden Era

The establishment of the Republic in the 1580s allowed political and economic security, and instigated the remarkable economic rise of the Netherlands, its citizens excelling in trade, science and exploration. All commercial aspects of Dutch life added great wealth and prestige to a small territory and gave its people, particularly the merchants, the means to enrich themselves, their homes, their families, their culture, their art. In the present day we see the creations of the artists of the Dutch Golden Age in galleries worldwide. Rembrandt, Vermeer, Steen, Ruysdael, Hals and Ruysch are artists' names as familiar as their Italian Renaissance counterparts. After them came a new generation of artists, but the Golden Age declined with the onset of the Glorious Revolution of 1688–89. The Revolution saw the overthrow of King James II of England, replaced with a joint monarchy of James's daughter Mary and her husband, the Dutch Stadtholder (executive leader) William III (1650–1702), Prince of Orange; otherwise known as King William III and Queen Mary II of England.

Above: *The Bull*, 1647, Paulus Potter (1625–54)

Art & Patronage

A Reformative Revolution

IT IS POSSIBLE to chart from the Reformation the change of direction in art in the Netherlands, away from religious paintings that had a restrictive market, towards commercially popular subjects in landscape, portraiture, genre and still life. Religious patrons, primarily the Catholic Church, and Catholic merchants were in a minority. The political, economic and social changes created a more democratic society, now controlled by stadtholders, the States General and the Regents, as previously described.

A New Framework

With watchful Lutherans and Anabaptists suppressing religious art – other than Biblical representations – artists turned to other forms of patronage, looking toward the rich burghers, wealthy civic officials, nobility and middling classes for commissions. Paintings were an acceptable form of luxury in the newly constrained Reformist period, and artists made capital from it, stepping away from the studio, and outdoors with a portable easel. Life in the newly formed Dutch Republic was captured on canvas, as in the bourgeoisie in *Family Group in a Landscape*, c. 1647–50 (*see* left), by the Antwerp-born painter Frans Hals, and also his informal marriage portrait,

Previous Page: *Winter Landscape with Skaters*, c. 1608, Hendrick Avercamp (1585–1634)
Left: *Family Group in a Landscape*, c. 1647–50, Frans Hals (1582/83–1666)

'The portrait of men and places, of bourgeois customs, of squares, streets, and countryside, of sea and sky – such was ... the programme adopted by the Dutch School.'

Eugène Fromentin

Portrait of a Couple, Probably Isaac Abrahamsz. and Beatrix van de Laen, c. 1622 (*see* page 178). The setting of both works, on country estates, was a new trend. These were intended as conversation pieces, set outdoors to portray the wealth and status of the landowners. The paintings, possibly briefly posed outdoors, would have been completed in the artist's studio.

Portraiture

In the Netherlands, portraiture, normally the reserve of nobility, increased in popularity amongst the rich merchant classes as well as the middling – *brede middenstand* – classes. At the same time the taste and inclination for private chapel decoration and religious icons waned following the onset of the Reformation and rise of the Calvinist-Protestant movement. Churches became bare of ornamentation, as a painting *Church Interior*, c. 1659 (*see* right), by Alkmaar-born painter of perspective Emanuel de Witte (1617–92), illustrates. Portraits initially recorded and documented nobility at historic moments; for example, a meeting with foreign nobility, a new reign, the betrothal of a bride and groom, a marriage portrait, the birth of a child, or to record a high-status dignitary in office. Now the reason for portraiture widened to include informal gatherings, or non-specific moments, as in *Curiosity*, c. 1660–62 (*see* left), by Gerard ter Borch (1617–81), born in Zwolle, northeast Netherlands.

Portraying Modern Life

Portraiture became a fashionable must-have for the upper middle classes, to acknowledge individual family members, or businesses, or civic groups, painted for posterity. Rembrandt's *Portrait of Jan Six*, c. 1654 (*see* page 29), epitomizes the wealthy private client-base that the most sought-after

Above: *Curiosity*, c. 1660–62, Gerard ter Borch (1617–81)

Above: *Church Interior*, c. 1659, Emanuel de Witte (c. 1617–92)

painters could expect. Jan Steen's informal portrayal of a burgomaster, a rich grain merchant and his teenage daughter, Adolf and Catharina Croeser, known as *The Burgomaster of Delft and His Daughter*, 1655 (*see* left), revealed much more than a likeness of the persons. Croeser is seated outside, on the raised doorstep of his house on the Oude Delft canal in Delft. The Oude Kerk church can be seen in the distance. Steen, a masterful portraitist of contemporary life, was a neighbour to Croeser. The painter depicts a commonplace occurrence with a poor woman and her young child seeking alms. Steen adds pathos, in her lined face and rough, worn hands, and the boy's hat, removed in respect, is riddled with holes. Steen contrasts the boy's apparel with the fine clothes of the young daughter, richly dressed in silk and lace. She is adorned with pearl earrings and necklace, symbols of wealth. In this one portrait Steen captures two differing circles of life, co-existing in Delft, yet far apart. He reveals his skill as a portraitist, landscape artist and still-life painter with a carefully placed, exquisitely detailed vase of flowers at the burgomaster's window.

In this new age artists felt freer to experiment. Frans Hals created an informal and superbly observed double-portrait, *A Young Couple, Probably Isaac Abrahamsz. Massa and Beatrix van de Laen* (*see* page 178). Depicting the richness of the couple's attire and their smiling, happy, relaxed demeanour, it was a breakaway from Dutch artistic convention and formal, dour depictions. Rembrandt, too, was a master of mood and emotion as well as opulent fabrics, as in the wondrous vision of colour and light in *The Jewish Bride*, c. 1667 (*see* right).

Portrait of Jan Six

Jan Six's merchant family, originally from France and of Huguenot heritage, moved to Amsterdam, where they owned silk-dyeing workshops.

Left: *The Burgomaster of Delft and His Daughter*, 1655, Jan Steen (1625/26–79)

Above: *The Jewish Bride*, c. 1667, Rembrandt van Rijn (1606–69)

Six worked in the family's business until the decade this painting *Portrait of Jan Six*, c. 1654 (*see* right), was created. He then chose a civic career, rising to burgomaster of Amsterdam in 1691. A cultured man, a friend and patron of Rembrandt, a collector of fine art and antiques, interested in art and literature, he also wrote poetry. His marriage to Margaretha Tulp (1632–1709), daughter of Dr Nicolaes Tulp (1593–1674), depicted in Rembrandt's *The Anatomy Lesson of Dr Nicolaes Tulp*, 1632 (*see* page 141), activated the rise in Six's social status. Rembrandt portrays Six as a serious, gentle man. He is depicted in a half-portrait viewed from below, close to the viewer, as if Six is entering the room and slowly taking off his gloves. His face is bathed in light. The use of chiaroscuro (light and shade) focuses attention on the man and his rich, colourful clothing. Six bought several works from Rembrandt and was depicted more than once.

Self-Portraiture

To artists, a self-portrait revealed a painter's skills. Gabriël Metsu (1629–67) painted a portrait of himself to confirm his art credentials and included his wife in *Self-Portrait of the Artist and His Wife Isabella de Wolff in a Tavern*, 1661. Rembrandt van Rijn, the most prolific self-portraitist, may have intended to paint himself to test his skills, as in the early *Self-Portrait as a Courtly Squire*, 1629 (*see* left). Forty years on and painted in the year of his death, *Self-Portrait at the Age of 63*, 1669 (*see* page 62), reflects an honourable man laid low by debt and family deaths.

A Taste for 'Tronies'

A popular type of portraiture in seventeenth-century Dutch art was the 'tronie', a head or half-length portrait of an anonymous person,

Above: *Self-Portrait as a Courtly Squire*, c. 1629, Rembrandt van Rijn (1606–69)

Right: *Portrait of Jan Six*, c. 1654, Rembrandt van Rijn (1606–69)

dressed in character, in the style of Rembrandt's *Young Woman with Earrings*, 1657 (*see* page 63), and Delft-born Johannes Vermeer's *Girl with a Red Hat*, c. 1665 (*see* left). Some tronies depicted characters with exaggerated expressions to connote low life. Examples include: *Bitter Draught*, c. 1635 (*see* page 146), by Flemish-born master of 'low-life' portrayals Adriaen Brouwer (c. 1606–38); or *The Procuress*, 1625 (*see* page 67), by Gerard van Honthorst (1592–1656); or models dressed as diverse characters in exotic or theatrical costume. Rembrandt, like many other artists, had a wardrobe of theatrical clothes to use for paintings. Tronies might depict persons ranging from soldiers to serving girls to flute players. Many painters used their family as models, or their domestic servants, as in *Girl with a Pearl Earring*, c. 1665 (*see* page 49), by Vermeer. It is possible that Rembrandt used his son, Titus van Rijn (1641–68), for *'Tronie' of a Young Man with Gorget and Beret*, c. 1639. One can see the appeal of the tronie in the dashing portrait *The Falconer*, 1647 (*see* above left), by Ferdinand Bol of Dordrecht. Other tronies include *Old Woman Reading a Book*, c. 1660–65 (*see* above right), by Gerrit Dou (1613–75). These are just some of the immensely popular subjects for Dutch tronie portraiture, all saleable, commercial works, mirroring public taste.

Left: *Girl with a Red Hat*, c. 1665, Johannes Vermeer (1632–75)

Above left: *The Falconer*, 1647, Ferdinand Bol (1616–80) **Above right:** *Old Woman Reading a Book*, c. 1660–65, Gerrit Dou (1613–75)

Landscape

Landscape art is surely most synonymous with Dutch Art of the Golden Age. In Haarlem between 1610 and 1630 a 'tonal' school of landscape painting evolved. The resulting portfolios of work were drenched in subtle colour and light. The high quality of finish created a detailed pictorial realism, expressing an evocative mood in subtle atmospheric scenes. *Wide Rivermouth with Boats*, c. 1660 (*see* right), by Salomon van Ruysdael is one example. Others include: Johannes Vermeer's timeless *View of Delft*, c. 1660–61 (*see* page 45); *View of Haarlem with Bleaching Grounds*, c. 1670–75 (*see* page 54), by the masterful Haarlem-born landscape artist Jacob van Ruisdael; and *The Avenue at Meerdervoort*, 1650–52, and *View of Dordrecht*, c. 1658 (*see* page 70), by the Dordrecht-born artist Aelbert Cuyp (1620–91). All reveal supreme talent for accurate realism.

Winter landscape views were immensely popular in Dutch society. *Winter Landscape with Skaters*, c. 1608 (*see* pages 20–21), by Amsterdammer Hendrick Avercamp (1585–1634) is typical of such a scene, showing Dutch citizens meeting, walking, selling, skating and travelling across frozen lakes and rivers. It was a scene of joy and gaiety, as depicted in *A Winter Landscape with Figures Skating on a Frozen River*, by Adriaen van de Venne (1589–1662) (*see* page 12). It was not unusual for the lowest-paid Dutch citizens to have copies of paintings or prints, such as these, adorning their homes, and a picturesque landscape of their homeland was a popular choice. Landscape painters in Europe, particularly in the art academies of France and Britain, suffered from the landscape art form being categorized as inferior to portraiture and history painting. Meanwhile, the Dutch artists prospered.

Right: *Wide Rivermouth with Boats*, c. 1660, Salomon van Ruysdael (c. 1602–70)

Above: *The Windmill at Wijk bij Duurstede*, c. 1668–70, Jacob van Ruisdael (1628/9–82)

Windmills and Canals

The Netherlands (meaning 'low-lying') has 90 per cent of its land below sea level, making it a challenge to farm. From medieval times the flow of water inland had been controlled by windmills, which are synonymous with the Dutch flat lands, both natural and those reclaimed from the sea. Dutch landscape paintings with windmills and canals were immensely popular, like *River Landscape with Ferry*, 1633, by Salomon van Ruysdael, or *Landscape with a Windmill*, 1646, or *The Windmill at Wijk bij Duurstede*, c. 1668–70 (*see* left), by Salomon's nephew, Haarlem-born Jacob van Ruisdael, considered by art historians as the greatest Dutch landscape painter. Their works convey what were everyday views for the Dutch as extraordinary places. In addition, their works illustrate how the Dutch used the rivers and canals as a daily ferry transport system, for people, animals and cargo. In *Winter Landscape with Skaters Before s'Hertogenbosch*, 1646 (*see* above), by prolific Leiden-born painter Jan van Goyen (1596–1656), the artist illustrates both geographical location and social pleasures, the skaters set against a backdrop of the wealthy southern town of s'Hertogenbosch (Den Bosch), in the Duchy of Brabant, the birthplace of the revered Dutch painter Hieronymus Bosch (1450–1516).

Above: *Winter Landscape with Skaters Before s'Hertogenbosch*, 1646, Jan van Goyen (1596–1656)

Genre – A Dutch Masterpiece

Genre painting – everyday scenes of life – became extraordinarily popular amongst all classes and incomes in the Netherlands. The domestic interior was a favourite subject for genre painting. The cessation of war against Spain allowed the people of the northern Netherlands to focus on their lives. Artists painted what they experienced, what they saw, like three musicians playing in *The Concert*, c. 1626 (*see* page 128), by artist Hendrick ter Brugghen (1588–1629) of The Hague. Contemporary life could be painted in the fields, in the taverns, on frozen lakes, in the scullery, or the drawing room, such as *A Game of Tric-Trac*, c. 1630 (*see* left), by Haarlem-born Judith Leyster (c. 1609–60).

Dutch life was explored by artists and consumed by the public. Jan Steen was a master of hectic, disorderly, often chaotically amusing scenes of everyday life, which created the Dutch adage 'a Jan Steen household'. Steen captured – with a little poetic licence – the intimate lives of people, from *Celebrating the Birth*, 1664 (*see* page 4), and *Grace before Meat*, c. 1665 (*see* page 17), both set in a domestic interior, to tavern scenes such as *Garden at the Inn*, 1663 (*see* right). This everyday life genre spread out from the Netherlands across Europe, visible in many artists' portfolios, including that of the English artist William Hogarth (1697–1764).

'...his paintings are like his way of life and his way of life is like his paintings.'

Arnold Houbraken on Jan Steen

Still Life

Still life is categorized as an assemblage of random objects, such as fruit, bowls, glasses, vases of flowers, kitchen utensils, dead animals or fish, manuscripts, paper and books, usually positioned on a cloth or table top and formed into a composition. The term 'still life', in use from the middle of the seventeenth century, comes from the Dutch expression *still-*

Above: *A Game of Tric-Trac*, c. 1630, Judith Leyster (c. 1609–60)

Right: *Garden at the Inn*, 1663, Jan Steen (1625/26–79)

leven, *still* denoting a motionless object, *leven* nature or life. The objects chosen were often placed to symbolize a visual language of intended meaning hidden within the painting but recognized by the onlooker. In art this meaning could be inferred from a variety of objects, such as a death-signifier in the form of human skulls, dead animals or birds, rotting fruit or fading flowers, or butterflies, connoting the passage of time, or a memento mori, denoting the transience of mortal life. They were called 'vanitas' paintings, meaning 'futility' or 'worthlessness'; in other words, they illustrated the pointlessness of earthly goods and pursuits and the need to consider one's own mortality and repent. The presence of a lute, or lute players, could signify lowly behaviour. Still-life vanitas paintings were extremely popular as morality tales, and it was usual for even poorer homes to have such pictures adorning the walls, most often bought from the markets, or door-to-door sellers.

Still-Life Painters

Outstanding Dutch exponents of still life include Rachel Ruysch, painter of the remarkable *Tree Trunk Surrounded by Flowers, Butterflies and Animals*, c. 1685 (*see* left), notable for its beauty and life-like, realistic depiction, and *Still Life of a Tulip, a Melon and Flowers on a Ledge*, c. 1695–1700. From 1679 Ruysch, daughter of a botanist, trained with still-life painter Willem van Aelst (1627–83). In the 1680s she was influenced by the work of another still-life painter, Otto Marseus van Schriek (c. 1619–78). Ruysch attracted international fame in her own lifetime, in a career that spanned six decades, creating exquisite still-life paintings that were in high demand. The oil-on-copper *Still Life with Flowers*, c. 1609 (*see* right), by Ambrosius Bosschaert (1573–1621) helped popularize the century-long fashion of hanging paintings of flowers to adorn the Dutch home. Balthasar van der Ast (1593–1657) was a pioneer of shell, fruit and flower paintings, as in *Still*

'Painters should go to the Dutch school to learn the art of painting...'

Sir Joshua Reynolds on Dutch Art

Left: *Tree Trunk Surrounded by Flowers, Butterflies and Animals*, c. 1685, Rachel Ruysch (1664–1750)

Above: *Still Life with Flowers*, c. 1609, Ambrosius Bosschaert (1573–1621)

Life of Cherries and Peaches, *c.* 1620 (*see* page 6). Van der Ast's *Floral Still Life with Shells*, 1622, signifies breakthrough Dutch scientific discoveries, enabling artists to depict microscopic detail of insects and flowers. The rich beauty of still-life painting exploded in popularity after the suppression of religious iconography in churches.

History Painting

Historical painting, in academic tradition, was the highest art form, reserved for the academies' most established, prized painters. This was not a rule in Dutch art, but the most gifted artists were commissioned for commemorations of historic events. Flemish artist Cornelis Bol (*c.* 1589–after 1666) painted *Naval Battle Between Dutch Men-of-War and Spanish Galleys*, *c.* 1633–50, which commemorated the tough sea battles between the Dutch fleet under Prince William of Orange and the war ships of the Spanish ruler, Philip II, during the Eighty Years' War. Gerard ter Borch recreated the monumental occasion of *The Ratification of the Treaty of Münster* (*see* right), a treaty signed on 15 June 1648 in the town hall of Münster to end an eighty-year war between the Dutch Republic and Spain. Ter Borch magnificently reveals the momentous event with Dutch delegates to the left and Spanish to the right.

Cities and Artists Flourish

A bird's-eye view of cities of the Dutch Republic would reveal new gatehouses and defence structures, expansion in canal infrastructures, newly built properties from town halls to commercial properties and private houses, more students' residents at universities and an increased number of print and publishing houses. For artists this meant many

Right: *The Ratification of the Treaty of Münster*, 1648, Gerard ter Borch (1617–81)

Above: *View in Amsterdam*, 1665–75, Jan van der Heyden (1637–1712)

commissions to portray the civic culture, and growing wealth of citizens, to be displayed on the walls of public buildings and private residences. Each city prospered and, with them, their resident artists.

Amsterdam in the Golden Age

The city of Amsterdam visibly grew both financially and physically – with increased trade, private houses and commercial buildings – when the shipping route to Antwerp on the Rhine-Meuse-Scheldt estuary was closed off by Holland in the late sixteenth century to favour Amsterdam. The city expanded beyond the original city walls. In 1528, when Flanders, Brabant and Zeeland were part of the Spanish Hapsburg Empire, Antwerp was the principal harbour for trade. In 1585 Holland controlled the Zeeuws strip of land on the left bank of the Scheldt river estuary and closed it to shipping, thus cutting Antwerp trade and increasing commerce for Amsterdam and Middelburg ports. This included a rising market in slave-trading in both cities. By the 1650s a visitor to Amsterdam would have beheld an expanded city for a population risen from 30,000 in 1580 to 210,000 by 1650. The city was now supported by a ringed canal infrastructure to harbour boats and to carry freight and people. The banks of the Prinsengracht, Keizersgracht, Herengracht and

Above: The 'Golden Bend' in the Herengracht, Amsterdam as Seen from the West, 1672, Gerrit Adriaensz. Berckheyde (1638–98)

Singel canals were lined with impressive houses and gardens and there were public, tree-lined paths alongside the canals, paid for by merchant commerce. The wealth of Amsterdam in this period is reflected in the portrait cityscapes of its buildings and squares, such as *The 'Golden Bend' in the Herengracht, Amsterdam as Seen from the West*, 1672 (*see* page 43), by Gerrit Adriaensz. Berckheyde (1638–98), and *The Herengracht, Amsterdam*, c. 1668, *Amsterdam City View with Houses on the Herengracht and the Old Haarlemmersluis*, c. 1670 (*see* page 165), and *Dam Square with Nieuwe Kerk (New Church) and Koninklijk Paleis (Royal Palace)*, c. 1668, all by Jan van der Heyden the Elder (1637–1712), one of the first artists to specialize in architectural cityscapes, particularly views of Amsterdam.

Above: *Vegetable Market in Amsterdam*, c. 1661–62, Gabriël Metsu (1629–67)

Amsterdam's Early Morning Market

Gabriël Metsu of Leiden was a master of many types of art. He captured Dutch life with Amsterdam backdrops, as in *Vegetable Market in Amsterdam*, c. 1661–62 (*see* left), the outdoor vegetable market established in 1658. Ferries transported goods while tradespeople, including farmers, brought fresh produce to the market every day by barge or handcart. Metsu portrays the shoppers and the vegetable produce all in fine detail, set against the backdrop of the beautiful Prinsengracht (Prince's Canal), the longest canal in Amsterdam, with houses built during the Dutch Golden Age along its banks. Metsu verifies the recent history of Amsterdam in this realistic painting. The Prinsengracht is the outermost of three canals surrounding the port of Amsterdam. It is part of the canal system begun in 1612 and completed in 1660, at the time this painting was created. Merchant houses were built on the canal banks. The canals and waterways accommodated the many hundreds of barges ferrying goods across the city from larger ships at port. The painting is just one example of artists' reflections on the contemporary life of Amsterdammers.

Delft

The picturesque city of Delft on the Netherlands' western coastline is famous for many historic events and cultural accomplishments. It was chosen as the residence of William I of Orange and his court in 1572, occupying the Prinsenhof, converted from the former Catholic convent of St Agatha. The city grew, in size and wealth. It was the power base of the Prince until his assassination in 1584. Today the name of the city is synonymous with blue and white pottery. Potters from Antwerp, forced to flee the city due to the Spanish invasion of 1585, chose to settle in Delft. From 1602 the potters produced a type of Chinese porcelain, which became immensely popular and features in many seventeenth-century Dutch paintings.

Above: *View of Delft*, c. 1660–61, Johannes Vermeer (1632–75)

Johannes Vermeer

View of Delft (*see* page 45), by Delft-born artist Johannes Vermeer epitomizes the peaceful landscape of the city in which he lived, one that has changed little to the present day. Informed by the art of the early Netherlandish painter Jan Van Eyck (c. 1390–1441), for example in Van Eyck's *The Arnolfini Portrait*, c. 1339–1441 (*see* page 52), and Italian master of the Baroque, Michelangelo Merisi da Caravaggio (1571–1610), Vermeer's superb use of intense light and chiaroscuro – highly visible in Caravaggio's *Boy Bitten by a Lizard*, c. 1595–1600 – focuses the viewer's attention on the subject through its remarkable realism. Only a few paintings by Vermeer are known, with a total of 36 attributed to the artist. Through his work Vermeer gives the spectator a glimpse into his life as a painter, portraying the interior domesticity of his everyday life in a comfortable Delft household. Vermeer introduces this life through light-filled room settings, cultivated décor mirroring the status of the property owner, refined yet fashionable dress, stylish or educational objects, musical instruments and the people who live in the house.

Private Moments

Vermeer's painting *The Guitar Player*, c. 1672 (*see* above), possibly a portrait of his daughter Maria, is a visual experience of Dutch middle-class life. The artist places the viewer in the private domain of a young woman. She is elegantly clothed, wearing a sun-yellow brocade jacket edged with ermine over her dress. She wears pearls at her neck and her hair is swept back and groomed into ringlets, symbols of high fashion. The young woman's fresh complexion reflects her youth, glimpsed as the shaft of warm light falls softly on her features. On the wall behind her a landscape painting hangs in an ornate gold frame. On her left is a table with books.

'Vermeer is not a sun painter, but rather a moon-painter … that's good, it is the pure, final stage of art, the moment when it becomes more real than reality.'

Arshile Gorky

Left: *The Milkmaid*, c. 1658–60, Johannes Vermeer (1632–75)

Above: *The Guitar Player*, c. 1672, Johannes Vermeer (1632–75)

She is playing a guitar but momentarily stops to look up, distracted by someone or something to her right. The guitar strings continue to vibrate. This interruption connotes the presence of another person, unseen in the room, adding mystery to the scene. To catch these private moments in time in the lives of a domestic household, Vermeer uses a pause – as in *Girl with a Pearl Earring* (*see* right), *Woman with a Lute*, c. 1662–63 (*see* page 79), *The Lacemaker*, 1669–70 (*see* left), *Young Woman with a Water Jug*, c. 1662 (*see* page 81), and *The Milkmaid*, 1658–60 (*see* page 46). An interruption highlights an interaction, between seen or unseen people, as in *The Guitar Player*, and *The Love Letter*, c. 1669–70 (*see* page 72).

Vermeer the Painter

Johannes Vermeer (van der Meer), born 31 October 1632, was the youngest child of Reformed Protestants, Digna Baltens (d. 1670) and Reynier Jansz. van der Meer (c. 1591–1652). His father, a member of the Guild of St Luke in Delft in 1631, was originally a weaver of fine silks and velvets in Amsterdam before moving to Delft to become an innkeeper of The Flying Fox (*De Vliegende Vos*) on the Voldersgracht, from c. 1627–30, and an art picture dealer. Perhaps influenced by his father's profession dealing in artworks, Vermeer began an art apprenticeship around 1647, possibly tutored by Delft-born Leonaert Bramer (1596–1674), although there is no documentation. He worked with painter Carel Fabritius (1622–54) to become a master of the Guild of St Luke in Delft in December 1653, a year after Fabritius. As a master Vermeer was able to sell his own art and that of other artists as a dealer in Delft and to tutor paying pupils. The untimely death of Fabritius in 1654 left Vermeer as Delft's foremost painter. Fabritius died in an arsenal explosion of gunpowder on 12 October 1654, known as the Delft Thunderclap, commemorated in a dynamic painting by Egbert van der Poel (1621–64), *A View of Delft with the Explosion of 1654*. Many died and the resulting fire destroyed much of the city of Delft, including Fabritius' studio and his paintings (only 15 survived).

Above: *The Lacemaker*, 1669–70, Johannes Vermeer (1632–75)

Right: *Girl with a Pearl Earring*, c. 1665, Johannes Vermeer (1632–75)

Domestic Life

From around 1660 Vermeer lived with his wife Catharina Bolnes (1631–87/88) in the sizable Delft house on Oude Langendijk of his mother-in-law, Maria Thins (c. 1593–1680). She was a descendant of a distinguished family from Gouda. During their marriage Catharina gave birth to 15 children – four did not live beyond infancy – a huge financial responsibility for Vermeer, which he did not manage well. The paintings, maps and prints reproduced in Vermeer's room settings may have belonged to Maria Thins, along with other pieces, the tapestries, chairs, paintings, maps, tables and musical instruments that appear often in Vermeer's oeuvre. He utilized the house as an interior location and family members and domestic staff as models.

'It is for this rare, precious quality of truthfulness that I delight in many Dutch paintings ...'

George Eliot from *Adam Bede*

The Art of Painting

Painted over 10 years after Vermeer's entry to the Guild of St Luke, *The Artist's Studio*, c. 1665–66, also known as *The Art of Painting* and *The Allegory of Painting* (*see* page 80), reveals a possible self-portrait of the artist at work. Vermeer had his studio on the second floor, at the front

Right: *The Glass of Wine*, c. 1658–1660, Johannes Vermeer (1632–75)

of Thin's house. In the painting the studio is filled with light and with props, from the dramatic theatrical curtain drawn aside to set the scene to the vast map on the far wall to draw the eye in. The artist, his back to the viewer, is perched on a stool in front of an easel, while a young, finely dressed woman, the subject of the painter's work, stands by a window.

A Camera Obscura?

The work has intrigued art and science scholars. Did Vermeer use a camera obscura (the forerunner to the modern camera) to create this optical illusion, of a painter painting himself? This remarkable painting is vastly different to a version by Carel Fabritius (1622–54) – painter of the exquisite *The Goldfinch*, 1654 (*see* right). In the simpler but equally noteworthy *An Artist in His Studio*, c. 1640s, Fabritius may have used one of his two brothers as model. Fabritius was a gifted pupil of Rembrandt van Rijn, and this painting is possibly informed by Rembrandt's own work, *Artist in His Studio*, c. 1627–28.

Informed by Van Eyck

In his work *The Artist's Studio*, Vermeer pays homage to the greatest early Netherlandish painter, a master of light and realistic illusion, Jan van Eyck. Both van Eyck and the Italian Baroque painter Caravaggio were constant sources for Dutch artists of the Golden Age. In Van Eyck's *The Arnolfini Portrait* (*see* left), with a chandelier centred between the couple, stand Giovanni di Nicolao Arnolfini, a merchant from Lucca residing in Bruges, and his wife. As in Vermeer's work, *The Artist's Studio* (*see* page 80), there is the illusion of other people in the room, including the painter, not seen except through van Eyck's convex mirror on the wall behind the couple.

Left: *The Arnolfini Portrait*, 1434, Jan van Eyck (c. 1390–1441)

Above: *The Goldfinch*, 1654, Carel Fabritius (1622–54)

'There is considerable poetry in its composition, its gloomy skies, and darkened lights.'

John Charles Van Dyke on Jacob van Ruisdael

Above: *View of Haarlem with Bleaching Grounds*, c. 1670–75, Jacob van Ruisdael (1628/9–82)

Haarlem

View of Haarlem with Bleaching Grounds, c. 1670–75 (*see* left), by Jacob van Ruisdael, tells the viewer much about the trade of Haarlem in the seventeenth century, a city of around 16,000 people in 1650. Ruisdael sets his view of Haarlem on the distant horizon, whilst revealing in the foreground the bleaching fields where linens are stretched out to dry in the open air. His painting denotes the peaceful landscape surrounding the city and connotes the profitable textile industry, the major industry of Haarlem, in which Dutch linens and linens from other countries were bleached. The profusion of this type of landscape became known as *Haerlempjes*, that is, 'little views of Haarlem'. In inventories the word was widely used to describe a small landscape painting of Haarlem.

Atmosphere and Light

Studying Dutch paintings of this era, one notices that the landscape becomes as important as the people in it. The sky often dominates two-thirds to three-quarters of the picture plane with light strongly reflecting the seas or rivers, as in *Boats in the Estuary of Holland Diep in a Storm*, c. 1640s (*see* right), by Aelbert Cuyp, and dark clouds crossing the landscape, broken by small shafts of light, as in *Landscape with Two Oaks*, 1641 (*see* page 91), by Jan van Goyen. Both artists were masters of atmospheric mood, created by the tonal use of light. Van Goyen trained under different masters. One was Esaias van de Velde (1587–1630), whose father had fled the south to settle in Amsterdam. Van de Velde, who moved to Haarlem in 1610, was one of the first Dutch realist painters of landscape. He ignored the more colourful properties of northern landscape painting to concentrate on realism, using natural colour tones,

Above: *Boats in the Estuary of Holland Diep in a Storm*, c. 1640s, Aelbert Cuyp (1620–91)

ÆTA. SVÆ 26
A° 1624

as seen in *Winter Landscape*, 1623, in which the sky dominates two-thirds of the picture plane. One can see van de Velde's influence in the vast sky that dominates Jan van Goyen's *Winter Landscape with Skaters Before S'Hertogenbosch* (*see* page 35).

Frans Hals

One of the greatest portrait artists to live and work in Haarlem was the Antwerp-born son of a weaver, the highly successful painter Frans Hals. Dutch painter and author Arnold Houbraken (1660–1719) included Hals in his artists' biographies, reporting that Hals' family fled from the Spanish in 1585, settling, like many others, in Haarlem. There he was apprenticed to Karel van Mander, the painter and biographer. In 1610 Hals joined the artists' guild of Haarlem, thus allowing him to sell his work, set up a studio with assistants and tutor students, one of them being Judith Leyster and briefly her husband, artist Jan Miense Molenaer (1610–68), both born in Haarlem. Leyster's artworks were frequently misattributed to Hals or Molenaer.

Captivating Portraits

Hals is noted for his captivating, sensual portraits of citizens of Haarlem, who sat for him in a private or public capacity, such as the tronie of the unknown civic guardsman portrayed in *The Merry Drinker*, c. 1628–30 (*see* right). He set the mood and characteristics of his sitters through fine and loose brushwork, rich colour and a perceptive eye for detail. *The Laughing Cavalier*, 1624 (*see* left), is one of his best-loved works. The sitter is unknown and is neither laughing nor a cavalier (a name given to the painting in 1888), but his age is inscribed on the work as 26 years. The half-length close-portrait, featuring the 'cavalier' in a three-quarter pose away from the viewer with left arm akimbo and resting on his body, is dazzling. He wears an embroidered doublet decorated with emblems in gold, red and white thread, which Hals finely paints. It is enriched with neck and sleeve ruffs of richly worked handmade lace, connoting wealth. The pommel of a gilded rapier is visible at his elbow. The richness of the young man's costume supports his animated, confident demeanour, a special talent of the painter, summarizing the essence of the sitter's personality.

Left: *The Laughing Cavalier*, 1624, Frans Hals (1582/3–1666)

Above: *The Merry Drinker*, c. 1628–30, Frans Hals (1582/83–1666)

Above: *Militia Company of District XI Under the Command of Captain Reynier Reael, Known as 'The Meagre Company'*, 1637, Frans Hals (1582/83–1666)

Warmth and Realism

Hals created new forms of portraiture, particularly the traditional marriage double-portrait, singly painted portraits of the bride and groom to hang side by side on a wall. Hals infused companionship, love and intimacy into his portrayals, particularly in the double depiction *Portrait of a Couple, Probably Isaac Massa and Beatrix van der Laen*, c. 1622 (*see* page 178). In addition, his ingenuity as a painter allowed him to produce superb large group portraits for official commemorations, such as *A Banquet of the Officers of the St George Militia Company*, 1616 (*see* page 101), *Militia Company of District XI Under the Command of Captain*

Above: *Malle Babbe (Witch of Haarlem)*, 1633–35, Frans Hals (1582/83–1666)

Reynier Reael, Known as 'The Meagre Company', 1637 (*see* page 58), for the civic guard, and the *Regents and Regentesses of Haarlem*, 1664, imbuing the people represented with both warmth and realism. His portrayals of people included a local witch Malle Babbe, in *Malle Babbe (Witch of Haarlem)*, 1633–1635 (*see* page 59), a loosely worked portrait of broad brushstrokes, depicting her cheerful demeanour.

Leiden

The city of Leiden (Leyden) in the western Netherlands is approximately 16 kilometres (10 miles) northeast of The Hague and situated at the convergence of two rivers, the old Rhine (*Oude Rijn*) and new Rhine (*Nieuwe Rijn*). It was a strategic location under serious siege by the Spanish troops from May to October 1574. The city was finally rescued from its plight by the Prince of Orange, when its dikes were cut, flooding the country between Leiden and Dordrecht, thus allowing supplies and reinforcements to be shipped along waterways. Leiden was the birthplace of many Golden Age artists, including Rembrandt van Rijn, Gerrit (Gerard) Dou, Willem van de Velde the Elder (1611–93), Willem van de Velde the Younger (1633–1707), Gabriël Metsu, the master of genre Jan Steen, and Jan van Goyen, whose masterful landscapes include *A View of Leiden from the North East*, c. 1650 (*see* right), amongst others.

Textiles and Print-Publishing

The city was second in size to Amsterdam, due to its successful textile industry. Another boost to the city's culture was the establishment of Leiden University, founded in 1575 by William I of Orange. The academic establishment, a cultural draw for its scholarly study of

Right: *A View of Leiden from the North East*, c. 1650, Jan van Goyen (1596–1656)

humanism and theology, attracted publishers, printers, booksellers and art dealers. Leaving their home in Leuven, in 1580, the Protestant émigré family of book publishers Elzevir (Elsevier), led by son Louis (*c*. 1540–1617), established a printing press in Leiden. It brought further business and wealth to the city and to the family, who became printers to the university. Artists benefitted through increased demand for etchings for series of prints and illustrations for texts, books and pamphlets. By 1650 the population of Leiden was 12,500 with many students crossing Europe to attend university classes, bolstering its community and also its cultural and monetary wealth.

Rembrandt van Rijn

Rembrandt Harmenzoon van Rijn of Leiden is arguably the most outstanding, most exceptional painter in the history of Dutch art. He was also the most prolific. In his career of around 45 years he created nearly 400 paintings, over 1,000 drawings and 300 engravings. His legacy to art is immeasurable. Rembrandt was born on 15 July 1606, the ninth of 10 children, into a comfortably well-off family. Rembrandt's father, Harmen Gerritsz. van Rijn (d. 1630), was a miller; his mother, Neeltgen Willemsdr. van Zuytbrouck, was the daughter of a baker. They owned a malt mill. Its position on the banks of the Old Rhine gave the family the name 'van Rijn'. In addition, his mother owned houses and land, bequeathed to her four surviving children on her death in 1640. Rembrandt attended the Latin School in Leiden and at age 14 he went to study at the University of Leiden.

Rembrandt's academic education highlights the established success of the middle classes. On leaving university Rembrandt chose to study art in Leiden, under the tutorship of Jacob Isaacsz. van Swanenburgh (*c*. 1571–1638), arranged by his father. Rembrandt's father supported his son's career choice even though it differed from what he wanted. There then followed a period of six months in Amsterdam, travelling with a young companion, the Leiden-born prodigy Jan Lievens (1607–74), aged about 10. Rembrandt and Lievens studied under the guidance of the renowned Caravaggisti, Pieter Lastman (1583–1633) of Amsterdam.

Left: *Self-Portrait at the Age of 63*, 1669, Rembrandt van Rijn (1606–69)

Above: *Young Woman with Earrings*, 1657, Rembrandt van Rijn (1606–69)

From Caravaggio to Elsheimer

Lastman had worked in Rome from 1603 to 1607. Since the sixteenth century northern artists had colonized a small quarter in Rome near the Porta del Popolo. Artists met and techniques and ideas were exchanged. There, Lastman's work was influenced by German landscape painter Adam Elsheimer (1578–1610). In Venice, Elsheimer had studied the works, amongst others, of Tintoretto and Veronese, extraordinary painters of dramatic light and atmosphere, before moving to Rome in 1600, where he was exposed to the works of Caravaggio. The chiaroscuro style of Elsheimer informed the paintings of Lastman, visible in *Bathsheba at Her Toilet*, 1619. This in turn influenced the style of Lievens and Rembrandt, the latter painting his own version of this Biblical narrative, *Bathsheba at Her Bath*, c. 1654 (*see* left). The young artists returned to Leiden in 1624–25 to set up a studio and establish themselves as independent painters. Apart from his many portraits and self-portraits, Rembrandt chose history painting, the highest form of art, to establish his career, revealed in his earliest extant work *Stoning of St Stephen*, 1625, clearly informed by Lastman's chiaroscuro technique.

Above: *Bathsheba at Her Bath*, c. 1654, Rembrandt van Rijn (1606–69)

The Hague

The Hague (s'Gravenhagge) or Den Haag, the capital of the province of Zuid-Holland, with a population of 6,000 in 1650, was a smaller and more tranquil city than Utrecht or Amsterdam. It was the birthplace of Prince William III, the Stadtholder of Zeeland and Holland, and King of England from 1688. In the seventeenth century it was home to courtiers, politicians and diplomats, including Constantijn Huygens (1596–1687) and his son Christiaan Huygens (1629–95), the pioneering scientist and astronomer. Painters born in the city include Jan Mytens (c. 1614–70) and the brothers Jacob, Mattijs and Willem Maris. *A View of the Princessgracht, The Hague, Looking Towards the Bezuidenhoutsebrug and the Oost Singlesgracht*, c. 1660 (*see* right) by Joris van der Hagen (1615–69), born in Arnhem or Dordrecht, epitomizes the city's quiet charm.

Undercurrents of Tension

The Hague's tranquil tree-lined streets, with their Baroque, Rococo and Neoclassical buildings, reflected the power and wealth of its inhabitants, visualized in Pauwels van Hillegaert's *The Princes of Orange and Their Families on*

Above: *A View of the Princessgracht, The Hague, Looking Towards the Bezuidenhoutsebrug and the Oost Singlesgracht*, c. 1660, Joris van der Hagen (c. 1615–1669)

Horseback Riding out from the Buitenhof, The Hague, c. 1621–22. This work, along with many others of The Hague, exudes a feeling of calm and quietude as the seat of the stadtholders and the king. Yet in the early seventeenth century the town witnessed the brutal public beheading of its senior statesman, Stadtholder Johan van Oldenbarnevelt, in 1619. Once the moderator of peace between the States General and Spain, he was accused of accepting bribes from Spain in 1618, put on trial for high treason, found guilty and summarily beheaded. Beneath the surface of sublime paintings of domesticity and serene landscapes, tensions between Catholic and Protestant were present. Towards the end of the century, the brutal slaying of the De Witt brothers, Cornelis and Johan, by an unruly mob in 1672 occurred when the Republic was attacked by France and England, and Cornelis de Witt was accused of conspiring against the Prince of Orange. The gruesome painting *The Corpses of the de Witt Brothers*, c. 1672–75, attributed to Jan de Baen (1633–1702) of Haarlem, who was living in The Hague at the time and was possibly an eye-witness, reveals their horrific suffering and deaths by torture.

Utrecht

The Union of Utrecht, a treaty drawn up in 1579, was to unite the seven northern provinces against the Spanish Hapsburgs, leading to the suppression of the city's Roman Catholics. Counter to that general feeling, a group of young Utrecht painters – Gerard van Honthorst, Hendrick ter Brugghen and Dirck van Baburen (c. 1595–1624) – travelled to Rome and studied the work of the Roman-Italian painter Michelangelo Merisi da Caravaggio, a master of Biblical depiction, the sculptural quality of figures and the use of dramatic light and shadow. His intensely religious paintings influenced them deeply. They launched their Caravaggisti group on return to Utrecht, copying the fluidity of his figures and introducing Italian Baroque into Dutch art in the early decades of the seventeenth century. Artists of different faiths managed to live peacefully side by side. After all, patrons, of whichever faith, were the painters' livelihood.

Right: *The Procuress*, 1625, Gerard van Honthorst (1592–1656)

Trade & Economy

Natural Navigators

IN JOHANNES Vermeer's The Love Letter (see page 72), a lady receives a letter, handed by a maidservant. On the wall, in the well-appointed house, one can espy two paintings, positioned one above the other. The lower work is a seascape with boat, the upper painting a landscape. Surrounded by water, with their land infiltrated by man-made and natural inlets and waterway canals, the Dutch have always been natural sailors with a strong naval presence, in war and peace, and intuitive overseas voyagers and explorers by sea.

New Horizons

In the late sixteenth and seventeenth centuries the Dutch looked further afield, ambitiously exploring overseas territories in the East and West Indies. This was done with a view to founding new colonies from which profitable commodities might be extracted, such as crops, merchandise and human slaves. Dutch exploration was highly lucrative for entrepreneurs and merchants. The 1590s, a watershed of change and development in the Dutch Republic, with a larger naval command and growing fleet of merchant ships, culminated in Dutch dominance of European and

Previous Page: *The Departure of a Dignitary from Middelburg*, 1615, Adriaen Pietersz. van de Venne (1589–1662)
Left: *View of Dordrecht*, c. 1655, Aelbert Cuyp (1620–91)

[Vermeer's] simplicity of theme, his fine light and atmosphere, his beautiful colour, place him apart as a rare man in Dutch art.'

John Charles Van Dyke

overseas trade. The success of the Dutch East India Company and the Dutch West India Company in establishing long-distance trading routes to colonies seized from the Portuguese aided a booming economy at home. The Dutch explored land and sea during the Golden Age, visually reflected in their love of marine and landscape paintings.

New Trade Routes

The blocking of Antwerp's seaport access accelerated Amsterdam's involvement in trade route imports and distribution. Hamburg had been an alternative route for suppliers, but Amsterdam was favoured after 1590, including imports from Portugal and Spain, after a block placed by Philip II was revoked. The establishment of profitable trade routes in Europe anticipated the founding of companies to directly trade with and import from the Indies.

Compagnie van Verre

In 1594 Compagnie van Verre (long-distance company), a predecessor to the Dutch East India Company, was founded in Amsterdam by a group of nine wealthy merchants, who wanted to set up a commercial enterprise to break the monopoly that Portugal held in the trade of pepper. It included two Regents, Reinier Pauw (1564–1636) and Hendrick Hudde (d. 1596). The group raised 290,000 guilders and commissioned the Dutch navigator Cornelis de Houtman (1565–99) to command a fleet of four ships – the Amsterdam, Duyfken, Hollandia and Mauritius – armed with 100 canons and 249 crew. The enterprise capitalized on de Houtman's time in Portugal, when he worked undercover to obtain crucial maps and nautical details of coastlines, winds, reefs and undercurrents of the Portuguese trade routes. Added to this were vital trade secrets and navigational maps

Above: *The Love Letter*, c. 1669–70, Johannes Vermeer (1632–75)

Right: *The Grocer's Shop*, 1672, Gerrit Dou (1613–75)

obtained in the 1580s by a Dutch merchant and spy, working as secretary to the Portuguese Viceroy in Goa from 1583 to 1588, Haarlem-born Jan Huyghen van Linschoten (1563–1611).

First Dutch Voyage to Indonesia

Cornelis de Houtman set sail from Texel in April 1549 bound for Indonesia. He travelled with his brother Frederick de Houtman (1571–1627), the Dutch explorer and respected astronomer. The fleet arrived in Banten (Bantam), Java, in June 1596, whereupon de Houtman concluded an advantageous sales treaty with the Sultan of Banten, which read:

> *'We are well content to have a permanent league of alliance and friendship with His Highness the Prince Maurice of Nassau, of the Netherlands and with you, gentlemen.'*

But relations soured due, it was reported, to the rude temperament of the Dutch. They were expelled. The first voyage, encountering disease, on board disagreements, deaths, lack of food, pirates and confrontation with Portuguese ships, was unsuccessful and returned with fewer than 90 men and three ships, but the trade route was established and set the course for future expeditions. Between 1594 and 1597 trade in imports from these expeditions with countries in Europe, Russia and the Baltic States accrued great wealth for the organization, and led to a trade monopoly for the Dutch Republic, which established further trade and colonization, thus ending Portugal's dominance. Once established on the coastal areas, the Dutch gradually expanded in each territory to control all trade, such as in Sri Lanka, where the Dutch East India Company, VOC (Vereenigde Oost-Indische Compagnie), eventually gained access to the whole island, taking over the cinnamon production with a ruling Dutch governor and administrative council in residence.

Left: *Palace of Amsterdam with Exotic Birds*, c. 1695, Melchior de Hondecoeter (1636–95)

Above: *Still Life with a Dead Hare, Partridges and Other Birds in a Niche*, c. 1675, Jan Weenix (1642–1719)

From Produce to Painting

Paintings of this era reflected produce imported from the new trade routes and exotic merchandise brought to the Netherlands, plus flora and fauna collected by explorers on the long-haul voyages. *Palace of Amsterdam with Exotic Birds*, c. 1695 (*see* page 74), by Melchior de Hondecoeter (1636–95) of Utrecht, a masterful painter of exotic birds and farmyard animals, reflects the popularity of newly discovered species, set against a backdrop of the Palace of Amsterdam, a cultural symbol of the Dutch Republic. It reflects the passion of wealthy merchants to ornament their country estates with collections of peacocks, pelicans, turkeys, macaws, parrots, exotic poultry and plants. *The Poultry Yard*, 1688, and *Birds and a Spaniel in a Garden*, c. 1660–95, also by de Hondecoeter, show the influence of his uncle and tutor, the Amsterdam-born Jan Battista Weenix (1621–59), an extraordinary painter of game birds and animals, who had spent four years in Rome working for Pope Innocent X. He also tutored his son, Jan Weenix (1642–1719). A fine example of his son's work is *Still Life with a Dead Hare, Partridges and Other Birds in a Niche*, c. 1675 (*see* page 75). *The Poultry Yard* highlights de Hondecoeter's immense talent for intense, precise realism, using rich reds, black, white and a cool yellow to capture the characteristics of the birds, sharply defining the feathers and body shapes. Paintings such as these were highly collectable by wealthy merchants and landowners. *A Still Life of Fruit with a Macaw*, 1628 (*see* right), by Jan Davidsz. de Heem (1606–84) and Rachel Ruysch's *Still Life with Fruit, Flowers, Reptiles and Insects*, c. 1711 (*see* page 140), similarly reflect this new wave.

Published Accounts

A record of the epic journey of Cornelis de Houtman and his crew, *Om de Zuid: de eerste schipvaart naar Oost-Indië onder Cornelis de Houtman*, 1595–

Right: *A Still Life of Fruit with a Macaw*, 1628, Jan Davidsz. de Heem (1606–84)

1597, was narrated by Willem Lodewycksz, a traveller with the fleet, and published in 1598. Illustrated with maps and plates, it guaranteed further investment in the Dutch East and West Indies enterprises. It followed Jan Huyghen van Linschoten's 1596 publication *Itinario*, illustrated with maps and trade voyage routes to the East Indies.

A Market for Maps

Dutch cartographer and astronomer Willem Jansz. Blaeu (1571–1638) of Alkmaar, who worked as a map merchant and publisher in Amsterdam in 1596/97, is credited with producing the finest atlases and maps of the Dutch Republic Golden Age era, in addition to the widely popular terrestrial and celestial globes made of plaster, wood and engraved paper, by the Blaeu workshop. The quality of maps and globes, town plans, wall charts and atlases was due to Blaeu employing the finest engravers and printers, colourists and publishers, and using only the best-quality paper for printing. In 1633 the States General of Amsterdam appointed Willem Blaeu the mapmaker of the Republic, followed by the prestigious position of official cartographer of the Dutch East India Company. Large and luxuriously detailed wall maps were created by Blaeu for the nobility and as diplomatic gifts to foreign dignitaries.

Joan and Cornelius Blaeu

Willem Blaeu had six children. The eldest Dr Joan (John) Blaeu (*c.* 1596/9–1673) joined his father's company in 1630 and by the following year the company was listed in their joint names. Following his father, Joan Blaeu became official cartographer for the Dutch East India Company. Their trade enlarged to include wall charts, town plans and atlases, and required a move to larger premises in Bloemgracht,

'Dutch painting ... was not and could not be anything but the portrait of Holland, its external image, faithful, exact, complete, lifelike, without any adornment.'

Eugène Fromentin

Left: *Officer and Laughing Girl*, c. 1657–58, Johannes Vermeer (1632–75)

Above: *Woman with a Lute*, c. 1662–63, Johannes Vermeer (1632–75)

Amsterdam, with increased printing presses. When Willem died in 1638 his youngest son Cornelis (d. 1644) joined Joan Blaeu, both men outstanding as cartographers and astronomers.

Cartography in Art

There was a substantial market for maps – regularly sold in art dealers' galleries and art shops and print-publishers – as working tools for merchants, informative sources for academics and the public, and as decorative and informative cultural objects in the home. Vermeer in *Officer and Laughing Girl*, 1657–58 (*see* page 78), includes a large wall map of Holland and West Friesland. The map is a focal point and was created by Balthasar Florisz. van Berckenrode in 1620, by permission of the States General, and published in monochrome by Blaeu mapmakers, headed by publisher Willem Jansz. Blaeu. Vermeer's depiction is a precise copy of the original by Berckenrode. The same map appears in the left-foreground of Vermeer's *The Love Letter* (*see* page 72), and more visibly in *Woman Reading a Letter*, 1662–63. The glimpse of a map in the backdrop of *Young Woman with a Water Jug* (*see* right), displayed hanging from a rod, depicts *The Seventeen Provinces of the Netherlands*, published by Huyck Allart. *Woman with a Lute* (*see* page 79), features a map of Europe, as its text EUROPAE indicates. The featured map is thought to have been created *c.* 1613 by Dutch cartographer Jodocus Hondius (1563–1612).

The Art of Painting

For his artwork *The Art of Painting*, *c.* 1665–66 (*see* left), Vermeer prominently placed a large map of *The Seventeen Provinces of the Netherlands* as a backdrop, using it in a decorative manner. The cracked surface on

Above: *The Artist's Studio*, *c.* 1665–66, Johannes Vermeer (1632–75)

the substantially sized map – held by two supports – reflects the sunlight that streams through the window on the left. It is slightly obscured by the metal double-headed eagle chandelier, the painter's easel and the head and shoulders of the young woman who is posing for her portrait. The cartographer of the map was Claes Jansz. Visscher (1587–1652), also known as Nicolas Joannes Piscator, of Amsterdam. Visscher, a young artist, draughtsman, engraver and mapmaker, initiated the Visscher family of publishers, which went on to become one of the most important publishing dynasties in the Dutch Republic. His print shop 'The Fisher' on Kalverstraat, Amsterdam – moved to larger premises in Dam Square by 1611 – was an intense industry of print output. Visscher, a print-publisher of diverse print subjects, including Dutch picture Bibles, and landscape, animal, and ornamental prints, was finely tuned to public taste. The business grew and profited, and Visscher was joined in his business by son Nicolaes (1618–79) and later generations of family members. Johannes Vermeer never sold *The Art of Painting*, which prominently showed Visscher's map. He regarded it highly and kept it in his studio to show to prospective patrons and prospective buyers of his other works.

'An interior by Vermeer is a cubic painting. The atmosphere is in it and the exact volume of the objects; the place of these objects has been respected...'

Auguste Rodin

Above: *Young Woman with a Water Jug*, c. 1662, Johannes Vermeer (1632–75)

Vermeer's Palette

Restoration of many Vermeer paintings has opened up knowledge of the colour pigments the artist used. He limited his palette to natural pigments: he used a green earth pigment for skin tones, quite a rare format in Dutch seventeenth-century paintings; a particularly eye-catching lead-tin-yellow for the deep yellows of fine silk clothes and yellow-lake, plus earth yellow pigments; his reds included vermillion red, earth red and red-lake; plus lead white, bone black and charcoal black. For blues, ultramarine – an expensive pigment made from lapis lazuli – was the one Vermeer preferred to all other blue-tone pigments. In *A Young Lady Seated at a Virginal*, 1670–72 (*see* right), the rich blue and yellow tones of her dress create a calm ambiance.

Above: *Dutch Shipping in a Heavy Swell with a Small Hoeker*, c. 1670, Willem van de Velde, the Younger (1633–1707)

Right: *A Young Lady Seated at a Virginal*, c. 1670, Johannes Vermeer (1632–75)

Above: *Shipping Offshore in a Breeze*, Jan Porcellis (1584–1632)

Portraying Wealth

Maps and globes were displayed in Dutch homes, State-owned buildings and commercial offices, as a statement of cultural wealth. Rich shipping magnates and owners of ships, cargoes and lands invested some of their profits in fine and decorative art. Paintings of ships, of maps, of sugar, spices, sweets and exotic fruits imported to the Dutch Republic would hang on their walls, scenes like *Dutch Shipping in a Heavy Swell with a Small Hoeker*, c. 1670 (*see* page 82), by Willem van de Velde the Younger, which captures the small hoeker (an unarmed fishing or merchant vessel), with a half-lowered mainsail, engaged in heavy seas. On the right is a herring buss with sail (a Dutch fishing vessel equipped for long voyages to catch herring and preserve them on board), to the left a fishing boat. Further boats can be seen in the far distance. In the foreground a school of porpoises dip through the waves. The painting was possibly owned

'Through our art we shall wrest ourselves from the voracity of mortality and triumph in spite of death, the strangler of all things, and shall flourish from one century to the next without withering.'

Philips Angel, Dutch artist and theorist

'Leiden … always nurtured and reared in equal measure many different artists, especially many renowned and excellent painters.'

Jan Jansz. Orlers

by Johan van Heemskerk, a Dutch poet and an advocate who worked for the Dutch East India Company and held public office in the States General. *Shipping Offshore in a Breeze* (*see* page 84), painted in the early seventeenth century by Flemish painter Jan Porcellis (1584–1632), who migrated to the northern Netherlands, captures the mariner life. Another artist who migrated from the south, the masterful, Berchem-born Pieter Claesz (1597–1660) painted *Still Life with a Peacock Pie*, 1627 (*see* right), denoting the fruits of merchant exploration in the plentiful abundance of exotic peacocks, to be admired, used decoratively and to be cooked. With access to luxurious foodstuffs and Asian commodities, the Dutch cook's peacock pie may well have contained spices such as ginger, mace, cinnamon and cloves too.

White Bread and Herring

At the relief of Leiden on 3 October 1574, during the Eighty Years' War, the first rations distributed to citizens of the besieged city were of white bread and herring, distributed by the rebel troops. Herring and bread was the staple diet of Netherlanders. The Netherlands' seafaring heritage, particularly the fishing industry with its long history and considerable commercial trade of herring, is one that is frequently mirrored in its art. Fish stocks were a fine export commodity. Fishermen caught the herring shoals and preserved them at sea with salt before packing the fish on board, in barrels of wood.

Poetic Praise

One of the most important features of Dutch culture relates to the natural resources of its seas, flanking two sides of its territories,

Left *The Fishwife*, 1672, Adriaen Jansz. van Ostade (1610–85)

Above: *Still Life with a Peacock Pie*, 1627, Pieter Claesz (1597–1660)

the North Sea and the Zuider Zee. Marine life has always been inextricably linked to Dutch life and integral to art and literature. The Dutch poet and playwright Joost van den Vondel (1587–1679), renowned as the greatest writer of the Golden Age, praised the life-giving resource of the herring, referring to it as a royal fish in 'Lofsangh op den Scheepsvaart' (1622).

> *'O, wat een gulden Neeringh en voedsel brengt ons toe de Conincklijke Heringh; hoe menig duysend ziel bij dezen handel leeft en winnende sin brood God dank en eere gheef.'*
>
> *'O what a golden industry is created for us by that food, the royal herring. How many thousand souls, thank God, live by this trade and earn their living from it.'*
> Lines 197–200, 'Lofsangh op den Scheepsvaart'

Artists painted all aspects of the fishing industry and marine life, as in *Stormy Seascape*, 1655, by Jan van Goyen and *Fishing Boats Coming Ashore*, c. 1660 and *Dutch Vessels Inshore and Men Bathing*, 1661 (*see* left), both by Willem van de Velde the Younger. The young and old of the fishing community were depicted, as seen in Jan Steen's *Fisherfolk Selling Their Catch on the Dunes at Scheveningen*, c. 1650s. *Fisherboy*, 1630, by Frans Hals, was a popular painting copied by other artists. Fish sold at market often featured, as in *The Fishwife*, 1672 (*see* page 86), by Adriaen Jansz. van Ostade (1610–85). Jan Porcellis is noted for adventurous seascapes, as seen in *Shipping Offshore in a Breeze*, c. 1620s (*see* page 84) and *Shipping in a Squall*, c. 1620s. This was popular subject matter. Artists capitalized on the pride of their nation and its energetic economic trade in positive depictions of life, on land and sea, in the post-Hapsburgian United Provinces.

Left: *Dutch Vessels Inshore and Men Bathing*, 1661, Willem van de Velde the Younger (1633–1707)

Above: *The Wedding Dance*, *c.* 1566, Pieter Bruegel, the Elder (*c.* 1525–69)

Painting Prosperity

Dutch artists sought commissions and sold works in commercial galleries and art markets. Painters were commissioned for portraits of the wealthy, their families, their houses and land. The demand pushed the boundaries of artistic innovation, focusing on Dutch artists' remarkable ability to depict emotion and mood, through naturalism in landscape and portraiture. Émigré painters from the southern cities of Antwerp, Bruges and Ghent, the heartlands of fine art in the fifteenth and sixteenth centuries, brought to the north their knowledge of fine painting techniques with a meticulous quality of finish. Their predecessors were predominantly creators of religious paintings and altarpieces, such as Jan van Eyck of Bruges, Rogier van der Weyden of Brussels, Hugo van der Goes of Ghent, German-born Hans Memling of Bruges, Hieronymus Bosch and Pieter Breugel the Elder of Brabant (*c.* 1525–69). Breugel's meticulous attention to detail and flawless painted finish is shown in *The Wedding Dance*, *c.* 1566 (*see* left), an example of the superlative maturity of Dutch art of the sixteenth century. In the north, the skill of artists like Anthonie Blocklandt van Montfoort (1533/34–83) of Utrecht and Maarten van Heemskerk (1498–1574), active in Haarlem, both of whom had spent time in Italy, was carried through to the Golden Age in the art of their followers, for example Blocklandt's pupil Abraham Bloemaert (1566–1651).

A Crowded Market

In his autobiography, dated to 1629–31, diplomat and art collector for Frederik Hendrik, Prince of Orange, Constantijn Huygens pondered on Dutch landscape artists:

'The crop of landscape painters (so I choose to call those who devote themselves chiefly to the painting of woods, meadows, mountains, and villages) in our country is so plentiful and so renowned that if one wished to list every one of them one would fill a notebook.'

The loss of religious art, a mainstay of artists' commissions, led to a free market in innovation, and a boost to the economy. Religious paintings were still commissioned but in less abundance, more in the domain of private collectors than the public spaces of churches. Realism was a touchstone. The style of new works broke old boundaries, for example in the depiction of group portraits, which became more natural, life-size, impressive. With the influx of southern Netherlands artists from the 1580s, all pushing for work, it made the art market more competitive, highly successful for some, and fraught for others.

Above: *Landscape with Two Oaks*, 1641, Jan van Goyen (1596–1656)

An Artistic Family

Huygens could name many prolific, creative painters of landscapes, each with a distinctive style. Many artists had a comfortable living, particularly when running family-owned workshops. Outstanding in the field was a family of painters: Jacob van Ruisdael was the son of frame maker, art dealer and accomplished artist Isaack van Ruisdael (1599–1677), born in Naarden, near Amsterdam, and Isaack's brother was Salomon van Ruysdael, a noted painter. Both artists probably tutored Jacob, who was accomplishing mature works at the age of 17. He was accepted into the Guild at Haarlem in 1648. Jacob painted dunes, woods, fields, seascapes and sublime panoramas, such as *A Panoramic View of Amsterdam Looking Towards the IJ*, *c.* 1670, which was accomplished from the scaffolding used to build the tower of Amsterdam's new town hall. It reveals Ruisdael's versatility and the possible influence of two painters and printmakers living in Haarlem, Hercules Pietersz. Seghers (1589–1638) and Hendrik Goltzius, as well as that of the accomplished landscape painter Jan van Goyen. Jacob painted close to home, as in the early work *View of Naarden*, 1647, his father's birthplace, which reveals his future as the greatest Dutch painter of landscapes, and the later *View of Haarlem with Bleaching Grounds* (*see* page 54). What is perhaps less well known is his second career as a surgeon, taking a degree in medicine at Caen, France in 1676. Many Dutch painters of landscapes came close to equalling Ruisdael, including his student Meindert Hobbema (1638–1709), as in *The Watermill with the Great Red Roof*, 1662–65 (*see* right), and Pieter de Molijn (1595–1661) and Hendrick Avercamp, two exceptional landscape artists.

Aelbert Cuyp

Dutch Master of landscape and portraiture, Aelbert Cuyp of Dordrecht is noted primarily for highly commercial, bucolic scenes of cows grazing in lush pastures

Right: *The Watermill with the Great Red Roof*, 1662–65, Meindert Hobbema (1638–1709)

Above: *View of the Maas in Winter*, c. 1650, Aelbert Cuyp (1620–91)

From this one turns to Cuyp's landscapes that suppress figures to focus on the natural world, of land and sea, as in the luminous sea and skies of *Boats in the Estuary of Holland Diep in a Storm* (*see* page 55), that exemplifies his skill of spacious interpretation. However, it is works such as *View of the Maas in Winter*, c. 1650 (*see* page 97), that remains the core of Cuyp's oeuvre, beautifully executed with its vast expanse of sky.

Groups as Individuals

A painting by the workshop of Adriaen van de Venne, *The Princes of Orange*, c. 1625, reveals the difficulty in creating a group portrait. The artist must make each prince equal in status. To either side of the princes on horseback, lower-status persons are portrayed smaller in size. The small horses look weighed down by their riders, but their movement is the thing that portrays a moment in time. Frans Hals broke the rules on group portraits. He gave individuals the status of their rank while remaining an integral part of the group. Artists usually created preparatory drawings and sketches, to outline positions, and painted each member separately. In some works, the more money an individual paid the better their position in the finished work.

The Dordrecht-born painter and art theorist Samuel van Hoogstraten, noted for his treatise on painting 'Introduction to the High School of the Art of Painting' published in 1678, remarked that from the linear stiffness of some official group portraits, one 'could … behead them all at once'. Possibly he had a conservative group portrait like *Captain Allaert Cloeck and Lieutenant Lucas Jacobsz. Rotgans, Amsterdam and Members of Their Company*, 1632, by Thomas de Keyser (c. 1596–1667) in mind. Painted long after Frans Hals had introduced an animated informality to portraiture

Left: *Captain Allaert Cloeck and Lieutenant Lucas Jacobsz. Rotgans, Amsterdam and Members of Their Company*, 1632, Thomas de Keyser (c. 1596–1667)

Above: *The Night Watch*, 1642, Rembrandt van Rijn (1606–69)

in 1616, de Keyser may have been following the wishes of the men depicted, who were after all paying for the work. Preliminary drawings show a more animated grouping. Hoogstraten also criticized Rembrandt's art for its excessive naturalism. *A Trompe L'Oeil of Objects Attached to a Letter Rack* reveals Samuel van Hoogstraten's own skill as a painter of still life.

Civic Guard Histories

An important physical, political, symbolic and social element of the protection of the States General was the formation of the Civic Guard. It had been in practice since medieval times and increased after the establishment of the Dutch Republic in 1581. Rembrandt van Rijn's painting, *Militia Company of District II under the Command of Captain Frans Banninck Cocq*, 1642, more commonly known as *The Night Watch* (*see* left), was inspirational in its informality. The vast canvas – later cut down in size – was made for the newly built Arquebusiers Civic Guard Hall. The artist created an historic moment in the lives of Amsterdam's Civic Guard, portrayed in an everyday street scene. Rembrandt depicted the guards company on their evening patrol of the city's boundaries, guns at the ready, dressed in their military attire. It was spectacular for its different approach, which normally showed civic militia in an interior room, either standing or seated around a table.

Frans Hals was equal in his ability to animate large groups, to draw attention and interest to the company, as in the earlier large-scale *A Banquet of the Officers of the St George Militia Company*, 1616 (*see* above). A later work by Rembrandt, a commission given to Dutch painter

Above: *A Banquet of the Officers of the St George Militia Company*, 1616, Frans Hals (1582/83–1666)

Govert Flinck (1615–60) but handed to Rembrandt on Flinck's untimely death, was *The Conspiracy of the Batavians Under Claudius Civilis*, c. 1666. It was one of several monumental history paintings by different artists, planned to decorate Amsterdam's new town hall. The decision to build a new town hall linked to the year of peace with Spain, 1648. The painting was not admired and soon returned to the artist.

'Shakespeare and Rembrandt have in common the faculty of quickening speculation and compelling the minds of men to combat and discussion.'

William Ernest Henley

Trade in Cloth

Six discerning, worthy officials, known as the 'Syndics' or Staalmeesters of the Drapers' Guild in Amsterdam, are portrayed at work in Rembrandt's impressive group portrait *The Wardens of the Amsterdam Drapers' Guild, Known as 'The Syndics'*, 1662 (*see* right). The powerful men look down from their raised dais. To maintain the reputation and high standard of cloth for sale, a trade of high importance to the economy, the Syndics monitored the quality and quantity of dyed woollen cloth traded in Amsterdam. The finished cloth to be traded had to match the quality and colour of the original sample in the logbook. The large painting was to hang in the headquarters of the Drapers' Guild in Amsterdam.

Superlative Realism

Such is the expressive, creative realism of Rembrandt's near life-size portrayal that the Syndics are readily identifiable. Seated at a table, which is covered with a heavy tapestry and on which rests their sampling book, they all look down and directly toward a spectator beneath them, who is perhaps in dialogue with them. One Syndic, Volckert Jansz, half-rises from his chair and turns to get a better look. They are wearing wide-brim hats and are dressed near identically in black with white linen collars. In the background a servant, bareheaded, also in black and white, stands. Rembrandt captures a moment in time. His preparatory drawings reveal that he moved the positions of the figures several times to obtain the right balance of heads and bodies in the portrayal.

Artist of the People

Rembrandt van Rijn was a man of few words on paper. Apart from official invoices and receipts, there is little to gauge his thoughts about clients. After his apprenticeship his first paintings focused on history painting, but portraits were his mainstay. In Rembrandt's superlative portrayals, which captured the essence of the sitter through his ability to create evocative mood, one sees the wealth of the Dutch elite finely detailed, through demeanour, fine clothing and surroundings. From his sketches and drawings of ordinary people, one can see that Rembrandt was a man familiar with street life whilst also mixing with the aristocracy.

Trading in Commodities

Lemons, spices, shells and exotic plants are a few of the wondrous foreign commodities that defined Dutch culture, foreign objects that symbolized

Above: *The Wardens of the Amsterdam Drapers' Guild, Known as 'The Syndics'*, 1662, Rembrandt van Rijn (1606–69)

·B· vander· Ast· fe 1623·

the success of overseas Dutch trade. Consequently they made their way into Dutch still-life paintings, often commissioned by wealthy overseas traders. Paintings denoting trade with the East and West Indies might include porcelain, pepper and tea; sugar, tobacco and salt. Material luxuries provided artists with commercial possibilities. Homegrown commodities were popular and ever-present, such as cheese, fish, ham and beer, as in *Still Life with Ham*, c. 1646–50 (*see* page 107). European imports featured in still-life paintings might include grapes, wine bottles, or Mediterranean fruits, as in *Still Life with Fruit, Flowers, Reptiles and Insects*, 1711 (*see* page 140), by Rachel Ruysch, and *Still Life with Fruit, Flowers and Seafood*, 1620–21(*see* left), by Balthazar van der Ast.

'The aim is to imitate what is, to make what is imitated charming, to clearly express simple, lively and true sensations.'

Eugène Fromentin

Tulip Mania

In *Still Life of a Tulip, a Melon and Flowers on a Ledge*, c. 1690 (*see* page 106) by Rachel Ruysch and *Flower-piece in a Wan-li Vase*, c. 1620s (*see* page 108), by Balthasar van der Ast the focus is on the coveted tulip flower. Its bulb was a lucrative commodity for Dutch traders. Tulips, imported to the Netherlands from Turkey in the sixteenth century, had

Left: *Still Life with Fruit, Flowers and Seafood*, 1620–21, Balthasar van der Ast (1593/94–1657)

fuelled a mania, particularly for rarer variegated varieties with fluted petals. So in demand were they, and such were the prices that they could fetch, that tulips became a symbol of wealth.

A Tulip Economy

In the seventeenth century demand for tulips outgrew supply, sending prices spiralling upward. Money-brokers invested in a futures market, gambling on the future selling-price of flowers, from bulbs not yet in flower. Speculators bought and sold bulbs. Tulip mania peaked in 1636 when a rare variegated tulip, the Semper Augustus, a star bloom, sold for 5,200 guilders, an equivalent to the purchase of a spacious house at that time. Early in the following year, traders decided to sell their tulip commodities, causing the price and value of tulips to wither. Nonetheless, the tulip remained a popular flower, still closely associated with Netherlanders – who cultivated on land reclaimed from the sea to plant and sell tulip bulbs. The fashion for tulips spread to ceramic wares, with special tulip vases, in Chinese wan-li porcelain – another expensive commodity supplied by traders – or Dutch blue and white china to hold single, prized stems. Emblems of tulips flowers appeared on furniture

Left: *Still Life of a Tulip, a Melon and Flowers on a Ledge*, c. 1690, Rachel Ruysch (1664–1750)

Above: *Still Life with Ham*, 1647, Pieter Claesz (1597–1660)

Above: *Flowerpiece in a Wan-li Vase*, c. 1620s, Balthasar van der Ast (1593/94–1657)

and furnishings, on embroideries, and in many paintings and prints. In Van der Ast's still life, *Flowers in a Wan-Li Vase*, c. 1610–15 (*see* left), possibly informed by, or in homage to the first Flemish artist to paint flower still life, Jan Brueghel the Elder (1568–1625), the most expensive variety of tulip, variegated in colour with fluted leaves, is depicted in microscopic detail.

Middelburg

In the seventeenth century, Middelburg, capital city on the central peninsula of Zeeland, was the most important city after Amsterdam. It was a trade centre of the Dutch East India Company and a city of cultural and financial wealth with a growing Protestant population. Furthermore, it was a centre for scientific discovery in the sixteenth and seventeenth centuries. Pioneers of optical microscopy were born in or moved to Middelburg. In 1581, the year of Dutch Republic emancipation from Hapsburg rule, a crystal glass factory was established in the city. Glass blowers from the Venetian island of Murano – famed for its glass and skilled glassmakers – were invited to Middelburg. By the 1600s it was the foremost producer of superior-quality glass in the Republic. Fine glasses and dishes (*tazze*) were represented in still-life paintings as items of luxury. *Still Life with the Drinking-Horn of the St Sebastian Archers' Guild, Lobster and Glasses*, c. 1653 (*see* right), by Willem Kalf (1619–93) of Rotterdam, and *Pronk Still Life, with a Roemer, an Upturned Silver Tazza, a Half-peeled Lemon on a Pewter Plate, with a Pie, a Timepiece and a Knife*, 1631, (*see* page 157), by Willem Claesz. Heda (c. 1594–c. 1680), are two of many examples.

Exploring a Trade in Slavery

The vast wealth of the Dutch Republic was not only accumulated through its exploration of new lands for commercial products, such as sugar, spices

Above: *Still Life with the Drinking-Horn of the St Sebastian Archers' Guild, Lobster and Glasses*, c. 1653, Willem Kalf (1619–93)

and tobacco. From the sixteenth century the city of Amsterdam grew into a profitable slave-trading port. It rose rapidly to a peak in the mid-seventeenth century, the period of the Golden Age, when it was trading vast numbers of slaves. The Dutch West India Company, operating from major Dutch ports such as Amsterdam, Rotterdam, Middelburg and Groningen, monopolized Dutch slave trafficking from the 1630s and for the next 100 years. At first trade focused on northern Brazil, Surinam and Guiana (Guyana) during Netherlands' rule from 1630 to 1654. It spread to the west coast of Africa, the Caribbean and New Amsterdam (New York).

Merchants, effectively human-traffickers, were sold African men, women and children to be shipped to Amsterdam and Middelburg. There they were sold on to owners of sugar plantations in the West Indies. Of the many countries trading in slaves – England, France, Portugal and Spain – the Dutch accounted for about six per cent yet had the highest mortality rate due to the lack of medical aid, accommodation and food for their slave prisoners on board the long voyages. Thousands died. Those that survived lived lives in captivity, far from their homeland, to work until they died. Those that were employed as servants were occasionally portrayed in paintings commissioned by their 'owners'. Domestic slaves were also used as subjects for a painter's commercial output. Gerrit Dou's *Portrait of a Black Courtier*, (*see* left), Aelbert Cuyp's *A Page with Two Horses* (*see* page 96), and *The Game of Cards*, c. 1660, by Hendrick van der Burch (1627–c. 1666), define the casual acceptance of African servitude by the Dutch nobility and wealthier classes. In Dou's portrayal, the young boy wears a lock and chain, possibly bearing the initial of his owner. The harrowing experiences of men, women and children sold into slavery, often living under harsh conditions in the colonies, helped to create and expand the wealth of the Netherlandish population in the seventeenth and eighteenth centuries, their sea-going vessels active in human-trafficking in the Atlantic and Indian oceans. Around 550,000 West Africans were trafficked. The trade did not cease until the nineteenth century, when slavery was abolished in 1800, continuing illegally until around 1830.

'The art of painting in our own land, as in a new Greece, is at the height of its glory.'

Samuel van Hoogstraten on Dutch art

Exploring the World

As Dutch merchants colonized Africa and the East and West Indies, setting up long-haul trade routes for commodities, which included slaves, Dutch scientists took advantage of the ocean-going ships that visited many countries new to Dutch exploration. Cartographers, geographic surveyors, botanists and astronomers took passage on the long voyages, using every opportunity to study the seas, coastlines, landmasses, flora and fauna, and the night skies. Their contribution put the Dutch Republic at the forefront of primary source study. Matching the Netherlands' wealth of knowledge, overseas trade and colonization brought great prosperity and created a booming economy.

Left: *Portrait of a Black Courtier*, Gerrit Dou (1613–75)

Art & Identity

N·TE· D MINE·SPERAVI
ON·CONI DAR·I·ÆTERNV.
INIS·
T·DOMINV

The Dutch At Home

THE INTRINSIC link between artists of the Golden Age, and the people of the Dutch Republic, is the plenitude of paintings that reveal their characteristics, as individuals at home, at leisure and work, in their communities, and part of societies and guilds, inhabiting the new nation of the United Provinces.

Artists portrayed Dutch everyday life in the interior of the domestic home, depicting the occupants from the Master and Mistress, the servants and children, and those who visited the house, such as friends, tutors and delivery boys. Dutch art of this era is filled with these imageries, such as *A Man and a Woman Seated by a Virginal*, c. 1665 by Gabriël Metsu (*see* left) and *Interior with a Woman Drinking with Two Men and a Maidservant*, c. 1658 (*see* page 123), and *A Boy Bringing Bread*, c. 1663 (*see* page 120), by Pieter de Hooch. Surrounded by rich, human resources, artists chose to paint contemporary life in its many forms. At its simplest it could be a servant carrying out household chores or doctors visiting the sick to the complicated procedure of a surgeon dissecting the dead.

Snapshot of Dutch Life

There was a vast market for artists and art dealers to sell paintings and prints of contemporary life in the Dutch Republic, from the inn to the asylum, leisured life on a noble's estate to the busy fish market. The

Previous Page: *Portrait of the Mennonite Preacher, Cornelius Claesz. Anslo and His Wife, Aaltje Gerritsdr. Shouten*, 1641, Rembrandt van Rijn (1606–69)
Left: *A Man and a Woman Seated by a Virginal*, c. 1665, Gabriël Metsu (1629–67)

present-day viewer steps inside this Dutch world, through the lives of the artists, and their portrayals of the Dutch people at home. An insight into the tastes of Dutch Republic citizens can be gleaned by looking at Dutch domestic interior paintings. Within them, the owners' choice of art hangs on the walls.

Two paintings, intended as companions, by Gabriël Metsu, both painted 1662–66, *Man Writing a Letter* (*see* right) and *A Woman Reading a Letter* (*see* left), reveal the sitters' taste in art. In the first painting we see a young man sitting at an open window, with light streaming in, on to the letter he writes, his writing materials laid out on the table before him. In the far corner, behind the open window, stands a globe, a sign of intellect and wealth. Metsu's painting informs the viewer with a variety of detail: a close glimpse of the interior room design of the Dutch home; the fine clothing of the man represented; and the traditional heavy wool tapestry that covers the table at which he sits. In this Dutch home the painting on the wall is of a landscape with animals, reminiscent of fine art by the Dutch artists Aelbert Cuyp and Paulus Potter. It is presented in a richly ornate Baroque gilt frame, fitting the décor of the house.

Hidden Messages of Love

In Metsu's *A Woman Reading a Letter*, a young woman seated by a window reads a letter that has just arrived from the young man in the companion painting. A maid with a bucket resting on her hip, has in her hand the envelope of the letter, just delivered and being read by her mistress. The maidservant casually takes a moment to draw back the curtain that covers a blustery seascape painting on the wall. She must have seen it and dusted it many times in her domestic household role. The curtain denotes a prized possession, the painting beneath it

Above: *A Woman Reading a Letter*, c. 1662/65, Gabriël Metsu (1629–67)

Right: *Man Writing a Letter*, c. 1662/65, Gabriël Metsu (1629–67)

protected from strong daylight. The relationship between servant and mistress appears relaxed, one of the mistress's shoes is off, her little dog is close by. The servant has the freedom and interest to view the artwork whilst waiting, perhaps not just to clean the work but study it, too. Metsu denotes affluence in both paintings, depicting a domestic scene typical of the Dutch middle class. The hidden reference is of love in these two paintings: letter-writing and letter-reading was a symbol of love and courtship, a familiar subject for artists to paint. Paintings showing a person tearing up a letter usually denoted the end of a relationship or death of a loved one.

'I find a source of delicious sympathy in these faithful pictures [Dutch paintings] of a monotonous homely existence...'

George Eliot from *Adam Bede*

House Servants

The intimacy of the well-appointed Dutch home, where the family relaxed, ate their meals, received visitors, painted, played music and wrote letters, confirmed the institution of married life, and the home as the heart of the family and the nation. Maintaining a beautifully furnished home was the occupation of a retinue of servants in the wealthiest houses, down to perhaps one or two in lower middle-class domains. Household servants were depicted in paintings carrying out their duties, in daily tasks such as pouring out milk, and looking after a baby, or attending the mistress, as in Vermeer's *Mistress and Maid*, 1666–67 (*see* left), where often an interaction highlighted the mistress-servant role. Other denotations of rank included the servant standing in the presence of the mistress or master seated, and the visual difference in clothing, hairstyling and shoes. Servants were an important part of Dutch domestic life and art reflected it.

Away from the domestic interior, in commercial premises, *The Tailor's Workshop*, 1661 (*see* right), by Quiringh Gerritsz. van Brekelenkam

Left: *Mistress and Maid*, 1666-67, Johannes Vermeer (1632–75)

Above: *The Tailor's Workshop*, 1661, Quiringh Gerritsz. van Brekelenkam (c. 1620–68)

'Pieter de Hooch was a painter of purely pictorial effects, beginning and ending a picture in a scheme of colour, atmosphere, clever composition, and above all the play of light and shade.'

John Charles Van Dyke

(*c.* 1620–68), shows tailors at work, sitting near large windows for maximum light. On the wall above their heads is a fine land and seascape painting. Art was a classless appreciation, bought, collected and displayed in Dutch commercial businesses, indicative of a cultured society. This painting by van Brekelenkam was popular, and as many as thirteen versions of it are extant.

The Gendered Space

Looking at Dutch art of this period, one notices that painters assign genders to particular settings, reflecting the social traditions of Dutch society. The woman's gendered space is within the home. The male is predominantly seen away from the house, in an office or workshop, or place of work, the interior domestic scenes being principally occupied by women, their servants and children. The male space is outside, in the city, or countryside, or acting in an official role. At leisure, young middle-class women play the virginals, or lute or guitar, or they sew, write or read letters, such as in Johannes Vermeer's *A Lady Writing*, *c.* 1665 (*see* page 186). Female servants are portrayed inside and outside, working, serving, preparing food, or looking after children, but staying close to the domestic space of the house. In Pieter de Hooch's serene architectural composition *A Boy Bringing Bread*, *c.* 1663 (*see* left) the border between the inside and outside of the house is defined. One can see beyond the female servant and the young boy to the courtyard and house beyond. A glimpse of Dutch domestic life is shown to the viewer.

When at home the male is often in a dominant position within the interior, such as a music teacher, as in Vermeer's *The Music Lesson*, *c.* 1662–65 (*see* page 122), or a male doctor visiting a female patient, or a husband talking to his wife, as in de Hooch's *A Gentleman Reading*

Above: *A Boy Bringing Bread*, *c.* 1663, Pieter de Hooch (1629–84)

Right: *A Musical Party*, 1677, Pieter de Hooch (1629–84)

a *Letter to His Wife (?) in an Interior*, 1670–74 (*see* page 125), and Rembrandt's masterful *Portrait of the Mennonite Preacher, Cornelius Claesz. Anslo and His Wife, Aaltje Gerritsdr. Shouten*, 1641 (*see* page 121), where th wife of the Mennonite preacher Cornelis Claesz. Anslo (1592–1646), seated at a lower level than the preacher, listens intently to her husband's rhetoric.

Pieter de Hooch

The Rotterdam-born artist Pieter de Hooch was a contemporary of Johannes Vermeer. Both painters were members of the Guild of St Luke in Delft, and both are noted for exquisite domestic scenes, representing quintessential Dutch family life among the wealthier classes. In de Hooch's works, gender identity, the male and female role, circulates in and around the domestic home. Access to the outside world is through open doors and courtyards and streets glimpsed beyond the interior. The substance of other lives beyond the home is connoted in light flooding through windowpanes, but it is the interior scene on which de Hooch focuses.

In *Interior with a Woman Drinking with Two Men and a Maidservant*, c. 1658 (*see* right), de Hooch focuses the viewer's gaze on the wineglass held up by the young girl. On the wall behind the drinkers is a map showing the 17 provinces of the Netherlands. Over the mantelpiece is a vast canvas of the *Education of the Virgin*, which may relate to the intentions of the male drinkers towards the young woman. De Hooch has framed a painting within a painting and made the whole work a morality tale. One can read it on different levels, as a domestic everyday scene of leisure in the home, or an invasion of the female domestic space with dangerous consequences.

Above: *The Music Lesson*, c. 1662–65, Johannes Vermeer (1632–75)

Right: *Interior with a Woman Drinking with Two Men and a Maidservant*, c. 1658, Pieter de Hooch (1629–84)

Above: *Basket of Flowers*, c. 1695–1700, Rachel Ruysch (1664–1750)

Each work by de Hooch brings seventeenth-century Netherlandish culture closer to the viewer, much like Hieronymus Bosch, whose paintings had a moral edge, even when comical, such as *The Garden of Earthly Delights*, 1504. De Hooch's approach was closer to that of Pieter Bruegel the Elder, who mirrored Dutch contemporary and traditional customs, as in *The Wedding Dance* (*see* page 90).

Female Netherlander Artists

In comparison to the vast number of male artists, in the Netherlands during the seventeenth century there were few females at work in a professional capacity. Many women of noble, aristocratic or middling class had the opportunity to paint in an amateur capacity at home from an early age. Paintings of the Golden Age depict the roles that women were given, generally that of homemakers, a wife, mother, mistress, sister, daughter, servant, child. Opportunities to train in the workshop of an artist, the normal route for a male apprentice, were rare, unless acquired through a male relation, who worked professionally as an artist, possibly the father, brother, cousin, or a tutor recommended to her family. Of the female artists we know from this period, Rachel Ruysch and Judith Leyster are two that stand out for their level of engagement with the age in which they lived.

Judith Leyster, Mistress of Genre

In 1633 Dutch painter Judith Leyster entered the artists' Guild of St Luke in Haarlem, accepted as an independent master. It meant that she could sell her art either herself or through an art dealer; she could run her own workshop and tutor paying students. Her status was a

'There were famous female painters who could well compete with the men in the graphic arts, amongst them the admirable Judith Leyster.'

Theodorus Schrevelius

Right: *A Gentleman Reading a Letter to His Wife (?) in an Interior*, 1670–74, Pieter de Hooch (1629–84)

rarity for a woman. In *Self-Portrait*, *c.* 1630 (*see* page 127), Leyster is seated in front of her easel on which there is an unfinished painting. She half-turns to greet her visitor and smiles at the observer. She is painting a three-quarter portrait of a male musician with a violin. His actions mirror hers. In his left hand he holds the instrument of his profession, a violin; in Leyster's left hand she holds her palette and at least 18 brushes, the tools of her profession. The musician holds the violin bow up high in his right hand. Leyster holds a paintbrush in her raised right hand. She has painted herself wearing fine clothes, including an exquisite neck ruff, painted in meticulous detail. Her porcelain skin gleams, highlighting the youth of her early twenties, as she smiles at the unseen guest. The musician in her easel painting is similar to an earlier work, *Three Boys Merry-Making*, *c.* 1629 (*see* left). Infrared of the self-portrait revealed another self-portrait that Leyster painted over with the content we see today. The work advertises her skill as a portraitist and a leading painter of merry genre scenes.

'She paints with a good keen sense.'

Samuel Ampzing on Judith Leyster

Leyster and Hals

A comparison between Frans Hals' *Portrait of a Jester with a Lute*, 1623–26 (*see* page 129) – possibly a vanitas painting of music and pleasure – and Leyster's *The Concert*, *c.* 1633, reveals similarities, both in composition and painterly technique. Hals' signature Caravaggesque

Above: *Three Boys Merry-making*, c. 1629, Judith Leyster (c. 1609–60)

Right: *Self-Portrait*, c. 1630, Judith Leyster (c. 1609–60)

use of dark and light and painterly informality informed Leyster's work in a positive, progressive approach. In Leyster's painting, the singer is thought to be a self-portrait, the violin player her husband and the lute player, a friend. Merry-making paintings were Leyster's forte and were sought after by patrons and dealers. But paintings by Leyster were often passed off as Hals' work by rogue dealers, to make more money from the sale. It was simply a matter of changing her signature mark to his. There are many similarities, from the animated composition to the broad sweep of brush, as well as the use of tonal colours and finish that make the deceit possible.

The Mark of a Star

In 1636 Leyster married fellow-artist Jan Miense Molenaer. Together they had five children. Leyster's paintings reduced in number after her marriage, and her contribution to Dutch art was largely forgotten by the nineteenth century. Some paintings were either mistaken or intentionally sold as by Hals or Molenaer to raise the purchase price. In 1893, the Dutch art historian and collector Cornelis Hofstede de Groot (1863–1930) identified the mark of a star on paintings. This was Leyster's own mark for her identity, a symbol reflecting the meaning of her name (in Dutch *leyster* means 'lodestar' or 'leading star'). Today Leyster is acknowledged as the finest female artist of her generation in the Netherlands, and her work is once again sought after.

Jan Miense Molenaer

Jan Miense Molenaer of Haarlem, the husband of better-known artist Judith Leyster, used genre painting to exercise his sardonic humour.

Left: *The Concert*, c. 1626, Hendrick ter Brugghen (1588–1629)

Above: *Portrait of a Jester with a Lute*, c. 1623, Frans Hals (1582/83–1666)

He moved from Haarlem to Amsterdam in 1637 to develop his talent and popularity as a peasant genre painter. His work was prolific and sought after by agents to sell both in the northern and southern Netherlands. Molenaer was tutored by Frans Hals and his younger brother Dirck Hals (1591–1656), noted as a painter of 'merry-company' scenes. The influence, in terms of composition and content, of Frans Hals filters through to Molenaer's works, such as *Self-Portrait with Family Members*, 1630s (*see* page 134).

Picturing Real Life

Card Players in a Sunlit Room, 1658 (*see* left), by Pieter de Hooch, is an example of Dutch painters' penchant for depictions of the leisure pursuits of contemporary life and its everyday occurrences, such as card playing, or relaxing outdoors, as in *Courtyard of a House in Delft*, 1658 (*see* right). De Hooch paints a scene of domestic bliss, where calm and order dominate the household and Dutch life. However, common human habits, such as vomiting and urinating, were sometimes included in artworks, particularly in 'merry company' scenes.

To art critics this raw detail of human, and animal, life in Dutch art compared unfavourably to Italian artists of the High Renaissance. Paulus Potter, a fine painter of animals, in *The Farmyard* (*see* page 133), included a cow urinating. Biographer Karel van Mander in *Schilder-boeck* (1604), on painters and painting, described figures and animals defecating as 'nice little jokes' (*aerdige boetsen*). Did Dutch and English painters view everyday life differently? Probably not. A greater sense of decorum was maintained amongst the higher-status patrons and painters in both countries. However, the English painter Sir Joshua Reynolds (1723–92), first President of the Royal Academy of Arts

'Dissect it [the Dutch school], and you will find painters of *conversations*, of landscapes, animals, marines, official pictures, still life, flowers...'

Eugène Fromentin

Above: *Card-players in a Sunlit Room*, 1658, Pieter de Hooch (1629–84)

Right: *Courtyard of a House in Delft*, 1658, Pieter de Hooch (1629–84)

verheven anno 1614
P·D·H·
A 1658

in England, in 1768, suggested that 'Painters should go to the Dutch school to learn the art of painting, as they would go to a grammar school to learn languages.' He considered Holland as a basic training school for artists and Italy as a university.

Reynolds' views of the genre painter, Jan Steen of Leiden, considered today the greatest comic painter of all, typify the thinking that suppressed greater appreciation of Dutch art in England in the eighteenth and nineteenth centuries by negatively comparing Dutch to Italian artists:

> *'Jean Stein seems to be one of the most diligent and accurate observers of what passed in those scenes he frequented … if this extraordinary man had had the good fortune to have been born in Italy, instead of Holland, had he lived in Rome instead of Leyden, and been blessed with Michel Angelo and Raffaelle for his masters, instead of Brower and Van Gowen … he now would have ranged with the great pillars and supporters of our Art.'*
> Reynolds: Discourse VI, an address to Students
> of the Royal Academy, London, 10 December 1774

Portraying the People

A marketable interest in paintings and prints of scenes of everyday Dutch life led Jan Steen, his peer group and followers to portray what they saw in the streets and inns and at home and embellish it. Genre painting included 'merry' scenes, which were often cruel, possibly to be viewed as morality paintings. Characters, not known individuals, portrayed social life, from young children to the elderly. They were pictured at a moment in time, as though the painter was present at the scene. Steen's *Children*

Right: *The Farmyard*, 1649, Paulus Potter (1625–54)

Above: *Self-Portrait with Family Members*, 1635, Jan Miense Molenaer (1610–68)

Teaching a Cat to Dance, c. 1665, focuses on a cat held forcefully by its front paws and made to 'dance' for fear of being burned by a lit clay pipe held near its body, or bitten by a large dog watching below, and all recognized as mischievous fun. Haarlem-born Jan Miense Molenaer portrays another scene of children at 'merry' play, in *Children Teasing a Dwarf*, c. 1635–46. His wife, Judith Leyster, painted a different, milder view in *Laughing Children with a Cat*, 1629 (*see* right).

A Wealth of Talent

Artists conveyed diverse lifestyles in 'merry' works, from the street and tavern to the drawing room. Molenaer's *Self-Portrait with Family Members*, 1635 (*see* left), included framed portrait depictions of the deceased relations of the merry-making participants in this music-making scenario. As the family gathers to play music, the longevity of the family and its beloved relations connote the permanency and heritage of Dutch kinsfolk. They are splendidly dressed and hold a variety of instruments, denoting talent and diversity. Painters focused on images of domestic harmony, and steadfast relationships, highlighting families enjoying life together, to mirror the moral aim of Dutch society.

Overseas Ventures

In many Dutch households the comforts of domestic life were borne out of the ambitions of merchant-traders seeking fortunes overseas. 'Wherever profit leads us, to every sea and shore', translated from a poem by Joost van den Vondel, the most prominent Dutch poet and playwright of the seventeenth century, sums up the ambitious mindset of the seaborne empire of the Dutch Republic. The Dutch East India Company (Vereenigde Oost-Indische Compagnie) was founded in 1602 to increase trade and simultaneously destabilize Spanish colonies, thereby reducing the Spanish campaign funds sustaining the Eighty Years' War. The Dutch West India Company (West-Indische Compagnie) was founded in 1621, with the aim of conquering Spanish and Portuguese territories in the West Indies and South America. Their exploits led ordinary Dutch people to take a great interest in overseas exploration, and collectors to buy atlases, globes, charts and maps to be proudly displayed at home, and in paintings, such as the globe in Gabriël Metsu's *Man Writing a Letter* (*see* page 117), and the large wall map in Johannes Vermeer's *The Artist's Studio* (*see* page 80).

Above: *Laughing Children with a Cat*, 1629, Judith Leyster (c. 1609–60)

Universal Man

Vermeer's painting *The Astronomer*, 1668 (*see* above), and its pendant *The Geographer*, 1669 (*see* right), are two works of inestimable quality that underlie Dutch interest in, and expanding knowledge of, astronomical science and world exploration, which accelerated during the Dutch Golden Age. These paintings link to the enormous contributions made to science by Dutch pioneers, particularly by the mathematician, physicist and astronomer Christiaan Huygens, one of the greatest scientists of the Dutch Republic.

The Astronomer

In his painting *The Astronomer*, Vermeer's astronomer leans over an open book. It is recognized as a publication by Adriaan Metius (1571–1635), of Alkmaar, (brother of Jacob Metius), and a useful guide on the subject and practice of geography and astronomy, open at the first two pages of Book III, 'On the Investigation or Observation of the Stars'. The astronomer consults his celestial globe, made by Dutch cartographer Jodocus Hondius (1563–1612), with a pair of dividers, with an astrolabe (to measure the position in the sky of a celestial body), to hand. So precise is Vermeer's replication of the book that the pages can be identified as from Metius's second edition of 1621, showing text and an astrolabe of Metius's invention. This book was obviously in Vermeer's possession, illustrating how Dutch interest in the sciences, including astronomy and geography, closely connected, enriched the lives of both amateurs and professionals. Metius' aimed his texts at sea-faring merchants, captains, pilots, and cartographers too, as 'clear instructions for the art of navigation', recognising, and mapping the celestial sphere, to fix a position in order to measure longitude and latitude, a necessity for the Dutch long-distance seafaring merchants.

The Geographer

Vermeer, like Metius, linked the two disciplines of geography and astronomy in a companion painting *The Geographer*. In this work, in a similar room setting, the geographer leans over maps. His terrestial globe, also made by Hondius, and usually sold as a pair (terrestial and celestial,) is on top of a high cupboard with the Indian Ocean visible. From Vermeer's detailed portrayal it is possible to identify it as a 1618 third edition of Hondius's globe. In Vermeer's companion paintings both men of science, astronomical and terrestrial, amateur or professional, strive to further their knowledge of the world. The paintings were sold together as companion works.

Above: *The Astronomer*, 1668, Johannes Vermeer (1632–75)

Right: *The Geographer*, 1669, Johannes Vermeer (1632–75)

I Ver-Meer
MDCLXVIIII

Pioneers of the Telescope

From the late thirteenth century, magnifying spectacles made from highly polished discs of glass – sheared from a globe of glass – were produced for reading. In October 1608 German-Dutch spectacle-maker Hans Lippershey (1570–1619), living and working in the city of Middelburg, invented a telescope through experimentation with lenses. He sought a patent for his invention in 1608, claiming that with his telescope 'even the stars which ordinarily are invisible to our sight … can be seen by means of this instrument'. His tubular design would become one of the most important inventions of the seventeenth century.

'[Vermeer] was a remarkable man for his handling of blues, reds and yellows; and in the tonal relations of a picture he was a master second to no one.'

John Charles Van Dyke

While Lippershey was applying for a patent, the States General in The Hague were examining a similar patent application from Jacob Adriaensz. Metius (d. 1628), of Alkmaar, an instrument maker and lens grinder. Some historians consider Metius co-founder of the telescope with Lippershey. Also exploring the potential of a telescopic-microscopic device were Zacharias Janssen (1585–1632), and his father Hans Janssen (active 1580s) spectacle-makers of Middelburg. Through the exploratory work of the Middelburg pioneering craftsmen, Lippershey, and the Janssens, and Metius in Alkmaar, it was lens-makers as craftsmen, not scientists, who revolutionized the world of science and astronomy. Through the exploratory work of these pioneering craftsmen, it was lens-makers, not scientists, who revolutionized the world of science and astronomy. By 1609 telescopic devices were in circulation across Europe.

Gerrit Dou

Artists were part of this exploration. Their paintings mirrored the fascination with new lunar worlds discovered through telescopes. Gerrit Dou visualized the astronomers' ability for new discoveries in two similar works, *Astronomer by Candlelight*, c. 1650, and the later *Astronomer by Candlelight*, c. 1660/65 (*see* right). In the earlier version, the astronomer is an old man, his bearded face intense and lit by a single candle. He is framed sitting at a table, looking up at the stars. In the later depiction, the astronomer is a younger man, leaning over the table and poring over a treatise whilst holding a compass in his left hand. The astronomers' tools are visible: a celestial globe, an hourglass and flask of liquid (linking astronomy to alchemy) and an astronomical treatise showing maps of the galaxies and constellations. Many of Dou's portraits are framed in the same way, substituting different props and clothing depending on the subject: a painter in his studio, a schoolmaster and pupil in the classroom, or a hermit praying. His candlelit scenarios, using intense tonal shades of dark and light, create an atmospheric mood of wonder and mystery.

Vermeer and Dou

A close study of Vermeer's astronomer reveals many similarities with Gerard Dou's works of the same subject, and he is considered the source of Vermeer's painting. The same props appear but Vermeer places his astronomer in a day-lit study, light pouring in through leaded glass windows above his desk. Astronomy was of immense interest in the Netherlands. Ships' mariners were guided by the stars on lengthy voyages. The opening of the trade route to the East and West Indies allowed astronomers to study the southern hemisphere's stars at length over long journeys, to write up their findings and to publish their records on return to the Netherlands.

Christiaan Huygens

The abundance of exploration overseas was matched at home by ground-breaking planetary discoveries by Dutch scientists. The mathematician, physicist and astronomer Christiaan Huygens, renowned for his wave theory of light, detected in 1655 the rings of the planet Saturn using one of his own

Above: *Astronomer by Candlelight*, c. 1660/65, Gerrit Dou (1613–75)

telescopic lenses. In 1659 he published his findings in 'Saturn's Ring', the first full announcement of Huygens' discovery of Saturn's rings and satellites, tracing the periodic changes in the rings. In addition, he discovered Titan, the largest moon of Saturn, and drew the first map of the planet Mars.

Life in Microscopic Detail

Hans Lippershey's workshop development of convex-concave lenses was taken further by the Delft-born amateur scientist Antonie van Leeuwenhoek (1632–1723). He had travelled to London in 1668, and there may have obtained a copy of *Micrographia*, published in 1664. It was written by English scientist, philosopher and biologist Robert Hooke (1635–1703). Its content studied various objects by means of microscopy. Superb illustrations included a large-scale drawing of a flea, details of its body normally indiscernible to the human eye. In Delft, Leeuwenhoek used microscopy to explore the content of water and found minuscule living organisms. It is for his discovery of bacteria that Leeuwenhoek is called the 'father of microbiology'. Artists were soon to make use of interest in the microscope, particularly for still life painting. Microscopic details of insects' bodies, hardly visible to the eye, plant leaves and flowers were painted in infinitesimal detail, accurate and beautiful, as in Rachel Ruysch's snails, lizard, beetles, butterfly and other insects in *Tree Trunk Surrounded by Flowers, Butterflies and Animals* (*see* page 38), and *Still Life with Fruit, Flowers, Reptiles and Insects* (*see* left) by Ruysch, and the microscopic realism of shells and butterflies in *Still Life with Fruit, Flowers and Seafood* (*see* page 104) by Balthasar van der Ast.

Medical Matters

Microscopic exploration of living organisms by Leeuwenhoek links to earlier studies in medical science by Dutch barber-surgeons. Two paintings by Rembrandt van Rijn, commissioned 20 years apart, are masterful works that reveal the intensity with which anatomical science was explored and recorded by Dutch doctoral guilds.

Anatomical Studies

Rembrandt van Rijn's large-scale commemorative works of two public dissections, *The Anatomy Lesson of Dr Nicolaes Tulp* (*see* right), and *The Anatomy Lesson of Doctor Joan Deyman*, 1656 (*see* page 142), demonstrate Dutch interest in medical advancements during the seventeenth century. Together, the paintings exemplify the increase in artwork patronage

Above: *Still Life with Fruit, Flowers, Reptiles and Insects*, 1716, Rachel Ruysch (1664–1750)

Right: *The Anatomy Lesson of Dr Nicolaes Tulp*, 1632, Rembrandt van Rijn (1606–69)

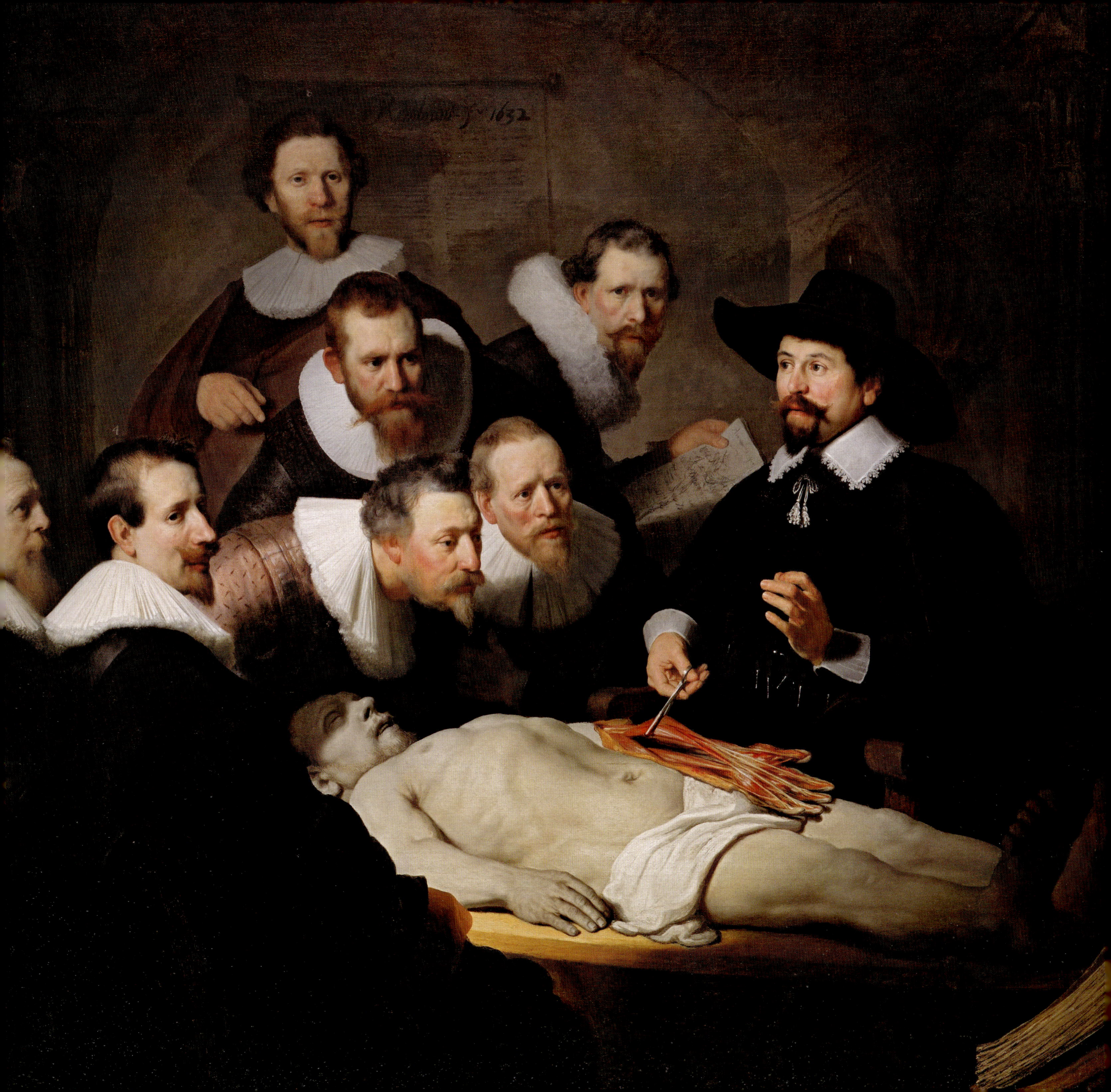

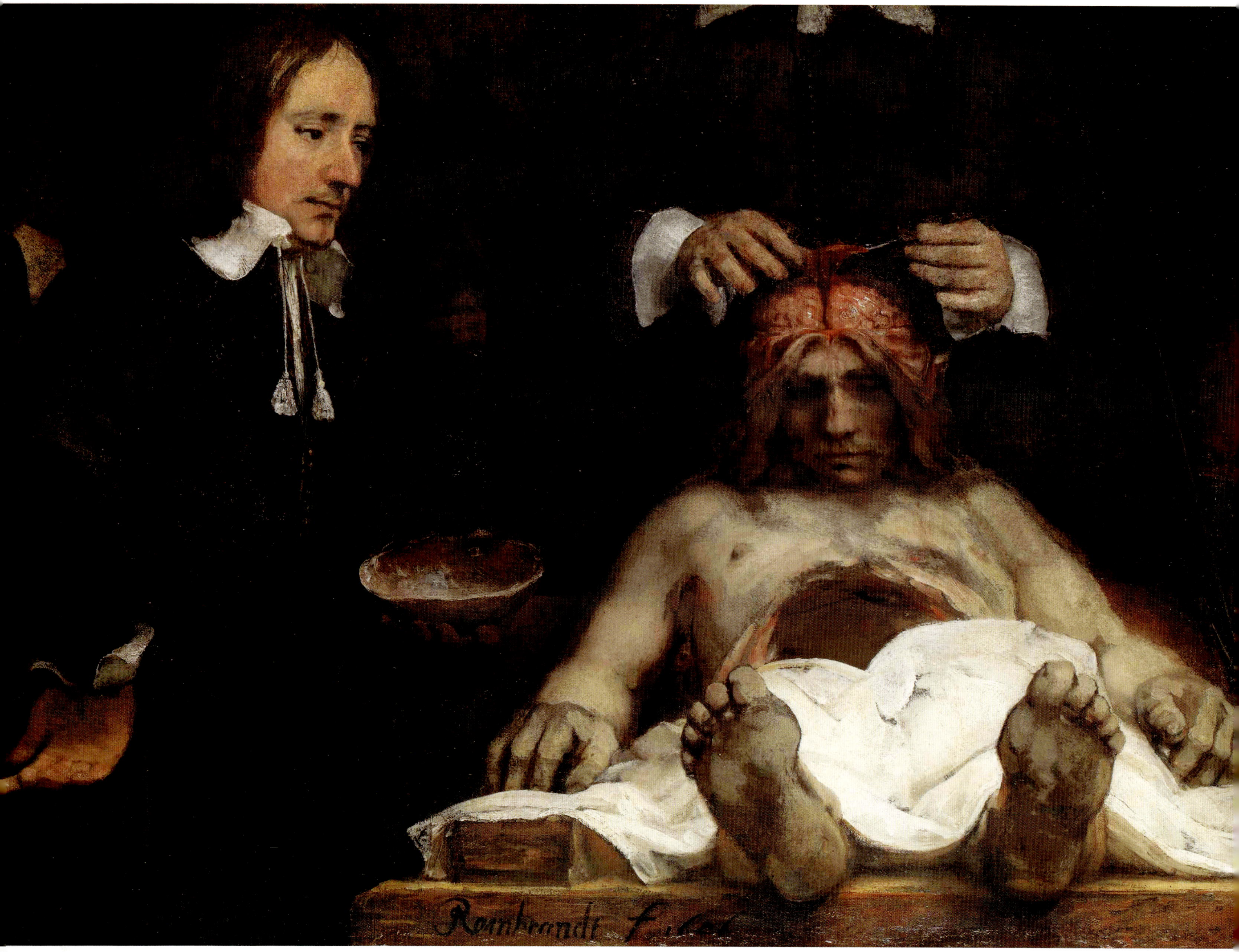

Above: *The Anatomy Lesson of Dr Joan Deyman*, 1656, Rembrandt van Rijn (1606–69)

related to physics, science and the universe in the Dutch Republic, simultaneous to its rise in economic power. Added to this, the study of philosophy, examining the nature of existence, humanity and knowledge, was a popular subject in artists' works, being of interest to patrons and art dealers, such as *A Philosopher*, c. 1640–55 (*see page* 144), by Salomon Koninck (1609–56) of Amsterdam.

'Practise what you know, and it will help to make clear what now you do not know.'

Rembrandt van Rijn

Amsterdam Surgeons' Guild

In January 1632 Rembrandt, aged 25, painted a large-scale work (169.5 x 216.5 cm; 66¾ x 85¼ in) in honour of the Praelector of the Amsterdam Guild of Surgeons and mayor of Amsterdam, Dr Nicolaes Tulp. It is a rare record of the dissection of a body in front of a group of guild members – barber-surgeons – and an audience invited to watch the examination at Dr Tulp's annual public lecture on anatomy. The painting, commissioned by members of the Surgeons' Guild, was to hang in their Guild room. The result was the remarkable work *The Anatomy Lesson of Dr Nicolaes Tulp*, 1632 (*see* page 141). Rembrandt was faced with a group portrait that had to include a cadaver. Each eminent person had to be clearly recognizable. In the composition Dr Nicolaes Tulp, the only one wearing a hat, was set apart on the right. Lit from above by an unseen source, the cadaver, an executed thief named Adriaen Adriaensz., and the faces of the members peering at him are bathed in light and, possibly with empathy on Rembrandt's part, a redemptive light to show respect for the deceased.

Scientific Progress

Dissections were frowned on by religious authorities and the Surgeon's Guild was allowed only one public dissection per year, which could be attended for a fee. Between 1619 and 1639 in Amsterdam they took place in the Weigh House, a small anatomy theatre used by the Guild. The corpses of executed criminals were used, although anatomist Frederik Ruysch (1638–1731) was portrayed dissecting a dead newborn child, its placenta still in place, in *The Anatomy Lesson of Professor Frederik Ruysch*, c. 1683, by Naarden-born painter Jan van Neck (1634–1714). In Rembrandt's work Dr Tulp is demonstrating the flexor mechanism of the muscles and tendons that control the fingers on the cadaver's left forearm and hand, which had been slit open. Tulp illustrates these movements using his own left hand. The guild members look on in wonder. Dutch scientists and surgeons were knowledgeable of the human body and familiar with the anatomical studies and theses of Aristotle (384–322 BC) and Galen (AD c. 129–c. 200). Dissections such as those carried out by members of the Surgeons' Guild put theory in action.

The Anatomy Lesson of Doctor Joan Deyman

Twenty years later Rembrandt received a second commission from the Amsterdam Surgeon's Guild to honour a public lecture given by Dr Tulp's successor, Dr Joan Deyman. The passage of time had lessened the artist's remarkable ability to shock and enthrall viewers of his work. *The Anatomy Lesson of Dr Joan Deyman* (*see* page 142), involved the examination of the two hemispheres of the brain, after sawing off the skullcap of the cadaver. For dramatic effect the half-skull is held in the hands of an assistant. The deceased is a criminal, Juris Fontieijn of Diest, hanged for armed robbery on 28 January 1656. Following the normal procedure for dissection, the stomach had been opened and organs removed. The ribcage is visible. Deyman dissected the cadaver over three days. Public dissections took place in winter for the better preservation of the body. Rembrandt creates a focal light to concentrate on Deyman and the cadaver, placing Deyman's contribution to the Surgeons' Guild of Amsterdam and the wider field of medical science centre stage. The foreshortened body with head pushed forwards onto the chest – the neck broken from hanging – accentuates the presence of Fontieijn, an unwitting participant in the advancement of medical science. What is not seen but felt is the audience. Rembrandt's skillful perspective of the feet, raising of the cadaver's head, and use of a low viewpoint, place the onlooker in the darkened anatomy theatre directly in front of Dr. Deyman and the cadaver. The painting today is a fraction of the size of the original, nearly destroyed in a fire in the eighteenth century. The painting's original content is known from Rembrandt's preliminary 1656 drawing, which illustrates six additional people with Deyman and Fontieijn.

Surgical Procedures

Surgery, c. 1630s (*see* right), by Adriaen Brouwer, a Flemish painter working in Haarlem, Amsterdam and Antwerp, is one of the artist's many doctor-patient genre scenes. Here he focuses on a doctor attending to a woman of the poorer classes, watched by an older woman. Is he a quack or a genuine physician? Brouwer lets the viewer decide as the doctor

'Conscious of the power as well as the necessity of shade, he took the utmost boundaries of darkness and allowed but one-third of light...'

J.M.W. Turner on Rembrandt van Rijn

Above: *A Philosopher*, c. 1640–55, Salomon Koninck (1609–56)

Above: *Surgery*, *c.* 1630s, Adriaen Brouwer (1605/6–38)

leans over his patient and peers through his glasses, possibly to lance a boil on the shoulder. His patient winces with pain as the doctor grasps her skin. Brouwer captures the immediacy of both the anticipation and the expression of pain. The chiaroscuro effect heightens the drama with light streaming onto the patient's bare shoulder and screwed-up face. The pain of medical treatment is expressed again on the face of a peasant grimacing as he drinks an apothecary's potion in Brouwer's comical work *Bitter Draught* (*see* left).

'The great Dutch school seemed to think of nothing but painting well.'

Eugène Fromentin

Rembrandt's Painterly Craft

Writing on art theory in 1690, the noted Dutch painter and etcher, theatrical designer, lecturer and author Gerard de Lairesse (1641–1711), of Liege, commented on Rembrandt's application of paint. He referred to the paint consistency as 'liquid mud', squishy and thick, applied as if with a trowel. Rembrandt's broad brushstrokes were loose, and freely applied, yet captured facial characteristics and features. It is evident in his Tulp-Deyman anatomical paintings. The thickness of the paint needed many layers of varnish to seal it. Lairesse went blind in 1690, turning to writing to continue his career, but around twenty years earlier he had moved to Amsterdam, where Rembrandt painted a portrait of him, sculpting the

Above: *Bitter Draught*, 1605 or 1606–1638, Adriaen Brouwer (*c.* 1605/06–38)

Right: *The Patient and the Doctor*, *c.* 1660, Jan Steen (1625/26–79)

Above: *A Mother Delousing Her Child's Hair, Known as 'A Mother's Duty'*, c. 1658–60, Pieter de Hooch (1629–84)

face in light and shadow. When the work was publicly viewed it created shock, for Rembrandt, with deft thick strokes, had accurately captured the painter's deformed facial features, visible since birth, and today widely recognized as congenital syphilis. Lairesse published two books from his lectures: *A Treatise of the Art of Drawing (Grondlegginge der teekenkonst)*, 1701, and *The Principles of Drawing (Het groot schilderboeck)*, 1707.

Visiting the Sick

Rembrandt's paintings of dissections explored the serious side of a surgeon's work open to public scrutiny, which the artist revealed in a restrained form, giving the cadaver an important role in the research. Other artists, not invited to record dissections, played on people's own experience of doctors, from home visits by professional practitioners, to quacks operating in villages and at country fairs or city markets, scenes that identified individuals in Dutch life, as portrayed in *The Quack*, 1650–60, by Jan Steen (*see* page 173).

Artists painted people receiving treatment, such as a test for pregnancy on a home visit, in Jan Steen's *The Patient and the Doctor*, c. 1660. Art buyers identified their lives with portrayals of Dutch everyday occurrences. Metsu, in *The Sick Child*, 1664–66 (*see* right), a work that highlights his superb gift for colour and light, focuses on a small child at home, half-dressed, lying across its mother's lap, the child's sad eyes directly set on the viewer. One sees in the body position of mother and child a parallel to the *pietà*, with the dead Christ in the arms of the Virgin Mary. In Metsu's work the mother's concern and devotion to the sick child is the focal point, more than the ailment of the child. In *A Mother Delousing Her Child's Hair, Known as 'A Mother's Duty'*, c. 1658–60 (*see* left), by Pieter de Hooch, a commonplace affliction is treated by the child's mother, no doctor required.

Above: *The Sick Child*, c. 1664–66, Gabriël Metsu (1629–67)

Meaning & Motif

Paintings as Signifiers

PUBLIC DEMAND for art in the Dutch Republic, allowed painters to create marketable, smaller paintings on wood or canvas. The content of popular works often carried hidden messages to the viewer, signifiers that were easily recognized in Dutch society. Still Life in particular was a two-fold visual experience. A vase of flowers would be painted exquisitely in microscopic detail, with the addition of subtle layers of meaning, from the rich luxury of rare exotic flowers, connoting wealth, to flowers and fruit slightly decaying, signifying the brevity of life. Paintings were a joy to 'read', and understood by the cultivated collector and less-educated alike.

Still Life

The term 'still life' came into use in the Netherlands from around 1650. Before that time a painting or artwork of inanimate objects would be referred to as *stilstaende dingen*, 'still standing objects', or more often by its content, such as fish, flowers, a vase, a skull, a banquet, or a porcelain bowl. The inclusion of inanimate pieces, often placed as symbolic motifs, was a custom in Dutch art from medieval times. Still-life paintings could be symbolic representations of many things: materialism, trade, religion,

Previous Page: *Orestes and Pylades Disputing at the Altar*, 1614, Pieter Lastman (1583–1633)
Left: *A Pie on a Pewter Plate, a Partly Peeled Lemon, A Silver Spoon on a Pewter Plate, Crayfish and Shrimp in a Wan-li Kraak Porcelain Bowl*, 1649, Jan Davidsz. de Heem (1606–84)

morality, death, love, honesty, virginity. They offered a wealth of meaning through visual interpretation, for example a night-setting often stood as a metaphor for ignorance, or a lack of knowledge, that needed enlightening. Patrons of art liked the metaphors, the allegories and symbols hidden within the paintings and the Dutch Republic produced masters of the art to accommodate the market.

Symbolism in Still-Life Objects

Placing objects as symbols in art has a long tradition. A painting could be read through layers of meaning by the objects depicted. In religious works, objects and plants were universally recognized for their religious associations, from the sun as divine light representing God to the apple symbolizing original sin. Thorns denoted the agony of Christ on the Cross, while bread, wine and cornstalks signified the Eucharist, the blood and body of Christ. Laurel and ivy, ears of wheat and wreathes placed on a skull were recognized symbols of the Resurrection. There are many more that were signifiers in religious works.

Vanitas Still Life

Symbols of the brevity of life are many and include books, torn papers, manuscripts, over-ripe and rotting fruit, butterflies, a candle, a lamp, an hourglass, an overturned goblet, a timepiece, soap bubbles, smoke, a half-empty glass and flowers, particularly pansies and roses, although a bouquet represented divine love. Death was often represented by a skull or skeleton, petals and shells. Immensely popular were paintings of still life with symbols of death or the transient brevity of life, or of luxurious items showing excess, referred to in Dutch as *pronk* (from *pronken* meaning 'to strut, show off'), indicating the ephemeral futility of material pleasures, collectively known as vanitas paintings.

Above: *Vase of Flowers with Ring and Diamonds*, Jan Brueghel the Elder (1568–1625)

Above: *A Vanitas Still Life with a Skull, a Book and Roses*, c. 1630, Jan Davidsz. de Heem (1606–84)

Above: *A Vanitas Still Life of Musical Instruments and Manuscripts, an Overturned Gilt Covered Goblet, a Jewellery Casket, a Candlestick, an Astrological Globe, a String of Pearls, Jewels, Shells, a Skull and Femur and an Hour-Glass on a Draped Table*, 1653, Pieter Claesz (1597–1660)

Depicting Material Life

In the Dutch Republic the Protestant Calvinist members of society, god-fearing upholders of moral standards, looked to the Old Testament for guidance. Many religious works of this period focus on the Old Testament stories. The Dutch Calvinists compared their emergence from the Roman Catholic Church, as a chosen people, with that of their religious forebears the Israelites (Old Testament: Exodus). The Bible's *Book of Ecclesiastes* was a favourite text of Calvinist ministers, which underlined the unimportance of materiality and was aimed at collectors of wealth, goods and possessions deemed immaterial when entering Heaven on the day of Resurrection: 'As he came forth of his mother's womb, naked shall he return as he came, and shall take nothing away of his labour' (Ecclesiastes 5:50). Artworks were not judged as cultural materialism, which aided the Dutch art market.

The underlying meaning of vanitas paintings was the importance of valuing a spiritual, non-materialistic life because death awaits all. There are many examples by Dutch masters revealing the temporary nature of a material life through wealthy objects, such as *Pronk Still Life, with a Roemer, an Upturned Silver Tazza, a Half-peeled Lemon on a Pewter Plate, with a Pie, a Timepiece and a Knife* (*see* above), by Willem Claesz. Heda, and A *Vanitas Still Life of Musical Instruments and Manuscripts, an Overturned Gilt Covered Goblet, a Jewellery Casket, a Candlestick, an Astrological Globe, a String of Pearls, Jewels, Shells, a Skull and Femur and an Hour-Glass on a Draped Table*, 1653 (*see* left), by Pieter Claesz.

Above: *Pronk Still Life, with a Roemer, an Upturned Silver Tazza, a Half-peeled Lemon on a Pewter Plate, with a Pie, a Timepiece and a Knife*, 1631, Willem Claesz. Heda (c. 1594–c. 1680)

'No painter knew so well the extent of his own powers and his own weakness.'

J.M.W. Turner on Rembrandt van Rijn

Memento Mori

Rembrandt van Rijn's *The Carcass of an Ox*, painted in the late 1630s, and *The Slaughtered Ox*, 1655 (*see* left), depict slaughtered oxen, strung up as if crucified, blood draining from the body, head and innards removed. The artist bares before the viewer the animal's flayed and disembowelled body, its muscles, flesh, fat and dripping blood. The motif of a slaughtered animal was a reminder of death, a memento mori. Rembrandt creates an evocative mood with shafts of light underscoring the isolation of the animal. It links to the Biblical parable of the prodigal son (Luke 15: 11–32), in which a fattened calf was slaughtered with the connotation of a life sacrificed for others, associated also with the death of Christ, crucified on the Cross. With this understanding, *Flayed Pig*, c. 1640–45 by Adriaen Jansz. Van Ostade can be read as either an everyday scene of Dutch life, or a religious motif. Many Dutch paintings of the seventeenth century portray the prodigal son, such as *The Departure of the Prodigal Son*, c. 1630 (*see* right), by Jan Miense Molenaer. Set in a spacious room of a seventeenth-century Dutch house, the family awaits the fashionable, finely dressed prodigal's departure. His conceited manner effuses *pronk*. To consolidate the moral message in the depiction, in the lower foreground vanitas and memento mori symbols spill out across the floor. The scattered possessions include overturned dishes and a flagon, human and animal skulls.

Jan Davidsz. de Heem

Battered books appear in many of the early works of Utrecht-born painter Jan Davidsz. de Heem such as *Still Life with Books*, 1625–30 (*see* page 161), and one which may be a self-portrait as a student, *Interior of a Room with a Man Seated at a Table*, 1628 (*see* page 160). The abandoned but well-

Left: *The Slaughtered Ox*, 1655, Rembrandt van Rijn (1606–69)

Above: *The Departure of the Prodigal Son*, c. 1630, Jan Miense Molenaer (1610–68)

Above: *Interior of a Room with a Man Seated at a Table*, 1628, Jan Davidsz. de Heem (1606–84)

thumbed books are scattered opened and unopened across a desk. A map on the wall may hint at an interest in geography. The inclusion of books in a vanitas painting was a motif for the transience of earthly life. In *Still Life with Books*, the lute, often associated with lewd or unseemly behaviour in Dutch genre works, here represents music's momentary earthly pleasure. The fleetingness of life is referenced again in the written page at the forefront, caught between a book's pages on the table. It states *finis* ('the end'). It is probable that de Heem was influenced by Balthasar van der Ast, when he lived in Utrecht, and possibly tutored by Pieter Claesz, both masters of still life. In 1628/29 de Heem painted a group of vanitas works featuring skulls, books and plaster casts of statuary, including *A Vanitas Still Life with a Skull, a Book and Roses*, c. 1630 (*see* page 155).

A *memento mori* in a monochrome tonal scheme, adding gravitas to the objects, while connoting the transient nature of material life, was repeated in the painting *A Pie on a Pewter Plate, a Partly Peeled Lemon, A Silver Spoon on a Pewter Plate, Crayfish and Shrimp in a Wan-li Kraak Porcelain Bowl*, 1649 (*see* page 152). De Heem used chiaroscuro – dramatic light and shade – to create intimacy. A table is piled with luxurious objects, pewter plates, flagons, silverware, glass, glistening crustaceans and delicious fruit, all depicted in meticulous detail, including a half-eaten pie – symbols of a wealthy household, and the brevity of life - as closely detailed as a fine portrait, masterpieces of trompe l'oeil, deceiving the eye with their realism. In the late seventeenth century de Heem emerged as one of the most sought-after artists of still-life and flower paintings.

Above: *Still Life with Books*, 1625–30, Jan Davidsz. de Heem (1606–84)

Popularity of Flower Paintings

Flowers have long been associated with religious symbolism, particularly noticeable in paintings of the medieval age. For example, a white lily and a blue iris are both associated with the Virgin Mary: the lily, always present in representations of the Annunciation, for the Virgin Mary; the iris for Mary, Queen of Heaven. This continued in religious works created during the Dutch Golden Age, but commercial flower paintings moved away from religious symbolism to outward signs of material wealth, in the exotic or rare flowers portrayed in still-life works. Simple still-life paintings had as their subjects bread and cheeses, or a laden breakfast table, or noticeboards with letters, or plain crockery on a sideboard, or tables near-collapsing under the weight of luxurious sweetmeats and exotic delicacies. However, for more expensive tastes, the simple flower displayed in a vase emerged on the art market from early 1600. It became a commercial product that gained in popularity, creating a passion for floral displays in art, as the sole subject, not as the contents of an expensive or antique vase, or placed as decoration in a window, or as a background addition to a painting. Soon the size of the floral bouquets overwhelmed the ornate vases, and became the focus, as seen in *Still Life with Flowers*, c. 1700 (*see* left), by Rachel Ruysch.

Rachel Ruysch

Rachel Ruysch, born in The Hague, was court painter to the elector palatine Johann Wilhelm von der Pfalz of Dusseldorf from 1708 to 1716. She was a prolific still-life painter, noted for her sought-after flower pieces, such as *Vase of Flowers*, 1695 (*see* right), *Basket of Flowers*, c. 1695–1700 (*see* page 124), and *Still Life with Flowers* (*see* left). At 15

Above: *Still Life with Flowers*, c. 1700, Rachel Ruysch (1664–1750)

Right: *Vase of Flowers*, 1695, Rachel Ruysch (1664–1750)

'...it is truly an unlooked-for spectacle to see ... in such a small space ... such a growth of painters, and such great painters.'

Eugène Fromentin

Above: *Still Life of Summer Flowers*, c. 1710, Rachel Ruysch (1664–1750)

Ruysch was apprenticed to Willem van Aelst from Delft, a painter of still life and game. Like van Aelst, Ruysch liked dark backgrounds for flower pieces to focus attention on the floral composition. Her richly detailed paintings of great realism and artistry forged her reputation and attracted high prices for her work.

Famed Father and Daughter

Ruysch painted throughout her life from an early age. Born into a wealthy family, she was the daughter of Frederik Ruysch, eminent professor of anatomy and botany, and Maria Post, daughter of the architect Pieter Post. Rachel Ruysch acquired a thorough knowledge of plants and flowers from her father. She helped to catalogue his natural history collection, which aided her scientific knowledge and meticulous accuracy in portraying plants, flowers and insects, seen in *Still Life of Summer Flowers*, c. 1710 (*see* left) and *Still Life with Fruit, Flowers, Reptiles and Insects* (*see* page 140). Frederik Ruysch was a pioneer in the practice of anatomical preservation and used art to enhance depictions of his embalming jars. Illustrations to advertise displays of his specimen collections included highly decorative representations of embalmed small animals, or skeletons, or parts of the body, placed in clear glass jars with lids of floral displays, shells, beads, insects and fruit.

Jan van der Heyden

The artist Jan van der Heyden was born in Gorinchem, south Holland, and at age 13 moved to Amsterdam with his parents. Noted as a fine draughtsman, glass painter and printmaker, with a good knowledge of classical architecture, he was also an engineer and inventor of firefighting

Above: *Amsterdam City View with Houses on the Herengracht and the Old Haarlemmersluis*, c. 1670, Jan van der Heyden (1637–1712)

PREDIKER,
KOHELETH.

equipment. He contributed to the safety of the city, becoming a city official. Van der Heyden was a wealthy man, occupying a house on the Herengracht with his wife and family. The canal features in several of his paintings, such as *Amsterdam City View with Houses on the Herengracht and the Old Haarlemmersluis*, c. 1670 (*see* page 165). In addition to around 40 landscapes, van der Heyden is best known for architectural cityscape views in the Netherlands and Germany, exact in their detail, and some popular fictional landscapes, such as *An Imaginary Town Gate with Triumphal Arch*, 1663, a picturesque architectural fantasy. Less well known are his fascinating *kunstkamer* ('cabinet of curiosities') still-life paintings, full of symbolism.

Kunstkamer

At the beginning and end of artist Jan van der Heyden's career he focused on still life. An early work, *Still Life with a Bible*, 1664, is painted with meticulous attention to detail. Its realism connects two subjects close to the hearts and minds of Catholics and Reformants, the religious content of fine art and religious belief. Van der Heyden paints the Bible open and the place held with a ribbon marker. A candle to read by, a symbol of enlightenment, is on the desk. *Still Life with Rarities*, 1712 (*see* left), painted in the year the artist died, aged 75, depicts a cabinet of curiosities (*kunstkamer*). The word *kunstkamer* has a double-meaning, and can be translated as a painting of a room of antiquities and art, or a museum of antiquities and art. The motif appeared in Antwerp at the beginning of the seventeenth century, linked to an interest in unifying Catholicism with philosophy and science. The Antwerp-born painter Frans Francken the Younger (1581–1642) introduced multi-faceted content to be unravelled by the viewer.

In van der Heyden's *Still Life with Rarities*, one enters the private room of a prodigious and cultured collector to look upon their material possessions.

Above the Italian marble mantelpiece is a painting by Italian artist Pietro Testa (1611–50), *The Suicide of Dido*, 1650–55. It depicts a mythological tragedy, the death of Dido, Queen of Carthage, who killed herself in despair after abandonment by Aeneas. From the mantelpiece hangs the shell of an armadillo. On a cabinet at the back right of the painting, one glimpses a Chinese porcelain bowl and cabinet drawers containing a collection of coins. There are globes of the terrestrial and celestial worlds placed on a richly embroidered Chinese cloth, on which Joan Blaeu's *Atlas Major* (1662–72) lies open. The connotation is man's exploration of the earthly world and the astronomical universe and his love of material objects. Close by, and to the forefront, propped on a chair, a Bible lies

Left: *Still Life with Rarities*, 1712, Jan van der Heyden (1637–1712)

Above: *Cabinet of a Collector*, 1617, Frans Francken the Younger (1581–1642)

open at Ecclesiastes, on the words of Solomon, which includes the text 'I have seen all the works that are done under the sun; and, behold, all is vanity and vexation of spirit.' (Ecclesiastes 1:14) The context, that these cultural vanities are worthless, and of limited time value in the immaterial earthly world would be understood by the onlooker to not forsake the infinite spiritual world.

Still-Life Classification

Symbols of status appeared continuously in Dutch still-life paintings, illustrating knowledge (items used by explorers, geographers or astronomers) and wealth (exotic fruit, birds, seashells, foods, spices, porcelain and glass). These were often strewn amongst an arrangement of

Above: *A Sleeping Dog with Terracotta Pot*, 1650, Gerrit Dou (1613–75)

Right: *Breakfast with a Crab*, 1648, Willem Claesz. Heda (c. 1594–c. 1680)

Above: *Still Life with Fruit and Flowers*, 1620-21, Balthasar van der Ast (1593/94–1657)

flowers, painted with meticulous detail and realism. Willem Claesz. Heda, born in Haarlem, was a master of still life and devoted his career to it. The realism of his paintings, such as *Breakfast with a Crab*, 1648 (*see* page 169), consolidated his reputation.

Still-life paintings had several classifications. One type was set in the kitchen or focused on a dining table filled with delectable breakfast, supper, or banquet ingredients, as well as plates, glass and silver and pewter wares, as in *Still Life with the Drinking-Horn of the St Sebastian Archers' Guild, Lobster and Glasses*, c. 1653, Willem Kalf. Other classifications included: still life in a peasant interior; still life with fish; *pronk* (excessive luxury); flowers and fruit still life; religious and moral symbolism in earthly pursuits and spiritual redemption; the brevity of life in transient objects; and *trompe l'oeil*. Works like Gerrit Dou's *A Sleeping Dog with Terracotta Pot*, 1650 (*see* page 168), served simply to highlight the talent of the artist to portray both live and inanimate objects, in exceptionally accurate detail with a great sense of realism.

Balthasar van der Ast

Balthasar van der Ast, born in Middelburg, southwest Netherlands, and working first in Utrecht and later in Delft, was an early exponent of still life, producing exquisite realism in his flower and shell paintings. Following the death of his father in 1609, the young van der Ast moved in with his sister and her husband, the flower painter Ambrosius Bosschaert the Elder, who greatly influenced van der Ast's style in its content, colour and form. Van der Ast was celebrated for his talent for realism in representations of reflective and textured surfaces and still-life depictions of shells and floral arrangements, as in *Still Life with Fruit and Flowers*, 1620–21 (*see* left).

The Quack Doctor

The quacksalver – a pedlar of fake cures – appears in many genre paintings, usually at fairs where he can trick a passerby or a small group of gullible people hoping for cures. Jan Steen's *Village Fair with Quack Doctor*, c. 1670–75, highlights the stupidity of the gullible in recognizable Dutch representations. The quack's assistant pulls hard with pincers at the skin of an old man's neck to remove a 'stone'. The 'stone-cutting', a fake operation meant to cure patients of madness, sometimes carried out on the top of the head to remove an imaginary stone, was a well-used motif in Dutch art and literature. Steen's 'patient' is left in agony whilst boys steal his eggs. On the left, another man, kneeling, is being bandaged after his 'operation'. Steen painted many exposés of fake doctors. In *The Quack*, 1650–60 (*see* right), the doctor holds up to a crowd of villagers a large molar, or 'stone', extracted from the head of a man tied to a chair. Steen makes many visual references to the fakery of the doctor.

'Jan Steen ... able to express with the brush and his wit things that deserve admiration because of their natural portrayal and manner of painting.'

Arnold Houbraken on Jan Steen

Right: *The Quack*, c. 1650–60, Jan Steen (1625/26–79)

Exposing a Fake

The 'quacksalver' doctor, derives from medieval Dutch *rederijkers*, theatrical players from the chamber of rhetoric (*rederijkerskammer*) dramatic society, and Italian *commedia dell'arte*. In plays, poetry, prose, and visual arts, theatrical characters like a love-sick young woman, an idler, a fool, a lecherous man, or a 'quack' – fake – doctor, amongst others, would be easily recognized. In Dutch paintings, visual signs and symbols guided the 'reader' of the work to what type of character they were seeing. In Steen's *The Quack*, the doctor stands above the audience, a theatrical, dramatic requisite, to gain respect and attention. His assistants are lowly characters, reflecting the dishonesty of the doctor. The removal of the 'stone' symbolized the empty-head of the patient. and gullibility of the believers watching. An assistant would hide a small stone, the 'doctor' would make a small incision in the forehead or back of head, slip the stone in to gather blood, then remove it with pincers, to hold up jubilantly to the crowd. Baskets of eggs, such as depicted here, could symbolize payment, and broken eggshells the emptiness or fragility of life. The inclusion of a monkey in the painting represented many things, from evil-doing to the wealth of the 'doctor' who could afford an exotic creature. The popularity of the subject is reflected in the many paintings produced in this era.

Picturing Senses

Highly popular genre depictions were those of the five 'senses', often made humorous, to expose the quackery of fake medicine sellers and sham doctors, often found at country fairs or in the city streets. Rembrandt highlights this practice in *The Sense of Touch: The Stone Cutters*, c. 1624–25 (*see* left), where two men remove a 'stone' from the patient's head. There is clearly pain involved, denoted by the patient's clenched teeth and clenched fists. Another in the series is Rembrandt's *The Spectacles Seller (Sight)*, c. 1624–25, which depicts an old man and woman being duped into buying spectacles that were useless to them. Rembrandt created a visual pun on the expression 'selling someone spectacles' which meant to deceive.

'...his pale blues, his bronze greens, like his lemon yellows and camellia reds, [Vermeer] derived them from Rembrandt.'

Théophile Thoré

Religious Symbolism

Although painters of religious art in the Golden Age had been suppressed by the Reformation, there was still a market for art with a religious content. Rembrandt was a master of religious symbolism, creating evocative, emotive works in chiaroscuro that moved and often surprised the onlooker. One such example is the remarkable *Belshazzar's Feast*, c. 1636 (*see* page 176), depicting Belshazzar, co-regent of the Babylonians (d.539 BC), from the Old Testament

Left: *The Sense of Touch: The Stone Cutters*, c. 1624–25, Rembrandt van Rijn (1606–69)

(Book of Daniel 5: 7–8). In it Belshazzar is holding his last great feast, when he sees a hand writing on the wall the Aramaic words 'mene, mene, tekel, upharsin'. The prophet Daniel interprets it as God's judgment that the corrupt city of Babylon will imminently fall and Belshazzar with it. A later work by Ferdinand Bol, a pupil of Rembrandt, *The Holy Women at the Sepulchre*, 1644, relates a moment in the Biblical narrative of the New Testament, with Christ's family visiting the tomb where he was laid after his death by crucifixion. On the third day after the Crucifixion, the family is greeted by two angels, bathed in celestial light, to tell of the Resurrection. Bol closely follows the Bible narrative (Luke 24:4) in his portrayal.

'I have had three masters, Nature, Velásquez, and Rembrandt.'

Francisco de Goya on Rembrandt van Rijn

Greek Myth Interpretation

In *Orestes and Pylades Disputing at the Altar*, 1614 (*see* pages 150–151), Pieter Lastman depicted a scene from Aeschylus' trilogy the *Oresteia*, a tale of love, hate and morality, and in so doing established himself as a painter of the highest form of art, historical. In the moment seen in the

Left: *Belshazzar's Feast*, c. 1636–38, Rembrandt van Rijn (1606–69)

painting, Pylades is persuading his cousin Orestes to avenge the death of his father, King Agamemnon, and murder his mother. Lastman pinpoints the moment of dispute in epic proportion with multiple persons present at the open-air altar. The Dutch Mannerist painter, Utrecht-born Joachim Wtewael (1566–1638), trained by Joos de Beer (d. 1591), ignored the Caravaggisti followers' appreciation of naturalism and chiaroscuro. He secured his status as a history painter with the remarkable *The Judgement of Paris*, 1615 (*see* right). The painting is filled with characters illustrating the Greek mythological tale of a beauty contest between the goddesses of Olympus – Hera, Aphrodite and Athena – but underlying it is a tale of corruption. The goddesses remove their clothes and begin to bribe Paris, a mortal, with worldly wealth in order to win the contest and be presented with a golden apple. Wtewael depicts the moment the prize is handed to Aphrodite, whilst a wedding feast organized by the king of the immortal gods, Zeus, in celebration of the marriage of Peleus and Thetis (parents of Achilles) continues in the background.

Marital Symbolism

It was often the wish of a patron to have symbolic messages included within a painting, to signify love, unity and steadfastness, particularly for a newly married couple. The pictorial context in Frans Hals' informal marriage celebration *Portrait of a Couple, Probably Isaac Abrahamsz. Massa and Beatrix van der Laen* (*see* left) is filled with symbolism related to the couple. Beatrix was a Regent's daughter, her husband a wealthy merchant and diplomat. Hals breaks the convention of the indoor formal portrait. Here the vivacious, smiling couple is seated close together outside under a tree in the landscape of their own estate, an unconventional setting in the seventeenth century. They are casually posed, at ease; she rests her left hand on her husband's shoulder, a display of informality.

Above: *Portrait of a Couple, Probably Isaac Abrahamsz. Massa and Beatrix van der Laen*, c. 1622 (detail), Frans Hals (1582/83–1666)

Above: *The Judgement of Paris*, 1615, Joachim Wtewael (c. 1566–1638)

The couple look fondly on the viewer, their heads and bodies positioned as a mirror image of each other, a symbol of togetherness and understanding. Hals entwines the couple with symbols of fidelity and love: in the vine in the tree behind them, a symbol of mutual trust and fidelity, and the eryngium thistle to the left, a symbol of male fidelity. In the background on the right is a garden of love.

'The best history is but like the art of Rembrandt; it casts a vivid light on certain selected causes ... [the] best and greatest; it leaves all the rest in shadow and unseen.'

Walter Bagehot

Rembrandt painted two portrait companion pieces *Portrait of Jean Pellicorne and His Son Caspar*, c. 1632 (*see* left), and *Portrait of Susanna van Collen and Her Daughter Anna*, c. 1632 (*see* right). In the portrait of Susanna, the couple's daughter, standing at her seated mother's knee, is depicted receiving money, a symbol of the dowry she will receive from her wealthy merchant father. The basket of grapes, a symbol of fertility, is included in expectation of future children from the daughter's later marriage. Gabriël Metsu's *Self-portrait of the Artist and His Wife Isabella de Wolff in a Tavern*, depicts the married couple, she seated, he perched, in the middle of eating supper at an inn. Metsu is depicted happy, jovial and

Above: *Portrait of Susanna van Collen, Wife of Jean Pellicorne, and Her Daughter Anna*, c. 1632, Rembrandt van Rijn (1606–69)

Left: *Portrait of Jean Pellicorne and His Son Caspar*, c. 1632, Rembrandt van Rijn (1606–69)

'The appellation 'genre painter' is indiscriminately applied both to painters of flowers, fruits, animals, woods, forests & mountains, as well as to those borrowing their scenes from everyday life.'

Denis Diderot

making overtures to his wife. His left arm is around her shoulders, whilst, in a mirror image, signifying a close relationship, she offers him berries in her right hand. The informal painting, in the style of Rembrandt's lively, marital work, *Self-Portrait with Saskia on His Lap (The Prodigal Son in an Inn)*, c. 1635, gives insight into Metsu's married life.

Sexual Symbolism

Sex was often alluded to in Dutch genre paintings, usually through allegory or symbolism, hidden meanings recognized by the viewer. It was rarely explicit, even in brothel scenes, but artists like Jan Steen, a Catholic working in a Protestant republic, painted the reality of what he saw or experienced. Some paintings had his signature mark 'memento mori', or 'in good times beware'. Steen's *A Woman at Her Toilet*, 1655–60 (*see* left), places the viewer as voyeur, intruding into a private space. A rarer depiction of sexual misconduct is *Tavern Scene*, 1635 (*see* right), painted by Adriaen Brouwer. The setting is a rowdy inn. Away from the main group on the right, a young woman seated to the left is being groped under her skirt by a drunk, lecherous man, who has loosened his breeches. The spectator knows it is not consensual behavior, as the girl kicks out at the lecher who screams – mouth wide open – when she pulls his hair to stop him. Sexual references include the liquid content of the lecher's tankard spilling over and the walking stick, an allusion to the male sexual organ. Brouwer's hidden meaning is a morality tale, in which he mocks the drunkard, the effect of alcohol and the people who frequent low-life inns, instantly recognizable to a conservative audience of Dutch genre paintings.

Brouwer painted many inn scenes, like *Boors Smoking and Drinking at a Table in a Tavern*, 1625 (*see* page 185). He depicted himself in the comical, lively work *The Smokers*, c. 1636. Steen, too, used humour to

Left: *A Woman at Her Toilet*, 1655–60, Jan Steen (1625/26–79)

Above: *Tavern Scene*, c. 1635, Adriaen Brouwer (1605/6–38)

Above: *Beware of Luxury*, c. 1663, Jan Steen (1625/26–79)

push a moral message. *Beware of Luxury*, c. 1663 (*see* left), a painting filled with connoted messages of calamity to follow, warns of the dangers of excess. A basket hanging from the ceiling, filled with crutches, a sword and a leper's bell, was a visual message to beware temptation.

Jan Steen

So well-known for his genre paintings featuring humorous scenes of merry-makers, thieves and cuckolds, adulterers and procurers, quack doctors and bad parents, Jan Steen turned in the second half of his career to history and religious paintings. Scenes from ancient mythology, the Bible and Roman history featured in his work. Steen, a genius of storytelling, painted scenes without solemnity, turning the concept of history painting upside down, and painted from his imagination, not historical fact, such as his interpretation of *The Mocking of Samson*, c. 1675–76. The subject is treated with a humour readily appreciated by his patrons, who paid high prices.

Steen's father was a brewer and Steen leased a brewery at Delft in 1654–57 and an inn at Leiden in 1672, so the effects of alcohol would be well known to him. In a rather sad depiction *The Effects of Intemperance*, c.

Above: *Boors Smoking and Drinking at a Table in a Tavern*, c. 1625, Adriaen Brouwer (1605/6–38)

‘Often in Vermeer, as in Jan Steen, the accessories, and especially the paintings hung on the wall, are highly revealing…’

Théophile Thoré

1663–65 (*see* page 188), Steen illustrates a woman’s young family going hungry, due to their mother spending money on alcohol.

Children on the Scene

In 1635 Jacob Cats (1577–1660), a Dutch poet, humorous writer and politician, published a proverb book titled *As the Old Sing, So Pipe the Young*. Jan Steen visualizes it in *The Way You Hear It, Is the Way You Sing It*, c. 1665 (*see* right). This is another genre work, a morality tale for parents highlighting that bad habits in adults lead to bad habits in their children, as shown by a young boy smoking. Steen includes three generations, a grandfather, a grandmother singing and the mother with a child on her lap. The father laughing, on the right, lighting a pipe for his young son, is a self-portrait of Steen.

Masterful Art

Steen’s merry depiction of a moral Dutch proverb brings together the art of Johannes Vermeer and the Dutch Masters of the seventeenth century, portraying Dutch life and traditions, through diverse depictions. In the work of artists who lived in a remarkable period in Dutch history, its Golden Age is laid before the viewer, revealing its people, its landscape, the expansion of its cities, its independence as a Dutch Republic, its scientific discoveries and wealth of knowledge shared throughout the world, its literature and art. Looking at Dutch art, one sees artists relying on their skills in the commercial world to sell in the art markets after religious patronage of the pre-Reformation period was reduced. Their art reveals to historians and art lovers alike the remarkable lives lived in the Dutch Republic during the seventeenth century.

Above: *A Lady Writing*, c. 1665, Johannes Vermeer (1632–75)

Right: *The Way You Hear It, Is the Way You Sing It*, c. 1665, Jan Steen (1625/26–79)

Above: *The Effects of Intemperance*, c. 1663–65, Jan Steen (1625/26–79)

Further Reading

Alpers, Svetlana, *The Art of Describing: Dutch Art in the Seventeenth Century*, University of Chicago Press, 1984

Franits, Wayne (Ed.), *The Ashgate Research Companion to Dutch Art of the Seventeenth Century*, Routledge, 2016

Gaskell, Ivan & Jonker, Michiel (Eds.), *Vermeer Studies*, National Gallery of Art, Washington, 1998

Heard, Kate & Whitaker, Lucy, *The Northern Renaissance: Dürer to Holbein* (Exhibition), Royal Collection Publications, 2011

van Helden, Albert; Dupré, Sven; van Gent, Rob; Zuidervaart, Huib (Eds.), *The Origins of the Telescope*, Amsterdam University Press, 2013

Israel, Jonathan, I., *The Dutch Republic and the Hispanic World 1606-1661*, Oxford: Clarendon Press, 1982

Israel, Jonathan, I., *The Dutch Republic: Its Rise, Greatness, and Fall 1477-1806*, Clarendon Press, Oxford 1995

Prak, Maarten & Webb, Diane (tran.), *The Dutch Republic in the Seventeenth Century: The Golden Age*, Cambridge University Press, 2005

Rowen, Herbert, R., *The Princes of Orange: The Stadtholders of the Dutch Republic*, New York: Cambridge University Press, 1988

Schama, Simon, *The Embarrassment of Riches: An Interpretation of Dutch Culture in the Golden Age*, Fontana Press, 1991

Schwartz, Gary, *Rembrandt's Universe: His Art, His Life, His World*, London: Thames & Hudson, 2006

Slive, Seymour, *Dutch Painting, 1600-1800*, Yale University Press Pelican History of Art Series, Yale University Press, 1998

van Suchtelen, Ariane, and Kloek, Wouter, *Jan Steen's Histories*, Netherlands: Waanders Art Books, 2018

Waiboer, Adriaan E., *Vermeer and the Masters of Genre Painting: Inspiration and Rivalry*, National Gallery of Ireland in association with Yale University Press, 2017

Westermann, Mariet, *A Worldly Art: The Dutch Republic* 1585-1718, Yale University Press, 2010

Wheelock Jr, Arthur, *Vermeer & the Art of Painting*, Yale University Press, 1995

Wolf, Bryan Jay, *Vermeer and the Invention of Seeing*, Chicago and London: University of Chicago Press, 2001

Acknowledgments

Rosalind Ormiston (author) is a researcher, lecturer and author in art, architecture and design history. She lectures in art and architectural history at Kingston University, London. Her publications include *Origins of Modern Art, William Morris: Masterpieces of Art, Art Deco: The Golden Age of Graphic Art and Illustration, Van Gogh: A Life in Letters & Art, J.M.W. Turner: Masterpieces of Art, Edward Hopper: Masterpieces of Art* and *Alphonse Mucha: Masterworks*.

Janet Tyson (foreword) is an independent writer, lecturer and researcher in histories of visual and material culture. Attracted by its attention to the minutiae of daily life, her interest in Netherlandish art spans the fifteenth to seventeenth centuries, and encompasses works by Flemish and Dutch painters, printers and sculptors. She devoted her Masters thesis to domestic interiors in Rogier van der Weyden's oeuvre, and has lectured on genre works by Pieter de Hooch, Johannes Vermeer and Pieter Saenredam, among other artists.

Picture Credits

Courtesy of **Bridgeman Images** and © the following: 1 & 49 Mauritshuis, The Hague, The Netherlands; 2 & 106, 12, 77, 84, 87, 159, 168 Private Collection/Johnny Van Haeften Ltd., London; 3 & 56, 4, 94, 120, 180, 181 Wallace Collection, London, UK; 6, 16 Johnny Van Haeften Gallery, London, UK; 7, 10, 11, 20–21, 26, 27, 34, 43, 46, 57, 58, 68–69, 72, 86, 91, 98, 100, 103, 119, 148, 149, 150–151, 161, 165, 178 Rijksmuseum, Amsterdam, The Netherlands; 8, 61, 65, 108, 125, 156, 157, 174, 185, 152 & back cover Private Collection/Photo © Christie's Images; 9 Purchased in honor of A. Ian Fraser with additional funding provided by the David L. Chambers, Jr. Fund for Dutch and Flemish Art, the Dr. V.K. Stoelting Fund, and Mrs. Jane W. Myers; 13 Thyssen-Bornemisza Collection, Madrid, Spain; 15 Universal History Archive/UIG; 17 Belvoir Castle, Leicestershire, UK; 18, 22, 41, 52, 62, 88, 109, 114, 121, 128, 131, 176, 179, 183, 188 National Gallery, London, UK; 19, 45, 53, 54, 141, 187 Mauritshuis, The Hague, The Netherlands; 24, 79 Metropolitan Museum of Art, New York, USA; 25 Private Collection/Courtesy of Thomas Brod and Patrick Pilkington; 28 Germanisches Nationalmuseum, Nuremberg, Germany; 30 & 192, 127, 186 National Gallery of Art, Washington DC, USA; 31, 63, 133, 147, 169 State Hermitage Museum, St. Petersburg, Russia/Tarker; 311 Suffolk Collection/© Historic England; 33 © Museumslandschaft Hessen Kassel; 35 Guidhall Art Gallery, City of London/Harold Samuel Collection; 36 Worcester Art Museum, Massachusetts, USA; 37, 97, 126, 135, 163 Private Collection; 38 Museum Boymans van Beuningen, Rotterdam, The Netherlands; 39 Johnny Van Haeften Ltd., London; 42 Cannon Hall Museum, Barnsley, South Yorkshire, UK; 44, 48, 55, 129, 136, 158 Louvre, Paris, France; 51 Staatliche Museen, Berlin, Germany/Artothek; 59, 101, 146 De Agostini Picture Library; 67 Centraal Museum Utrecht, Netherlands/Tarker; 70 National Trust Photographic Library/John Hammond; 73, 96, 122, 130, 167 Royal Collection Trust © Her Majesty Queen Elizabeth II, 2018; 74 Private Collection/Roy Miles Fine Paintings; 75 Museum of Fine Arts, Houston, Texas, USA/Museum purchase funded by Brown Foundation Accessions Endowment Fund; 78, 118 Frick Collection, New York, USA; 80, 184 Kunsthistorisches Museum, Vienna, Austria; 82 National Trust Photographic Library; 83 National Gallery, London, UK; 90 Detroit Institute of Arts, USA/City of Detroit Purchase; 104 Musee des Beaux-Arts, Lille, France; 110 Private Collection/Photo © Rafael Valls Gallery, London, UK; 112–113 Gemaldegalerie, Staatliche Museen zu Berlin, Germany/© Leemage/Bridgeman Images; 134 On loan to the Frans Hals Museum, Haarlem, The Netherlands; 137 De Agostini Picture Library/M. Carrieri; 139 J. Paul Getty Museum, Los Angeles, USA; 144 Laing Art Gallery, Newcastle-upon-Tyne, UK/Bridgeman Images; 145, 154 De Agostini Picture Library/A. Dagli Orti; 155 Nationalmuseum, Stockholm, Sweden; 160 Ashmolean Museum, University of Oxford, UK; 164 Private Collection/Johnny Van Haeften Ltd., London. Courtesy **Getty Images** and © the following: 14t De Agostini Picture Library; 29, 47, 93, 107, 142, 166, 173 Fine Art Images/Heritage Images/Hulton Fine Art Collection; 64 Fine Art/VCG Wilson/Corbis via Getty Images; 123 Art Media/Print Collector/Hulton Fine Art Collection; 124 Alinari Archives; 140 DEA/G. NIMATALLAH; 162 Hallwyl Museum, Stockholm, Sweden; 170 Universal History Archive; 182 Rijksmuseum, Amsterdam, The Netherlands. © **akg-images**: 116, 117. © Quint & Lox Limited/**SuperStock**: 14b. Courtesy **The Metropolitan Museum of Art**, New York, Marquand Collection, Gift of Henry G. Marquand, 1889: 81 & front cover.

Index

Page numbers in *italics* refer to illustration captions.